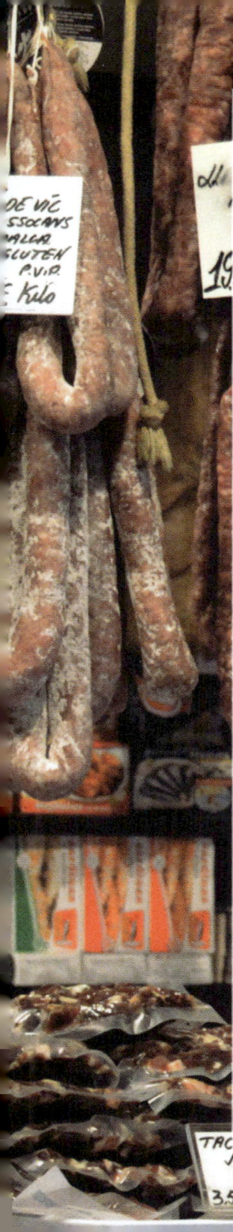

Introduction

This book got its start, naturally, over lunch, when we asked ourselves a simple question: Why are small, traditional eateries – where some of the best meals in any city await – so often overlooked? Why, in a city like Barcelona, with such rich culinary districts, are some of these areas and their bounty of good food rarely explored and celebrated?

In response, we launched Culinary Backstreets™, devoted to collecting the best undiscovered local eateries you might not always find on your own. We're talking serious food for serious eaters, hold the frills.

Beyond tapas – and what you will find listed in most guidebooks – lies a wide range of unique Spanish regional cuisines and restaurants and, more importantly, spots that reflect Barcelona's role as the heart of Catalan identity. With this booklet as your trusty introduction to the culinary backstreets of Barcelona, you will know what to eat and where to eat it.

Because prices tend to change, we have decided to generally not include them in our reviews. Most of the spots covered vary from very inexpensive to modest. More importantly, we consider all of our selections high in value. Alcohol is generally among the offerings, unless otherwise indicated in the review. In general, we recommend making reservations for dinner.

Welcome to Barcelona's Culinary Backstreets,

Bon Profit!!

Ansel Mullins & Yigal Schleifer

Founders, Culinary Backstreets

CONTENTS

SANTS-MONTJUÏC

SANT MARTÍ & SANT ANDREU

THE URBAN WINE ROUTE

SPECIALS

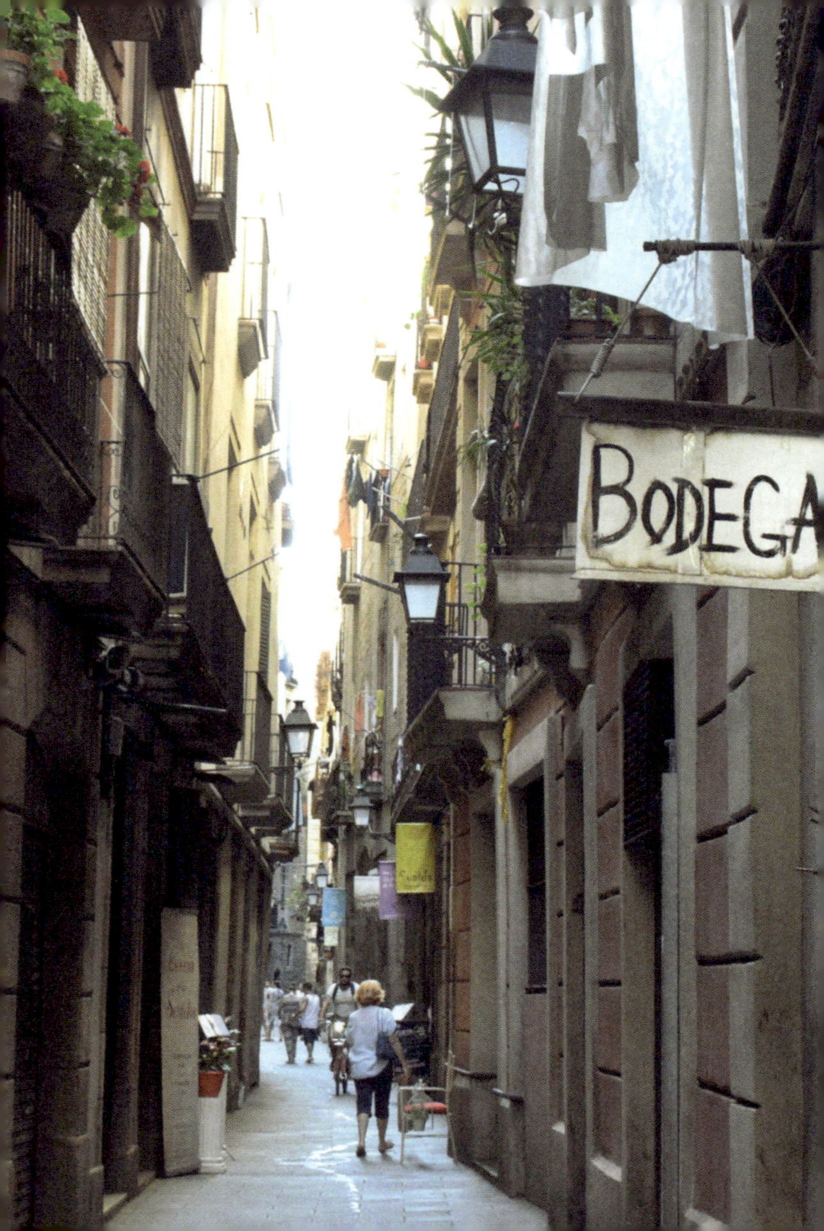
BODEGA

THE OLD CITY

CAN SOLÉ

From Fishermen to Famosos

Address: Carrer Sant Carles 4, Barceloneta
Telephone: +34 93 221 5012
Hours: Tues.-Sat. 1pm-4pm & 8:30pm-11pm; Sun. 1pm-4pm; closed Monday

Since the late-18th century, this quiet corner in the salty seaside neighborhood of La Barceloneta has borne the name Can Solé. Its conversion from a shop to a restaurant in 1903 set in motion a 114-year trajectory – from fisherman's tavern of humble stature to famous culinary institution, offering some of the best classic Catalan cooking, rice dishes and seafood in Barcelona. Throughout the elegant downstairs dining room, framed photos of celebrities (*famosos*) who have visited Can Solé give guests a glimpse back at more than a century of Barcelona's most celebrated citizens.

Chef Mari Carmen Durán follows the seasons, so when the artichokes of Catalonia flood into Barcelona in late winter/early spring, she serves a heaping plate of golden, paper-thin slices of crispy-fried artichoke hearts, blanketed in shaved foie gras *mi cuit* (semi-cooked). This was soon followed on our visit by a platter of the famous *trompetes de la mort amb xipirons* (black trumpet mushrooms with baby squid), along with a plate of ultra-fresh *navalles a la planxa*, razor clams grilled and served plain to allow the flavor of the sea to shine.

Can Solé has a multitude of rice dishes from which to choose – from the *arròs negre* (black rice, creamy and jet black due to the addition of squid ink) to the restaurant's signature dish, the *arròs caldós Can Solé*, which is more brothy than paella and cooked in a wide iron *cassola* (casserole). When ordering the arròs caldós, you choose your protein from an extensive list, be it sea cucumber, sea urchin, prawns, scallops, crab or clams. We ordered the luxurious lobster paella, with perfectly tender rice and delicious bits of *socarrat* (crispy rice grains) that become crusted around the edges and the bottom of the pan. Paella is all about the rice and the broth, with the seafood or meat playing a supporting role, and the version here pays the utmost respect to tradition.

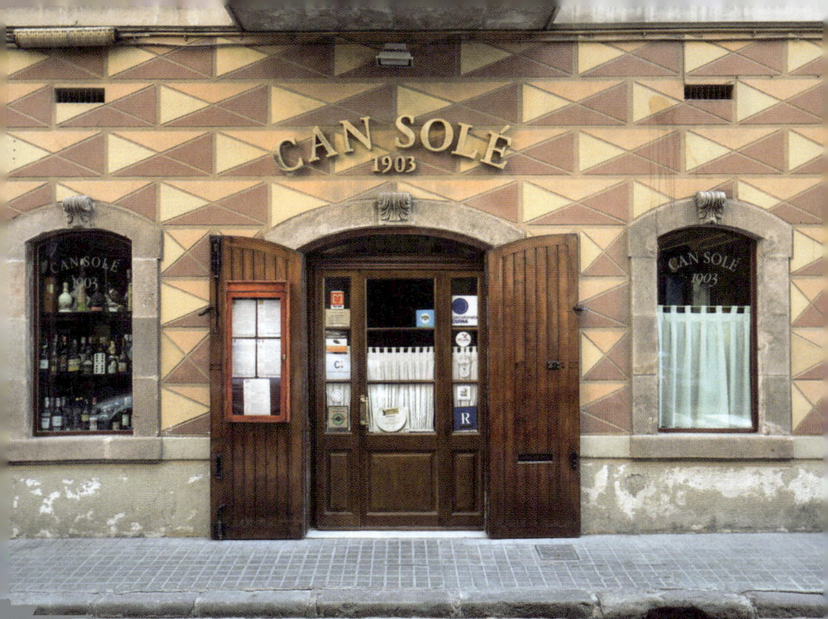
CAN SOLÉ
1903

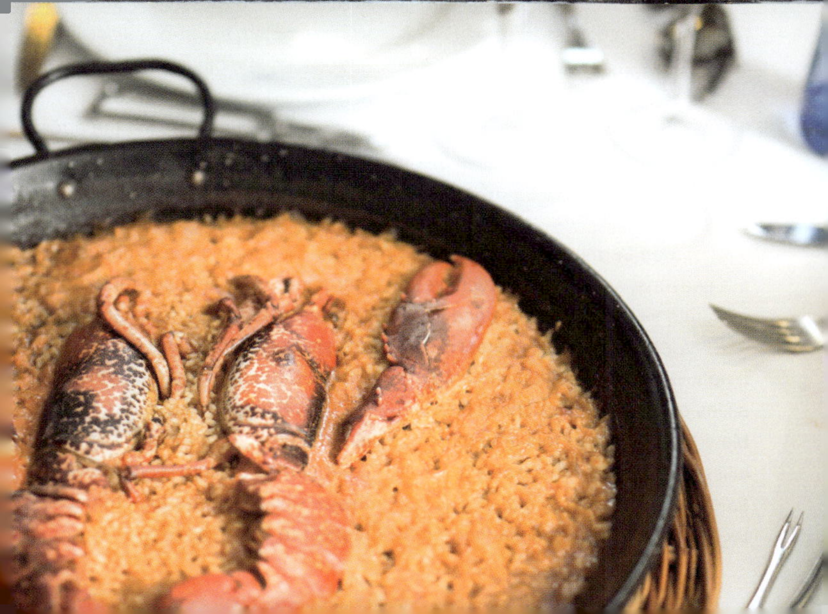

EL PASSADÍS DEL PEP

Address: Plà de Palau 2,
La Ribera-El Born
Telephone: +34 93 310 1021
(reservations recommended)
Hours: 1:30pm-10:30pm;
closed Sunday & Monday

Simple Pleasures

El Passadís del Pep may be located in one of the most visited quarters of Barcelona, but it's out of sight down a long corridor for anyone who isn't looking for it. From the moment you sit down, the house offers you your first bottle of cava, and the celebration of food and life begins. There is no menu and there are no daily specials, just whatever they decide to cook that day.

The restaurant, whose name means "Pep's Corridor," was opened in 1979 by the late Joan Manubens, an iconic local restaurateur, and is still run by his family. It specializes in *cocina de mercado*, or market cuisine, prepared in a simple, traditional Mediterranean style. As if in a ballet, the show begins when the waiters start to dance around you and the food arrives at the table in a continuous flow of abundance: Iberian cured ham, anchovies and typical Catalan bread rubbed with tomato; sautéed baby squid with rice and garlic; and choice shellfish such as *cañaíllas* (a kind of sea snail), velvet crabs or spider crabs prepared in such a delicate way that all the natural flavor is retained.

The long first act ends and the second act begins. Stewed chickpeas with ham, artichokes and Basque peppers in olive oil might appear, or perhaps a delicious stew of wild rabbit with mushrooms. Or how about *caldereta de bogavante*, a traditional dish with squid and clams in olive oil, a tiny touch of garlic, parsley and a little bit of lard to add intensity and richness to the flavors, all of which complement the star of the dish: a fresh lobster from the Bay of Biscay, cooked in salty seawater.

The choice of wine from the excellent cellar is the only aspect of the meal that is left up to you. The house will also make recommendations of wine pairings, but feel free to combine them as you like. The important thing here is to enjoy the meal, which the warm, comfortable atmosphere encourages.

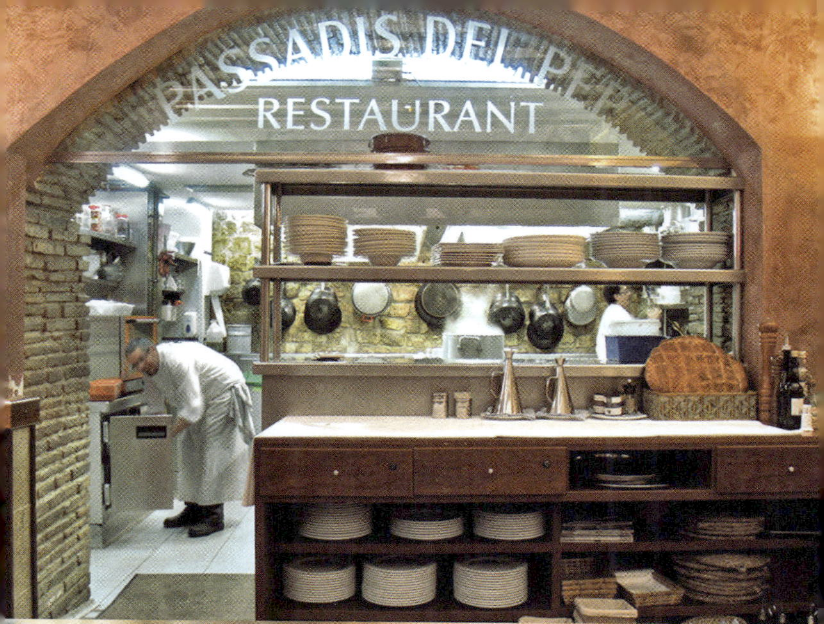
PASSADIS DEL
RESTAURANT

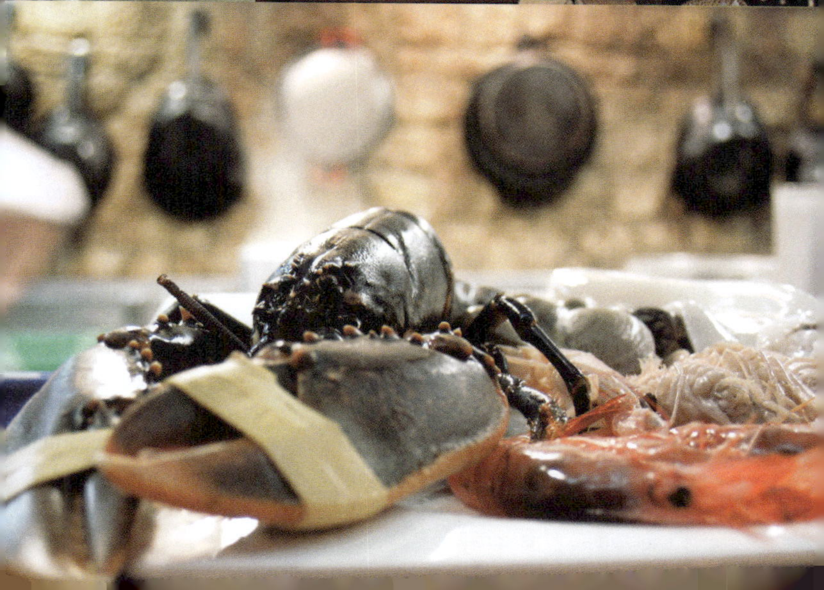

LA COVA FUMADA

The Bomb Squad

Address: Carrer del Baluard 56,
Barceloneta
Telephone: +34 93 221 4061
Hours: Mon.-Fri. 9am-3:45pm;
Sat. 9am-2pm;
closed Sunday, holidays & in August

One of the most beloved gastro-nomic icons in Barcelona's port area, La Cova Fumada is a place to take off your tie, eat with your hands and relinquish your smartphone, lest the screen get covered with grease from your fingers.

The atmosphere has remained almost unchanged since the 1940s. In those difficult years just after the Spanish Civil War, the customers were people from the neighborhood and workers at shipyards and the nearby factories who came to have a glass of wine and to heat up their own food in the open "cheap kitchen." The same spirit still pervades the tiny venue today, from the seven old, marble-topped tables and the cramped open kitchen to the almost prehistoric blackboard.

La Cova Fumada is legendary for its food. María Pla, grandmother of the current owners, brothers Josep María and Magí Sole, is said to have invented the famous and now ubiquitous potato bomb, a breaded and deep-fried ball of mashed potato with pork served with aioli or a spicy cayenne sauce. It's just one of many classics on the menu, which includes tender and tasty fried artichokes, cooked chickpeas, stewed beans from Cartagena, *butifarra negra* (black sausage) and salt cod. Sardines, mackerel, prawns, squid and octopus are all served with a touch of olive oil and are best eaten with some *pa amb tomàquet* (bread rubbed with oil and tomato). The only change in the menu in the last 70 years is the introduction of seasonal seafood, such as fresh clams or crayfish.

La Cova Fumada is a place with what Spaniards call "solera," a sort of vintage character and maturity. And nobody in the Sole Pla family would ever think of changing this.

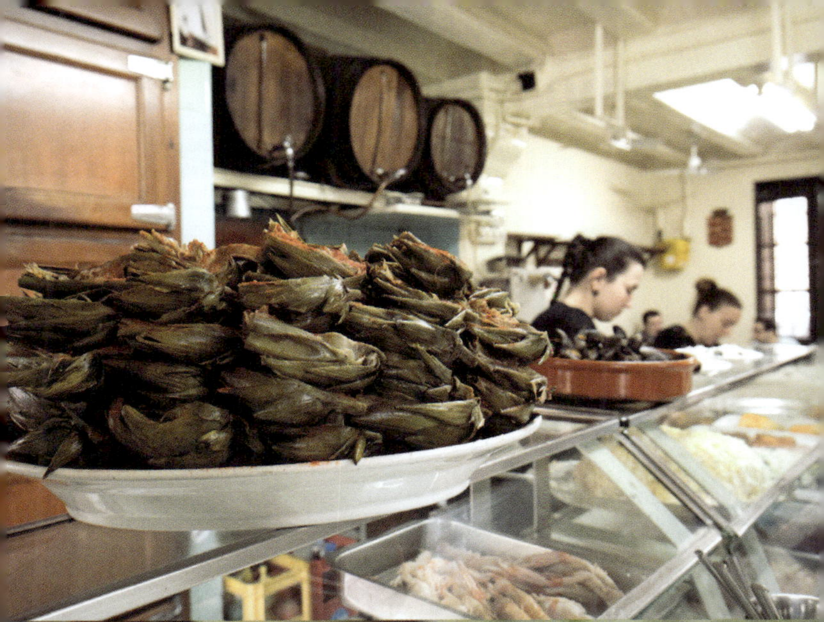

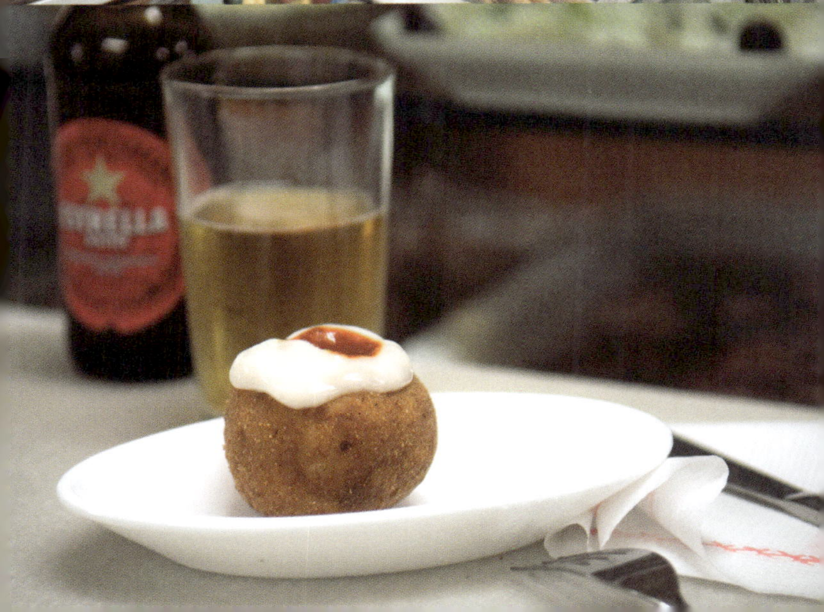

LA ESTRELLA

Grand Dame

Address: Carrer Ocata 6,
La Ribera-El Born
Telephone: +34 93 310 2768
Hours: 1:30pm-3:30pm &
8:30pm-10:30pm;
closed Sunday & Monday

Josefa Chiquillo opened La Estrella in 1920 as a kind of travelers' inn and began cooking for guests in 1924. Her great-grandson, Jordi Baidal, and his wife, Josefa Villada, run the restaurant today, serving simple but refined Catalan cooking, with a little French and Italian influence, thoughtfully prepared from quality local products. The atmosphere is formal but relaxed, quiet and friendly. Eating here feels like eating in someone's home.

One of La Estrella's most beloved specialties is the starter of chickpeas with prawns, served in a ceramic casserole dish. The chickpeas have been divested of their papery skins and are tender and delicate; the grilled prawns offer their sweet, marine flavors; and everything is bound by a rich, earthy garlic confit mousseline. The last time we visited La Estrella, Baidal surprised us with some *canyuts*, small razor clams from the Ebro Delta, which he grilled and served with a traditional *picada* of toasted almonds and hazelnuts crushed in a mortar with olive oil. This technique has been used since medieval times to thicken sauces and intensify flavors.

Cod, a cornerstone ingredient of Spanish and Catalan cooking, is another standout at La Estrella. Baidal cooks the *morro*, considered the best part and found along the back, close to the head, of specimens that are more than 10 years old. (The very best morro usually comes from cod that's between 20 and 30 years old.) Many of his cod preparations are based on old Catalan recipes, such as those served with that garlic mousseline or *romesco* sauce (made from red pepper, almonds and bread) or with spinach and pine nuts. The wonderful Lenten cod, stewed with artichokes, chickpeas, hard-boiled eggs, olive oil, onion, garlic, tomato and paprika, is a masterpiece.

Like an aged cheese or cellared wine, La Estrella has only gotten better with time.

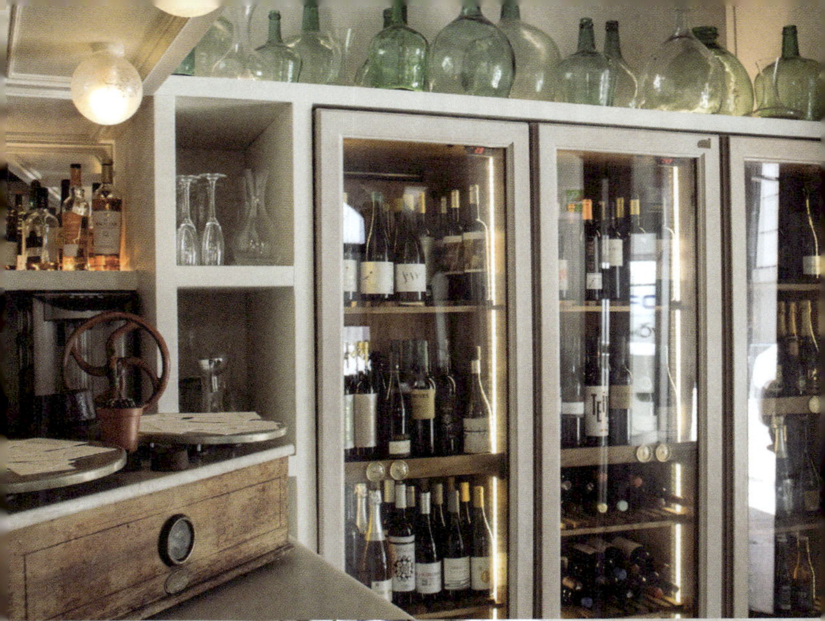

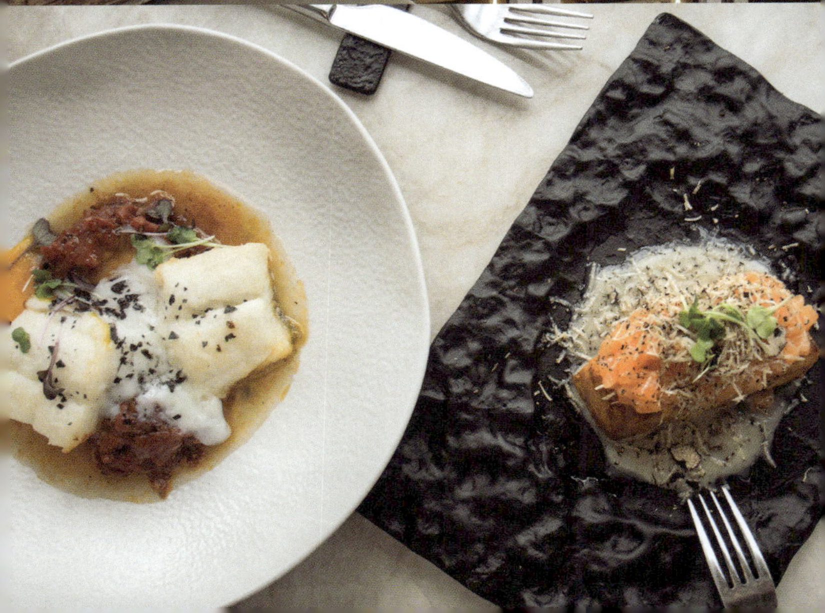

LA PINEDA

The Sausage Club

Address: Carrer del Pi 16,
Barri Gòtic
Telephone: +34 93 302 4393
Hours: Mon., Wed.-Sat. 9am-9pm;
Sun. 11am-4pm;
closed Tuesday

The sign over the entrance says La Pineda was established in 1930, but it has actually been around much longer. In the 19th century, it served as a place to slaughter pigs and prepare meat. Around the turn of the century, it became a *colmado*, a small store selling dry goods and *conservas* (tinned or jarred foods). As the years passed, La Pineda began to focus more on selling *embutidos* (sausages) and cheeses along with the conservas. The proprietors also installed a marble-topped bar in the back and started serving snacks and drinks.

In 1976, Antonio Segovia, then 14, arrived in Barcelona and began working at La Pineda. After a few years, he was joined by his younger brother José, and now, nearly 40 years later, they run the place. The brothers have put together a top-notch list of suppliers, and their meats, cheeses and tinned seafood are all of excellent quality. There is *morcón*, a cured, paprika-flavored sausage from Jabugo; white and red *longaniza* from Murcia; and *chistorras*, fast-cured, fat-laced sausages from Pamplona.

But what we really can't resist are the *butifarras*, traditional Catalan sausages made with pork, salt, pepper and other spices. A seemingly infinite number of other ingredients can be added, including honey, pine nuts and *calçots* (spring onions). On any given day at La Pineda there are at least four different varieties of butifarra on offer. Our favorite, the butifarra with *ceps* (porcini mushrooms), is succulent and rich, accented by a spicy, mushroomy depth that makes us close our eyes and sigh with contentment. It's even better washed down with a glass of the house-made *vermut*.

We're not the only butifarra fanatics at La Pineda. In 2010, a group of younger customers went so far as to form the Buticlub, a "butifarra appreciation society," with La Pineda serving as club headquarters.

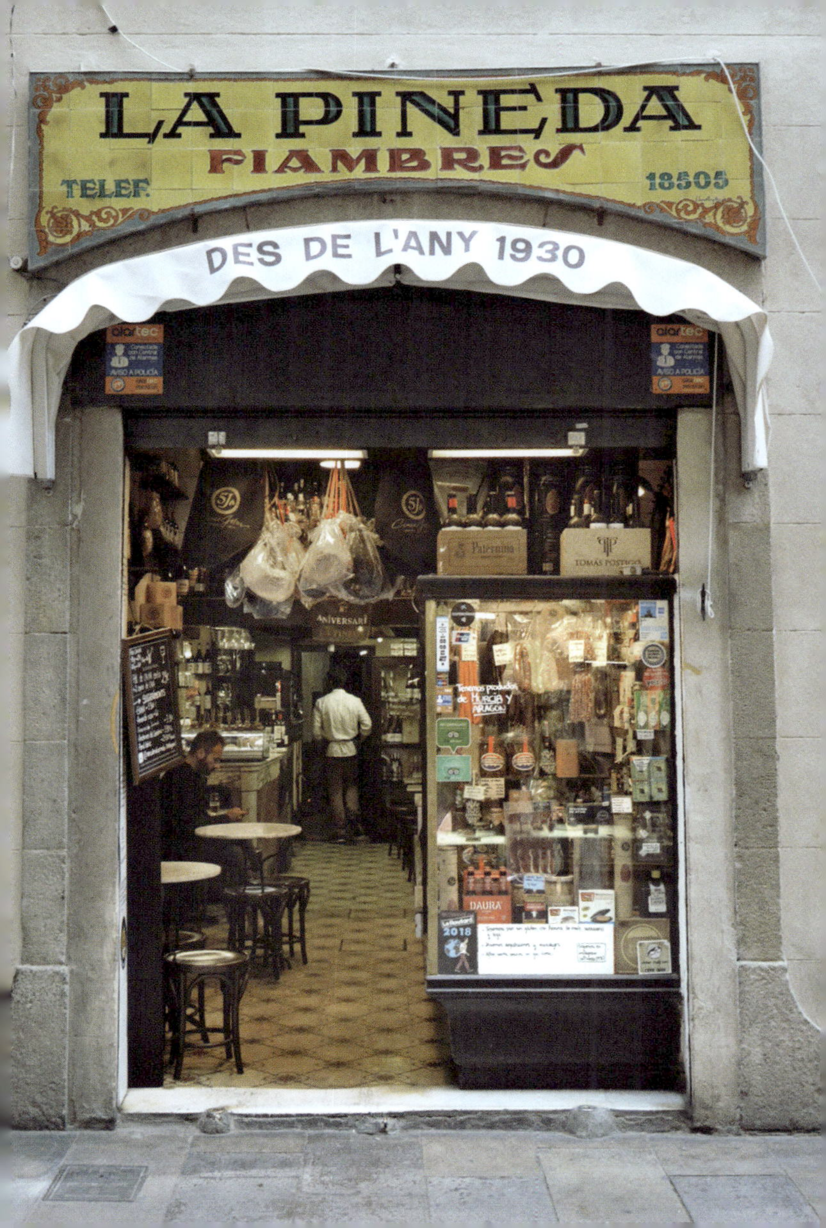
LA PINEDA
FIAMBRES
TELEF.
18505
DES DE L'ANY 1930

LA SOSENGA

Modern Medieval

Address: Carrer de n'Amargós 1, Barri Gòtic
Telephone: +34 93 750 5820
Hours: Tues.-Thurs. 1pm-4pm;
Fri.-Sat. 1pm-4pm & 8pm-11pm;
closed Sunday & Monday

The first cookbook written in Catalan is one of the oldest in Europe: *El Llibre de Sent Soví* (1324). Inside is a recipe for a meat stew herbed and spiced with parsley, clove and marjoram and cooked with lard and honey. This is a variation of *sosenga*, an old Catalan word for "sofrito," and the inspiration for chef Marc Pérez and Tania Doblas's restaurant in the Gothic quarter. "We do it with beef cheek," Marc says about their medieval sosenga, "now a very traditional ingredient in Catalonia."

Modern culinary candy wrapped in cute vintage paper, La Sosenga is a fantastic contemporary addition to the Catalan culinary tradition. The restaurant offers attractive daily lunch specials for less than 20 euros, in which you can choose from a seasonal selection of first and second dishes. The main dishes are preceded by unexpectedly sophisticated tiny appetizers. The tapas include all the classics, such as Sosenga's special spiced *patatas bravas*, seasonal *croquets* or mussels marinated *en escabeche* (pickled). Everything comes with bread baked in-house and an excellent selection of Spanish wines.

The more elaborate plates ("platerets") include dishes like cod confit with Idiazábal cheese or the traditional Catalan *caneló* (cannelloni), made with *poularde* chicken and béchamel. As for the medieval sosenga *de vedella*, it tastes perfectly modern. Mission accomplished here. The cohesion of Catalan roots and the use of local ingredients is Marc's main motivation, but he keeps an eye toward new combinations or the addition of foreign ingredients – like the seasonal *calçots* (local spring onions) omelet with Mexican salsa *tatemada*.

For dessert, don't miss the luscious house-made cheesecakes waiting temptingly on the counter. While not a medieval recipe at all, it's certainly one for the history books.

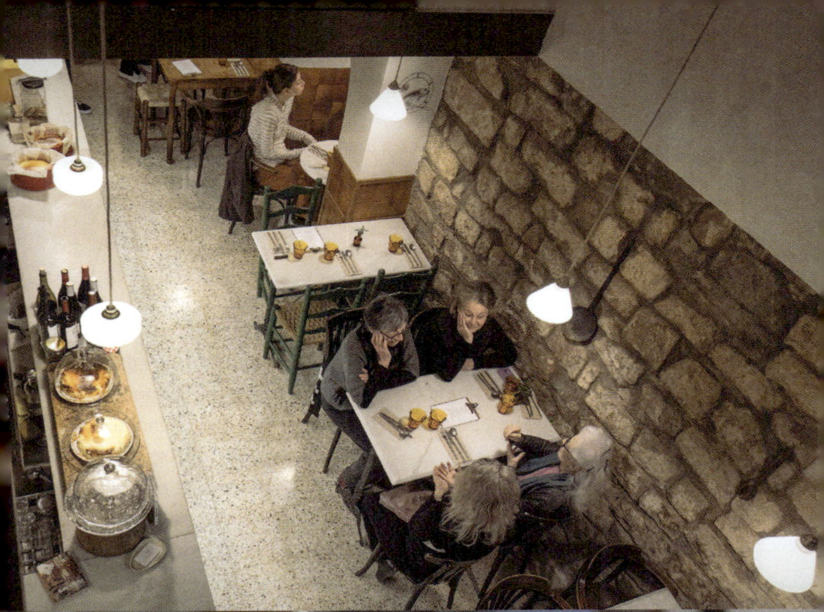

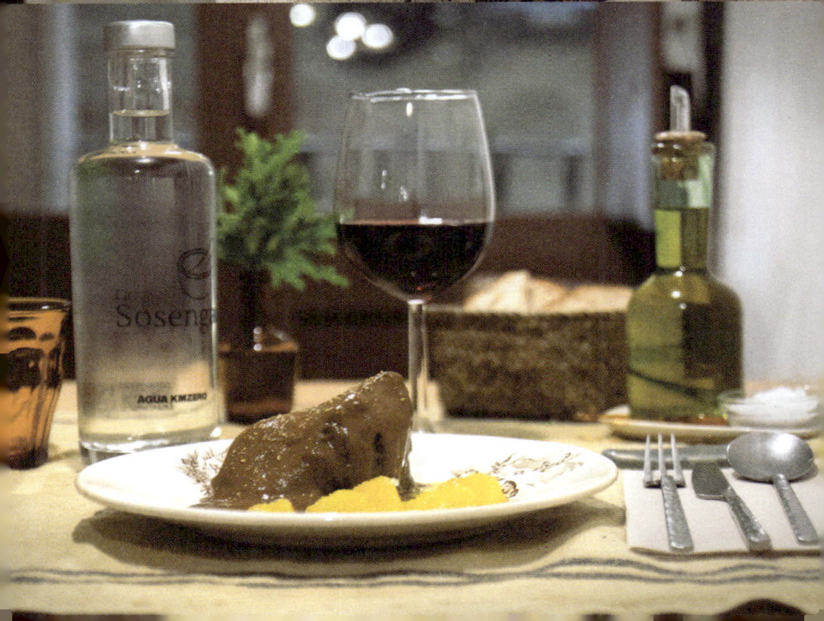
AGUA KMZERO

MESCLADÍS

Address: Carrer dels Carders 35,
El Born, Ciutat Vella
Telephone: +34 933 19 8732
Hours: Mon.-Fri. 1pm-9pm;
Sat.-Sun. 11am-9pm

Cooking Up Opportunities

The entryway of Espai Mescladís del Pou is jam-packed with people: neighbors, workers and visitors who come and go all day long, and waiters walking from the kitchen to the tables on the terrace. But there are also dozens of people staring out from black and white photos that cover the restaurant's walls; some are alone, others in couples, families or groups, smiling and laughing.

All the people pictured at one point immigrated to Barcelona, and whether they're still living in the city or have moved elsewhere, their stories are always present through Mescladís. The Mescladís Foundation is a multifaceted Barcelona initiative that provides tangible and sustainable economic programs – mostly in job training or work at one of its three restaurants – to people at risk of social exclusion, with a focus on migrants and refugees.

The first restaurant integrated into the project was Mescladís del Pou, a colorful, open-air terrace in the Born neighborhood, which has grown to be the foundation's most well-known location. Here, you'll find some of Mescladís's most celebrated food and drinks, like the Middle East trio of hummus, baba ganoush and muhammara with Moroccan bread, or the refreshing *bissap*, an African Hibiscus-infused drink from Senegal.

Whether at evening tapas or dinner, you can taste some of their excellent Catalan savory *cocas* (pastries), as well as creations from much farther afield. The Mescladís projects, including the restaurant and school in L'Eixample, currently share a similar culinary offer of regular snacks and seasonal daily specials, all made mainly with local, organic products. Even more, these products come from providers with similar social visions.

Mescladís defies fusion that focuses on one or two cultures, or that is made by chefs far removed from either. Here, the kitchen teams work together on menus that celebrate their diverse ideas and backgrounds, making every plate something truly unique.

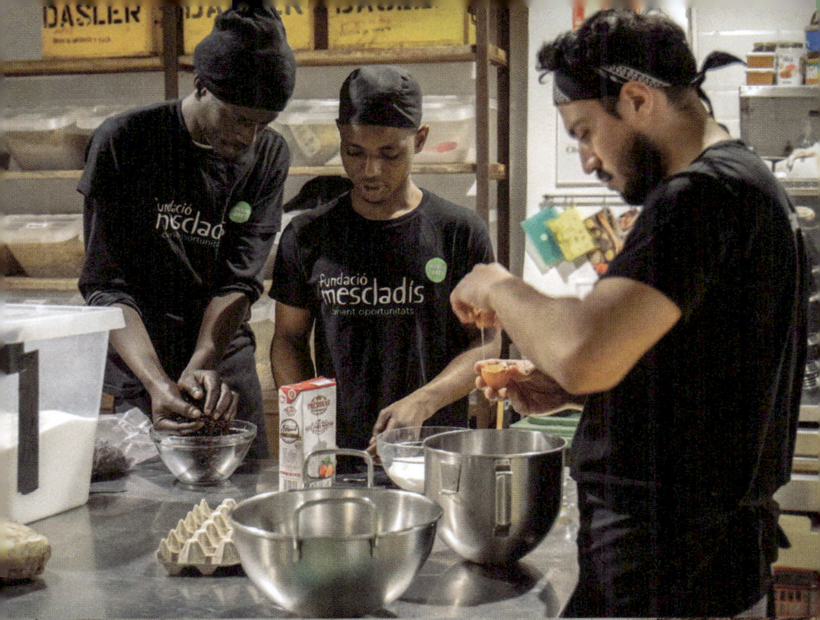
DASLER
fundació
mescladís
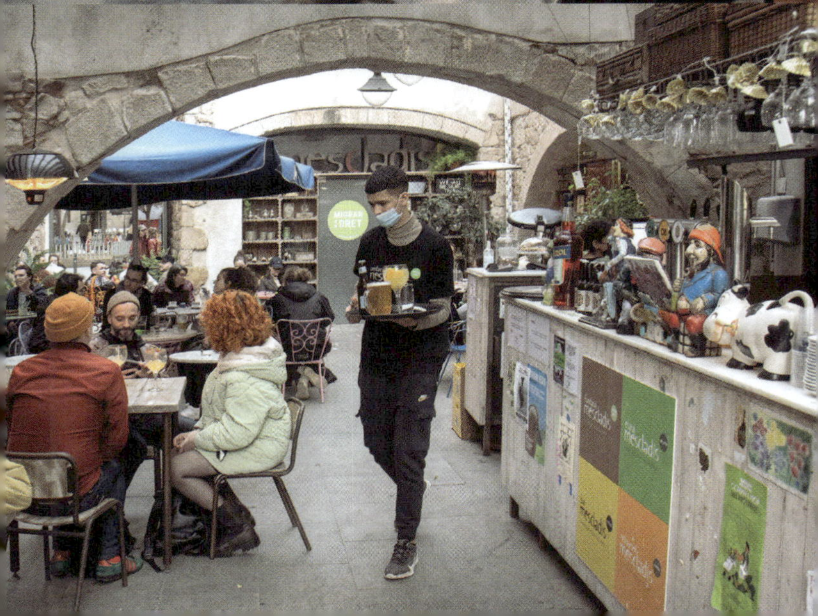
mescladís
mescladís
mescladís

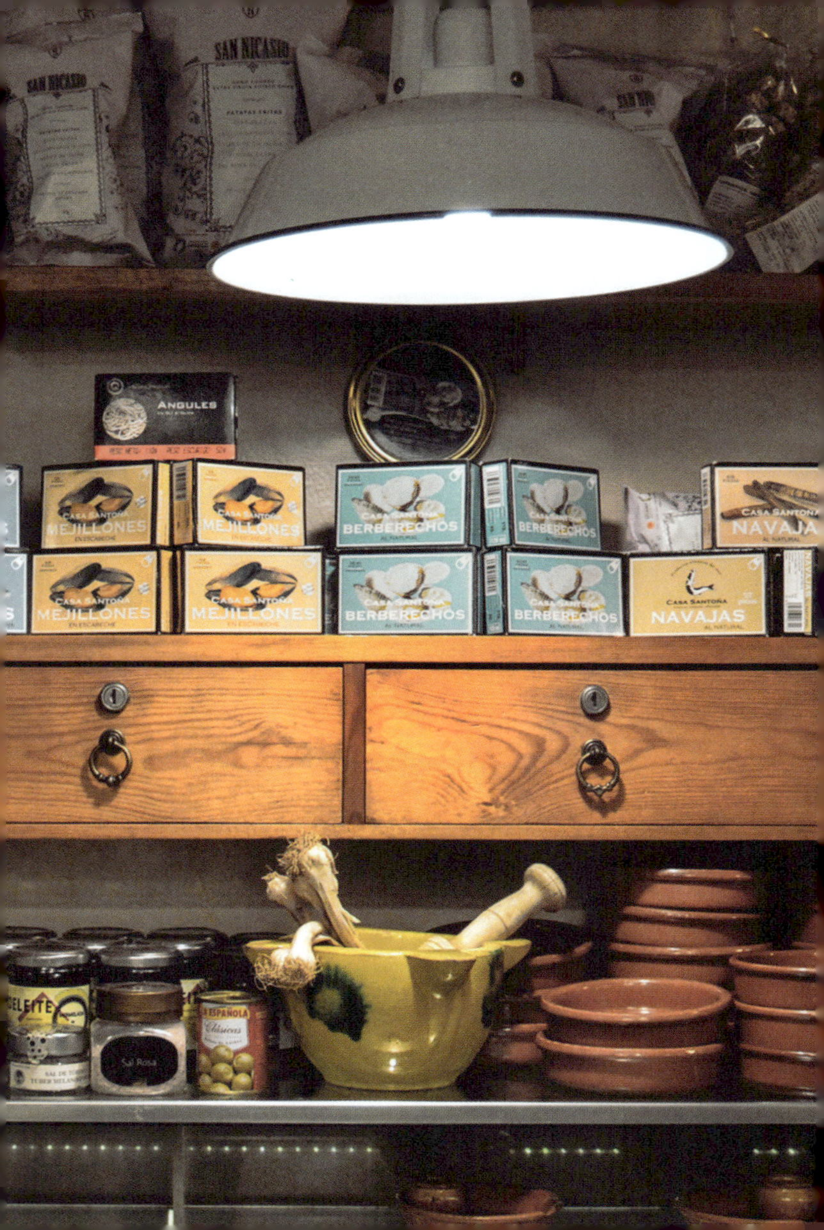
SAN NICASIO
SAN NICASIO
ANGULES
CASA SANTOÑA
MEJILLONES
EN ESCABECHE
CASA SANTOÑA
MEJILLONES
EN ESCABECHE
CASA SANTOÑA
BERBERECHOS
AL NATURAL
CASA SANTOÑA
BERBERECHOS
AL NATURAL
CASA SANTOÑA
NAVAJAS
AL NATURAL
LA ESPAÑOLA
Sal Rosa

L'EIXAMPLE

BAR BODEGA GELIDA

Address: Carrer Diputació 133,
L'Eixample
(corner of Comte d'Urgell)
Telephone: +34 93 453 7997
Hours: Mon.-Fri. 7am-10pm; Sat. 8am-4pm; closed Sunday, holidays & in August

Old Faithful

At the beginning, Gelida was just a bodega where Joan Llopart Pujó, who came from the village of Gelida in Penedés, offered Catalan wine, cold cuts and a few traditional Catalan dishes cooked by his grandmother, like *butifarra amb mongetas* (boiled sausage with beans).

These days, Gelida, now run by Llopart Pujó's son Alberto, is a modest yet charming old-school "all in one," where you can buy bulk wine, have a drink with tapas or sit and enjoy a complete meal with dessert. The atmosphere is homey and pleasing, relaxed between meal times but hectic at lunch and dinner. The day begins early with *esmorzars de forquilla,* traditional hearty "fork breakfasts," and the same dishes are offered all day. Customers can come in for a *callos* (tripe stew) fix whenever they need it. Gelida's specialty is traditional Catalan cooking, particularly stews, but there are also a few salads, soups, grilled fish and salt cod dishes, plus tapas, omelets and sandwiches.

Paella is served on Tuesday and here, it's a surf-and-turf version with ribs, squid, mussels, prawns and peas. On Friday and Saturday, Gelida serves *cargols* (snails) stewed in a spicy sauce made with chorizo, ham and herbs. On Wednesday, there's pig feet. The restaurant's most iconic Catalan dish might very well be *cap i pota*, the famous cartilaginous stew made with beef head and leg, plus some chorizo and a powerful *sofrito* to make a dense and soft spicy sauce, perfect for dipping bread in.

Another great classic is *fricandó*, a dish with medieval origins – a very different version of which turns up in French cooking – made with thin beef chops that are fried, coated in flour and then stewed with a sofrito of garlic, onion and tomato (the original went without), ranci wine (a fortified sweet wine) and *moixernons* (St. George's mushrooms), the delicate fungi that give this recipe its distinctive flavor.

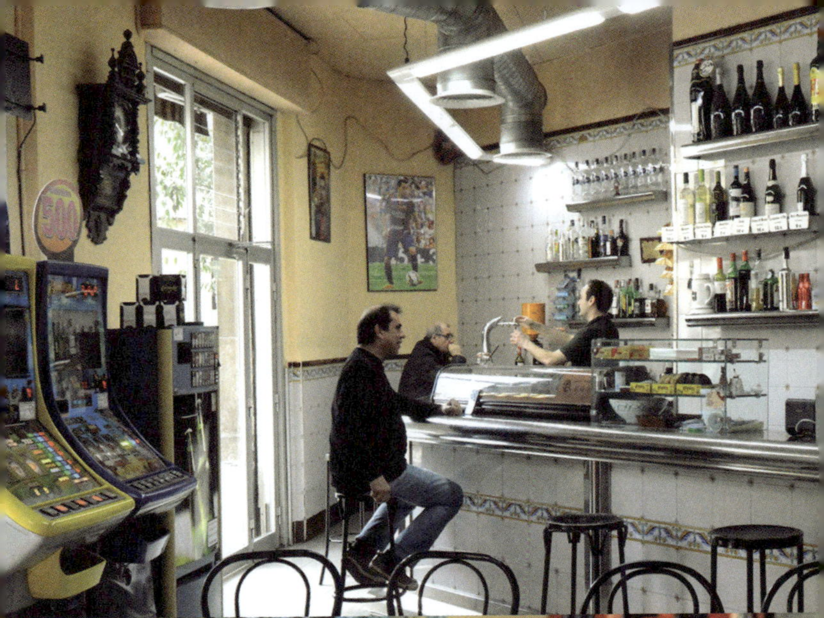
500

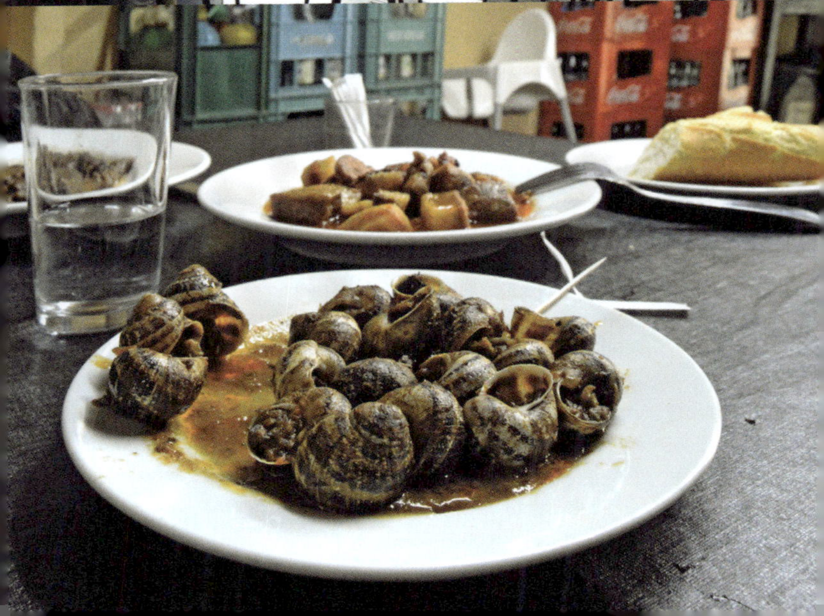

CAN VILARÓ

Address: Carrer Comte Borrell 61,
Sant Antoni-L'Eixample
Telephone: +34 93 325 0578
Hours: 8am–3:30pm;
closed Sunday

No Guts, No Glory

Can Vilaró, a third-generation traditional eatery located in front of Sant Antoni market, pays tribute to offal, cuts of pork, lamb and beef that most Catalan people seem to have turned their backs on these days. The interior is bare-bones, but owner Dolors; her über-friendly husband, Sisco; and their hardworking daughters, Aida, Alba and Anna, make regulars and newcomers feel like they are eating at Grandma's house.

The faces of Dolors's legion of fans certainly glow with happiness when they have her superb *cap i pota*, a traditional Catalan stew made with calf's head and leg and chickpeas, as well as *lletons amb mongetes* (sweetbreads with baked beans), *fetge amb salsa* (liver with sauce), *tripa amb cigrons* (tripe with chickpeas), *peus de porc amb bolets* (pig's trotters with wild mushrooms), *cervells a la romana* (battered lamb brains), *callos* (beef tripe and pork feet stew) or *conill amb herbes* (rabbit with herbs) for breakfast or lunch.

For not-so-adventurous eaters, this popular restaurant offers more everyday dishes, such as breaded chicken, pork rib stew, sardines, cod salad, baked cod and squid in sauce. There isn't a set lunch menu but there are daily specials: *escudella* (a traditional Catalan soup) and *carn d'olla* (a stew of seasonal vegetables, beef bones and pork sausages) on Mondays; *fideus a la cassola* (casserole noodles) on Tuesdays; *llenties amb xoriç* (lentils with chorizo) on Wednesdays; *arròs a la cubana* (rice with fried egg and tomato sauce) on Thursdays and Fridays; and *fricandó* (beef fillets with wild mushrooms cooked in a beef broth sauce) on Saturdays.

When asked about Can Vilaró's future, Dolors says: "If this market becomes a tourist trap like La Boquería, I don't think Can Vilaró will last another 100 years, to be honest. Tourists want to eat paella, not offal." We hope she's wrong, but in the meantime, we plan to eat as many bowls of cap i pota as we possibly can.

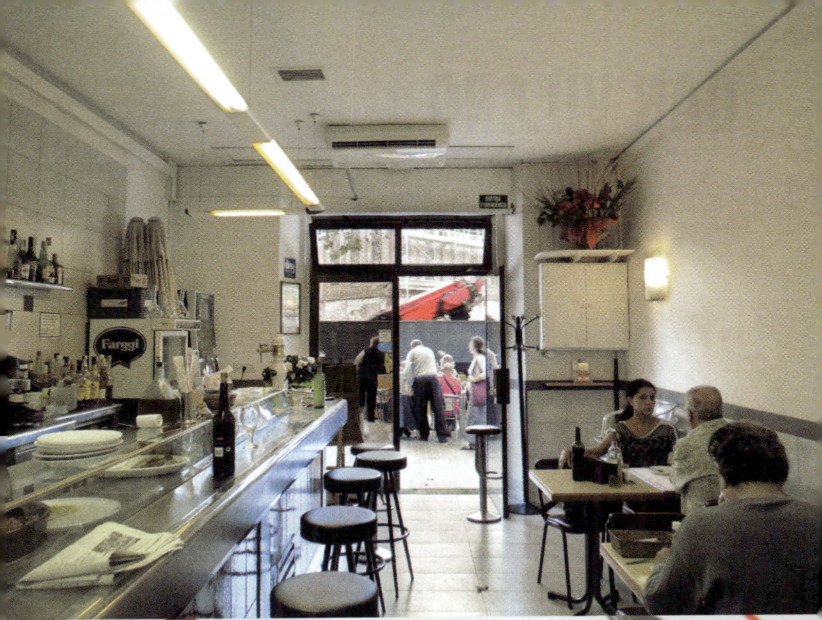
Farggi

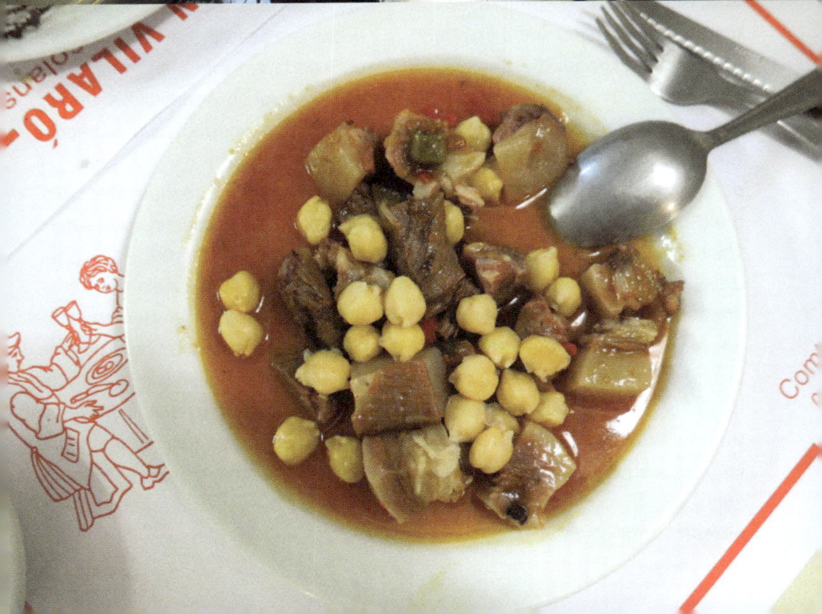
VILARÓ

CONTRACORRENT

Address: Carrer de Ribes 35,
El Fort Pienc
Telephone: +34 61 784 0060
Hours: Mon. & Thurs. 7pm-11pm;
Fri.-Sun. 1pm-4:30pm &
7:30pm-11pm;
closed Tuesday & Wednesda

Against the Flow

On a pleasant pedestrian street just by the Estació del Nord and close to Arc de Triunf sits Contracorrent ("against the flow" in Catalan). Since the owners first met more than a decade ago, Nicola worked in Michelin-starred Celler Can Roca and Anna at Barcelona natural wine flagships like Bar Brutal. Now, at Contracorrent, both streams flow together to create a small spot with a focus on produce, the environment and community.

There are 50-60 different wines on the menu, depending on the week, mostly natural wine from Catalan and Spanish small producers. Their blackboard menu usually lists around 10 dishes and tapas, plus some daily surprises that always follow the seasons, the products available in their garden or the stores of their trusted providers. We were recently wowed by the grilled local beach squid, served with dry algae, garden vegetables (including aromatic rapini and mustard leaves) and *bagna cauda* sauce made with anchovy paste. The dish felt like an intense sea wave crashing down on a field of greens.

We also loved the refreshing *ventresca* (tuna belly) salad with fennel and citrus fruits, a beautiful and colorful composition with a Mediterranean spirit. A smaller but no less delicious bite was the extremely delicate "taco" made of marinated chopped beef with pickled vegetables wrapped in a nasturtium leaf.

But the showstopper of our most recent lunch on the Contracorrent terrace was a fantastic small ceramic plate with a tiny grill. On top sat beef slices and pickled onions, while below the grill was an aromatic bed of thyme and rosemary that Nico torched at the table to create the smoke and heat needed to cook the meat slightly and give it a great mountain flavor. Phenomenal. With all the pandemic closures in Barcelona, new spots like Contracorrent prove that not all hope is lost.

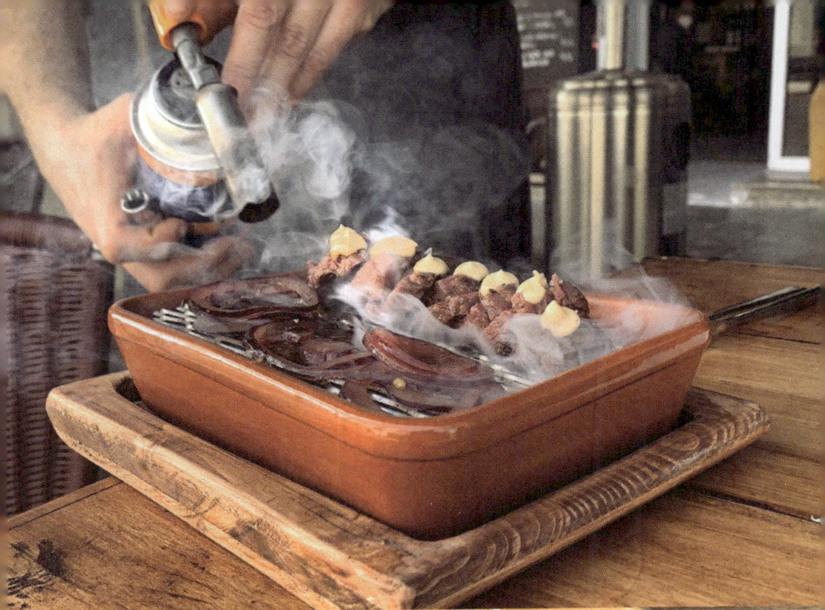

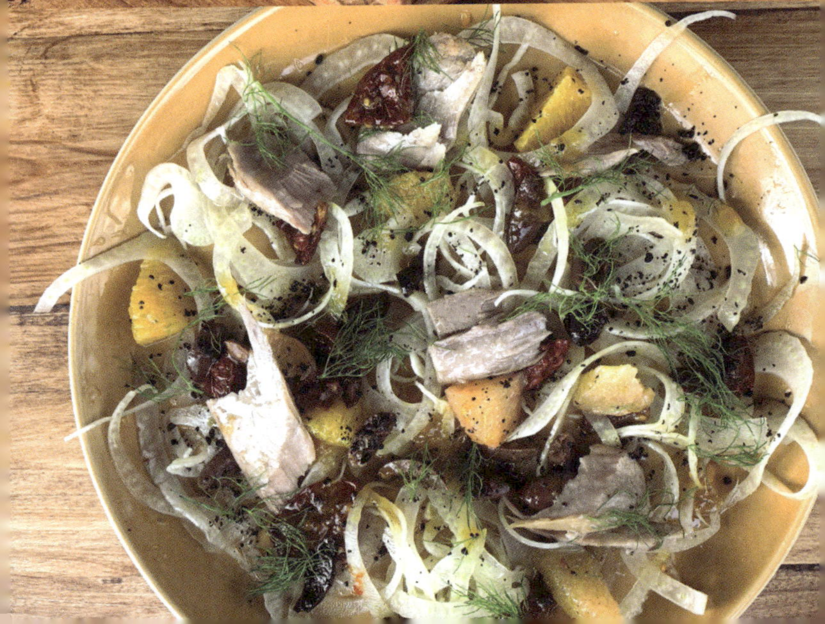

CRUIX

Address: Carrer d'Entença 57, La No
Esquerra de l'Eixample
Telephone: +34 935 25 2318
Hours: Wed.-Sat. 8pm-10:30pm;
Fri.-Sun. 1pm-3:30pm;
closed Monday & Tuesday

Crunch Time

When you hear something go *crunch* on the left side of L'Eixample, whether crispy bread or churros, croquettes or *socarrat* (the toasted bottom of paella), there's a good chance it came from the kitchen of Cruix (Crunch).

At this relaxed spot, chef Miquel Pardo creates excellent sides and main rice dishes from Castellón, a province in the Valencian Community. A native of this region, Pardo mixes his granny's *sofritos* with a creativity inspired by the celebrated Adriá brothers. "In all of eastern Spain, you can eat wonderful rice dishes," he says, whereas in Barcelona that's often not the case anymore. "Here we have too many pizza places and very few quality rice places. I want to offer great rice at a pizza price."

Though Miquel is dedicated to traditional Spanish rice dishes, he also incorporates powerful flavors from Asia, North Africa and even Mexico into the menu. We start our crispy path with a semi-salted anchovy with *pane carasau*, very thin and crispy Sardinian bread, and some hollandaise sauce, all together a contrast of freshness, umami and rich fats.

The roasted beet hummus with mushrooms and *tartufo* was a creamy vice in which we dipped the Sardinian bread (this time smoked), while the cod churro that followed was a fun twist. Instead of chocolate, we dipped it in a soft garlic foam.

Next up was another Cruix classic, the Peking duck croquettes with kimchi sauce – a tiny bite with explosive flavor. From Asia we moved on to Mexico with a ray fish and trout eggs taco accompanied by a shot of very green tequila and completed with coriander, cucumber and lime.

After all that traveling, we come back home with a bang: bomba rice served socarrat, and flavored with a sensuous cut of Iberian pork. Perfectly balanced and excellently crafted, no, this is definitely not pizza.

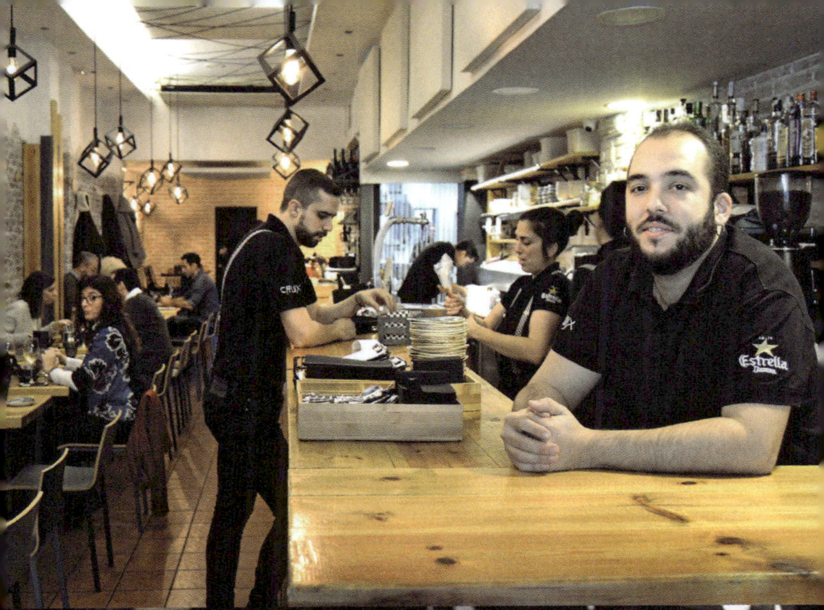
CRUX
Estrella
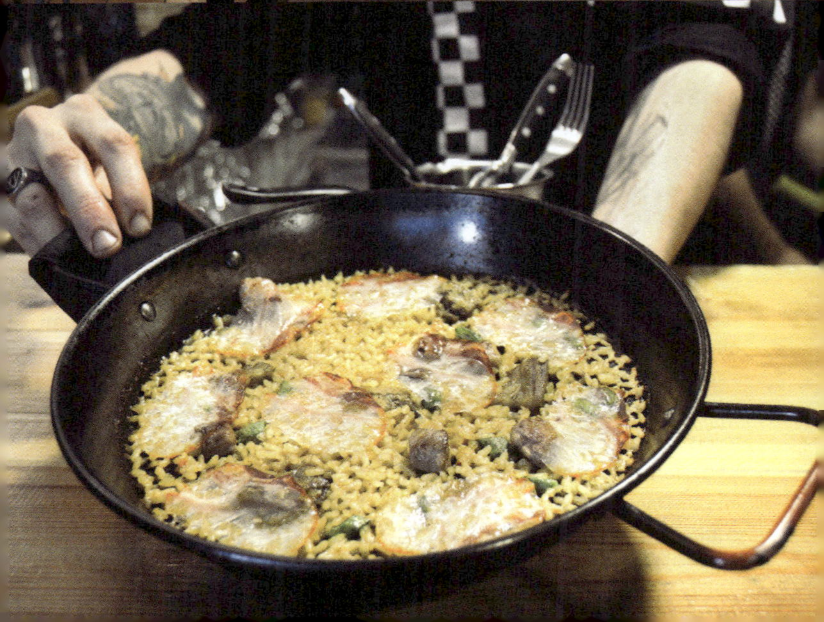

EL CHATO

The Basque Truck Stop

Address: Gran Via de les Corts
Catalanes 697, El Fort Pie
Telephone: +34 93 245 2169
Hours: Tues.-Sat. 1pm-3:30pm &
8:30pm-10:30pm;
Sun. 1pm-3:30pm;
closed Monday

When El Chato, considered to be Barcelona's oldest Basque restaurant, opened in 1941 in El Fort Pienc, the neighborhood was a decidedly industrial one. In fact, the restaurant's main clientele for decades were Basque truck drivers who were dropping off or picking up goods in the area.

Much has changed since the 40s. El Fort Pienc is now home to office workers as well as families, lured to the area by its proximity to the center of town. Meanwhile, Basque cuisine has gone on to become one of the world's most celebrated, its home region filled with numerous Michelin-starred joints.

El Chato has evolved to reflect both of these changes, but in many ways it remains as it was when it first opened – a warm and welcoming place to taste traditional Basque market cuisine, still run by the same family. One of their most classic fish dishes is the Basque style hake stew. Composed of a succulent flour-thickened sauce of garlic, onion and white wine, it is accompanied by peas and asparagus. Another iconic Basque recipe is cured cod chunks, with garlic and spicy chile fried and served in creamy pil-pil sauce that is made with the cod juices – rich in albumin – emulsified with olive oil. Then there are the baby squids in their ink, clams with beans, and the *morcilla* (Spanish blood sausage) with piquillo peppers (sweet preserved red peppers). Mushrooms are a passion shared by Catalans and Basques, and another classic menu item that has remained over the years is the *butifarra amb bolets*, yellow chanterelles with stir-fried Catalan pork and black pepper sausage.

Like the Basque dishes, septuagenarian Agustín Jr. has inherited the restaurant from his family. What are today intimate dining rooms in the back and upstairs of El Chato were at one time bedrooms, where the younger Agustín says he used to take naps during the work day. "I have no intention of retiring," he says. "I'm happy here." After all, he's known no other home.

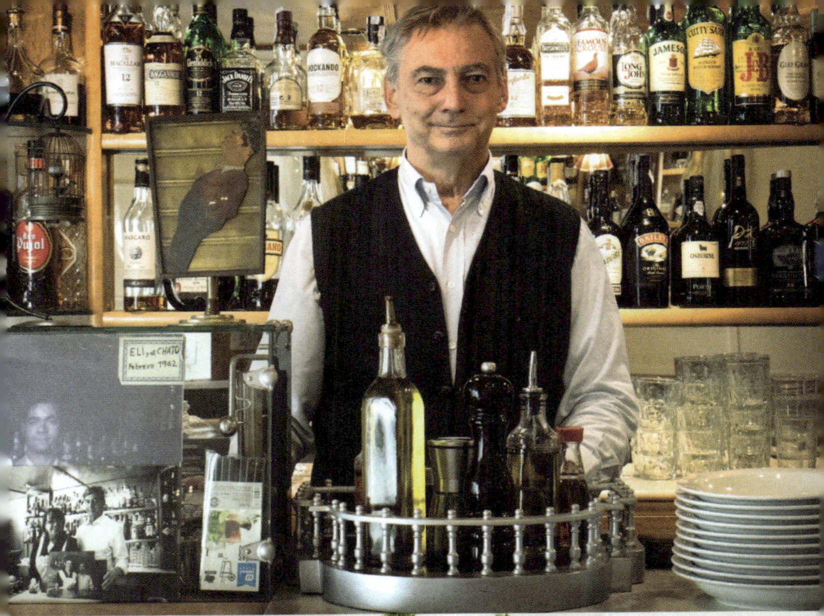
JAMESON
CUTTY SARK
J&B
BAILEYS
OSBORNE
Febrero 1942

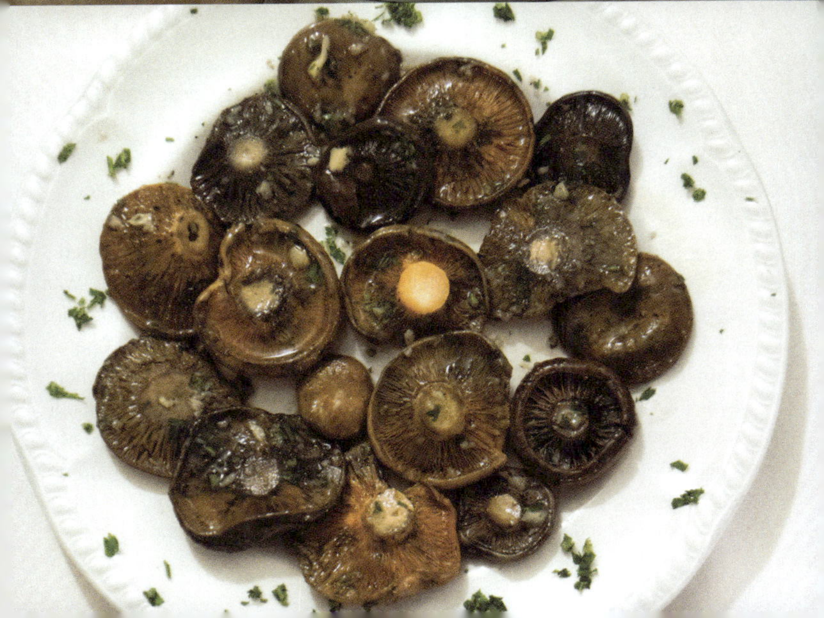

EL RACÓ DE L'AGÜIR

Address: Carrer de Tamarit 117, Sant Antoni
Telephone: +34 934 26 6839
Hours: 1pm-4pm; closed Sunday

All the Rice Moves

El Racó de l'Agüir ("Agüir's Corner") in Barcelona's Sant Antoni neighborhood is a family affair. Mom (Roser) and dad (Ferran) opened the restaurant in 1990 but, after two years, their sons Iván and Ferran took the reins. All four are well-versed in Iberian and Mediterranean flavors, and while the restaurant is perhaps best known for their rice dishes, it also offers contemporary takes on a number of traditional Catalan and Valencian recipes.

The long and narrow dining room is decorated with wooden accents and traditional Valencian tiles, geometric beauties in blue, green and yellow. Beyond this warm space lies a small open kitchen, where younger Ferran, now the head chef, works his magic. Next to him, his mother and mentor oversees the stoves with her trained and expert hands. The elder Ferran, meanwhile, presides over the bar with a smile and an inexhaustible energy, while Iván manages everything else.

Depending on the day, you can find *fideuàs* (noodles with seafood) and rice dishes of all kinds: seafood rice, *arròs caldós* (brothy/soupy rice), *arroz a banda* (rice cooked in fish stock) and other seasonal dishes created on the go. We tried their rice with *sepionets* (baby cuttlefish), tender garlic and clams, served in an iron paella on the table. The rice texture was perfect and the sepionets tender, while the clams were like small and delicate bites of the sea.

Beyond rice, their salt cod is excellent, served with a romesco sauce and *picada* (minced almonds). Their monkfish *croquets* are also standouts, but even simple comfort food dishes, like their lentil stew, are terrifically restorative. We appreciate how their dishes deftly navigate the territory between familiarity and modernity: healthy, made with top-quality ingredients and impeccably presented.

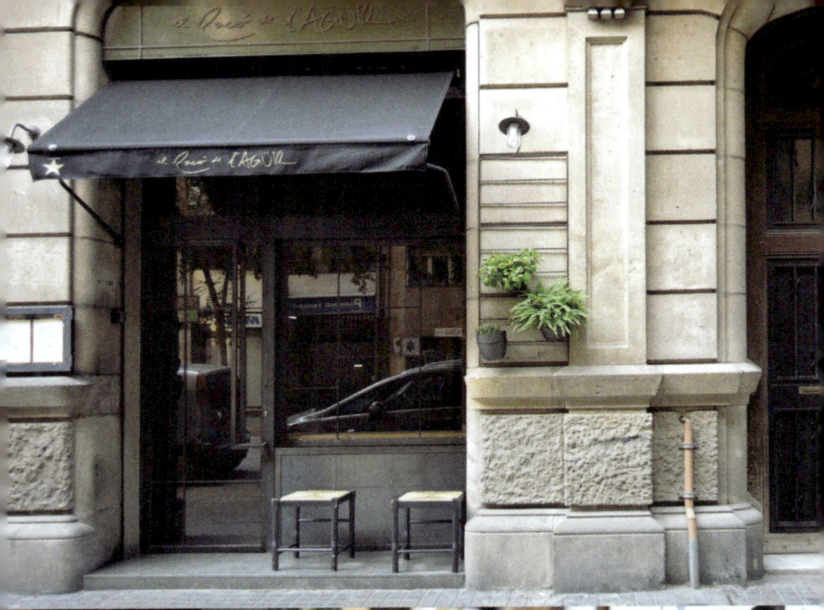

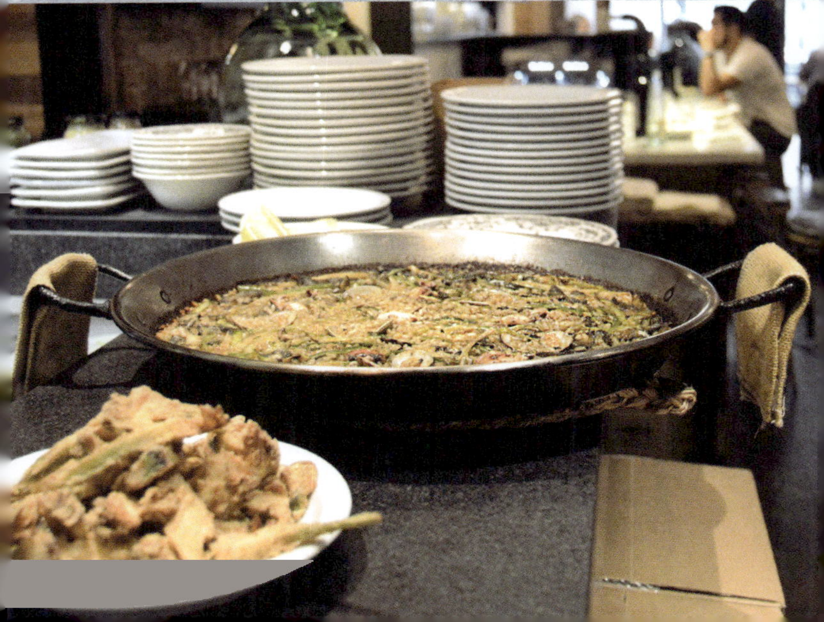

ENTREPANES DÍAZ

Address: Carrer de Pau Claris 189, L'Eixample
Telephone: +34 93 415 7582
Hours: Tues.-Wed. noon-midnight; Thurs.-Sat. noon-2:30am; closed Sunday & Monday

Sandwich Central

Kim Díaz, a well-known local restaurateur and owner of Bar Mut tapas bar and El Mutis cocktail bar, wanted to pay tribute to one of the most humble and sadly underrated Spanish snacks, the sandwich, by giving it the respect it deserves.

It took months for Kim to find the right bread rolls, at Forn de Sant Josep, an old bakery a few blocks away. Then came the right chef, Víctor Lema, able to turn classic plated dishes into nearly 20 absolutely mouthwatering gourmet sandwiches. Customers' top five favorite sandwiches are *calamares* (calamari with squid ink mayonnaise), *rabo de buey* (oxtail), *cochinillo* (roast suckling pork), *kokotxas al pil-pil* (cod chin cooked in parsley and garlic) and Antxón (red pork sausage and poached egg).

Despite the sandwich being the main theme of this bar, Kim hasn't neglected to include a wide range of equally delicious non-sandwich offerings on the menu. Among the tapas are classics such as *croquetas, callos* (pork tripe cooked with chorizo and paprika) and *patatas bravas,* as well as more Andalusian ones: *ortiguillas* (deep-fried anemones), *cazón en adobo* (marinated school shark) and *tortitas de camarón* (deep-fried shrimp pancakes). Brunch at Entrepanes Díaz means eggs: eggs Benedict, scrambled eggs and omelets. Among the daily specials there are always meat, fish and pasta options. Desserts are as delicious as the rest of the menu: Amaretto ice cream, *crema catalana* and chocolate marquise are the highlights. Drinks include *caña* (a small glass of draft beer), Spanish red and white wine, French rosé and champagne, Catalan cava and homemade vermouth.

Black-and-white photos, a marble bar and tables, red stools, mirrors and blackboards fill up this little corner joint while the chatty and cheerful veteran waiters offer impeccable service and lively conversation to regulars and newcomers. Businesspeople and the 30-something hipster crowd congregate here throughout the day, giving it a classy and yet informal vibe.

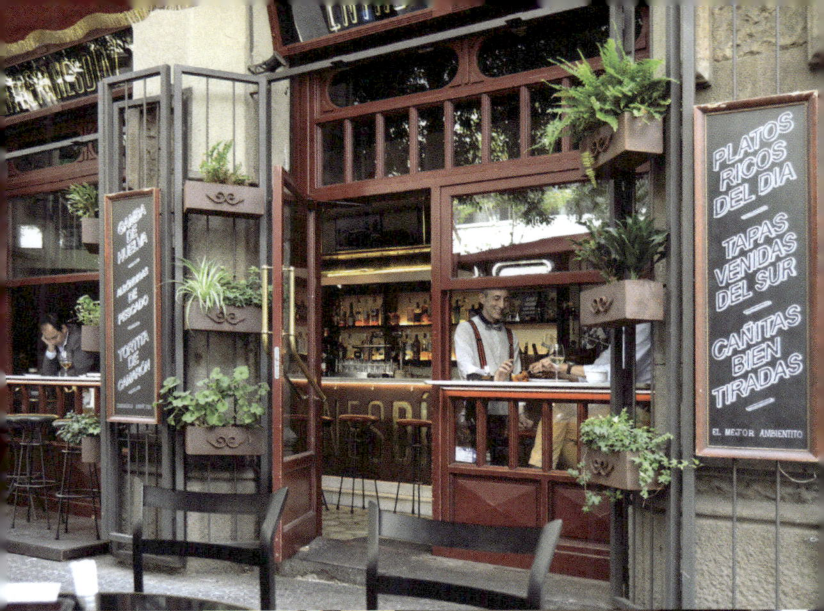
GAMBA DE HUELVA
TORTITA DE CAMARÓN
PLATOS RICOS DEL DIA
TAPAS VENIDAS DEL SUR
CAÑITAS BIEN TIRADAS
EL MEJOR AMBIENTITO

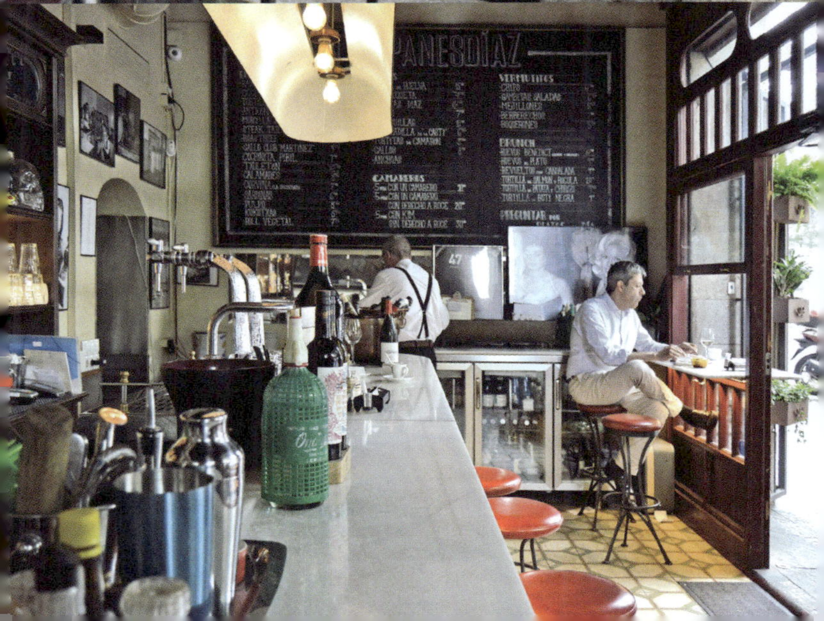
PANESDÍAZ
VERMUTITOS
BRUNCH

GATBLAU

Vegetable Worship

Address: Comte Borrell 122,
L'Esquerra de l'Eixample
Telephone: +34 933 25 6199
Hours: Tues. 8:30pm-midnight;
Wed.-Sat. 1pm-5pm &
8:30pm-midnight;
closed Sunday & Monday

Vegetables often get short shrift at restaurants – greens, legumes and tubers are relegated to being the same tired sides or become just one component of many, lost in the sauce. Not so at GatBlau (BlueCat in Catalan), located in the Left Eixample. This restaurant is a shrine to vegetables, showcasing them anew in all their complexity. Here, the personality of a parsnip, a kohlrabi or any other delicious weirdo from the garden is taken to the next level, refashioned into carpaccio, cake or even rillettes.

Back in 2010, "nobody thought that a good top restaurant should also be conscious with their products," GatBlau co-owner Pere Carrion says. But by 2013, his new restaurant was certified as Km0, a Slow Food designation for food that has been locally grown and produced. In the restaurant's open space, with its natural colors and easygoing atmosphere, they serve up almost exclusively organic products – not just vegetables but also meat and fish, although they are used sparingly.

Over the last decade, GatBlau has matured, developing Pere's personal Km0 philosophy, which resulted in good food, into a higher gastronomic concept: creating dishes that spotlight one seasonal vegetable in all its unique glory. Some of their creations mix land and sea, including a green hummus made of chickpeas and Galician algae. Sometimes they get creative with traditional meat dishes, like their fennel *fricandó* (originally a stew of thin beef filets with St. George's mushrooms) and parsnip rillettes with Marcona almonds.

On a recent visit, we loved their creamy and luscious gnocchi made of sweet potato and served with aromatic *rossinyols* (Cantharellus cibarius, a mushroom that is very common in Catalonia) and a chestnut pesto that gets its zing from a subtle touch of garlic. It's true vegetables are having a moment, gaining new importance on our tables and in our restaurants, and GatBlau is giving tasty shape and color to this renewed gastronomic world.

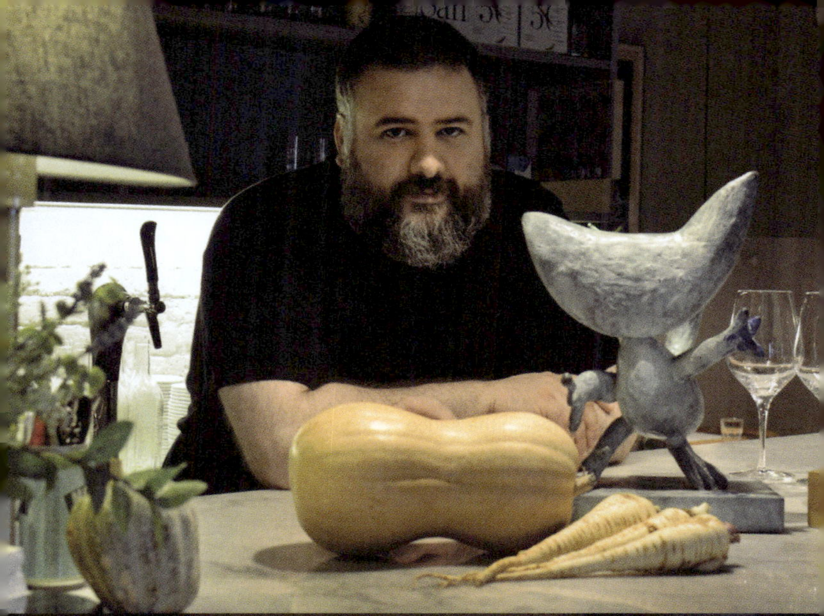

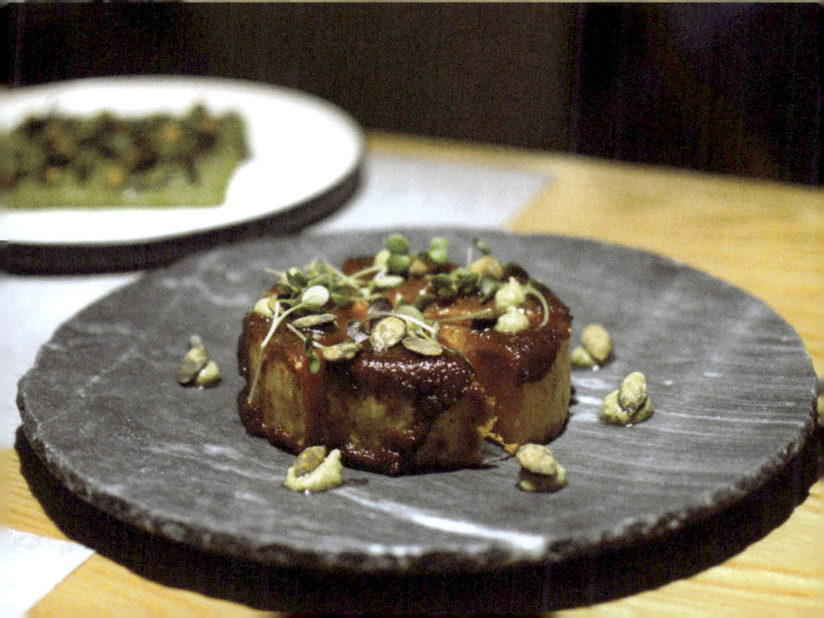

PIRINEU EN BOCA

Address: Carrer Girona 17,
L'Eixample
Telephone: +34 931 29 6987
Hours: 1pm-5pm & 7pm-11pm

Down the Mountain

There are many legends and myths surrounding the Pyrenees. Some claim that the divine hero Hercules created the mountains by piling up rocks as a tomb for his love Pyrene. While a romantic story, the Pyrenees are much more than a symbol of mythic love – they are also the birthplace of Basque culture, crisscrossed by Roman roads and architecture, a key point in the Camino de Santiago and a legendary land for the Catalans. More importantly for us, we find an equally rich culinary culture of edible treasures produced in a still pristine natural environment.

It was an intense process to find and select all the different vinegars, marmalades, yogurts, honeys, wines and amazing cheeses with PGI (Protected Geographical Indication) recognition for restaurant-shop Pirineu en Boca ("Pyrenees in the Mouth"). Even harder still was sourcing free-range meat – the restaurant's specialty – from different mountain hamlets. In total, they work directly with around 70 producers.

Diners can choose from a menu of tapas and sharing plates or a menu of meat and fish mains. There is also the option to select your cut of meat from the butcher and have it cooked right there. We went with the specialty, and while we were slicing through the tender beef, which had been grilled to rosy, juicy perfection, dressed simply with some salt from Basque Country, we saw other dishes flying out of the kitchen; the grilled pork loin of a Latón de la Fueva pig, served with rice and caramelized pears, caught our eye.

But not everything here is meat. We also had a succulent eggplant stuffed with veggies. And for dessert, there are artisanal cakes and exclusive mountain dairy products, like Pyrenean ice creams and yogurts. The Herculean love for the Pyrenees can really be tasted from start to finish.

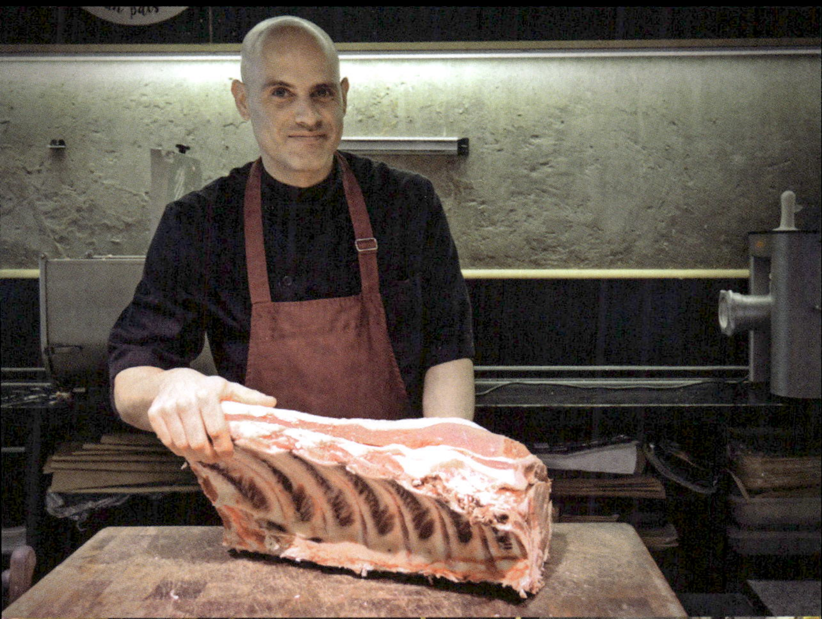

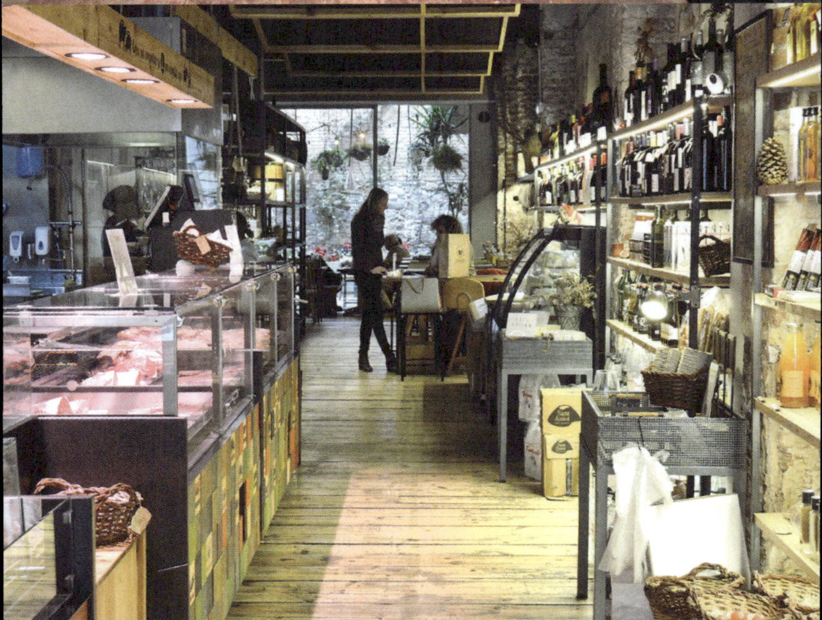

PULPERÍA A GUDIÑA

Address: Carrer d'Enteca 2,
Sant Antoni
Telephone: +34 93 426 5631
Hours: 11am-1am;
closed Sunday

Pulpo Paradise

An icon, a national symbol venerated by Galicians and Spaniards across the country, *pulpo* is more than just a staple food. In Galicia, the autonomous community in northwest Spain, octopus is consumed at traditional village fairs and is sold on weekends at street stalls. In cities all over Spain, there are temples fully dedicated to the octopus culinary cult, specialized pulpo restaurants called *pulperías*. Pulpería A Gudiña, located in Sant Antoni, is one of those shrines in Barcelona, a place where *pulpo a la gallega* (fair-style octopus with potatoes) is the most frequently ordered dish and at the heart of the restaurant's origin story.

What owners Jose Luis Sierra and Andrés Flórez knew best was how to reproduce this magnificent tradition of the Galician pulperías, and they have been doing just that at A Gudiña. Here, the cephalopods are boiled to perfection in a large copper pot, then served a la gallega – cut in slices with potatoes, served in a wooden dish with paprika and olive oil, and available in three different sizes, from a little tapa to a big plate to be shared. You can also order octopus in *salpicón* (a kind of vinaigrette salad with onion, tomato and capsicums).

The rest of the menu, closely supervised by Jose Luis and Andrés in person, is based on small plates and tapas to taste and share, and has expanded to explore the diversity of traditional Galician Atlantic recipes beyond octopus, plus a few Mediterranean dishes like the grilled *tallarinas* (clams) or the cod *esqueixada* (desalted cod salad). They also serve other seafood such as grilled razor clams, cockles, mussels, oysters and velvet crabs.

Here you can also try some of the most classic Galician comfort foods, as well as seasonal delicacies like hake eggs. The extensive menu is best washed down with Pulperia A Gudiña's house wine served in traditional clay jars – just another of the many touches of Galicia.

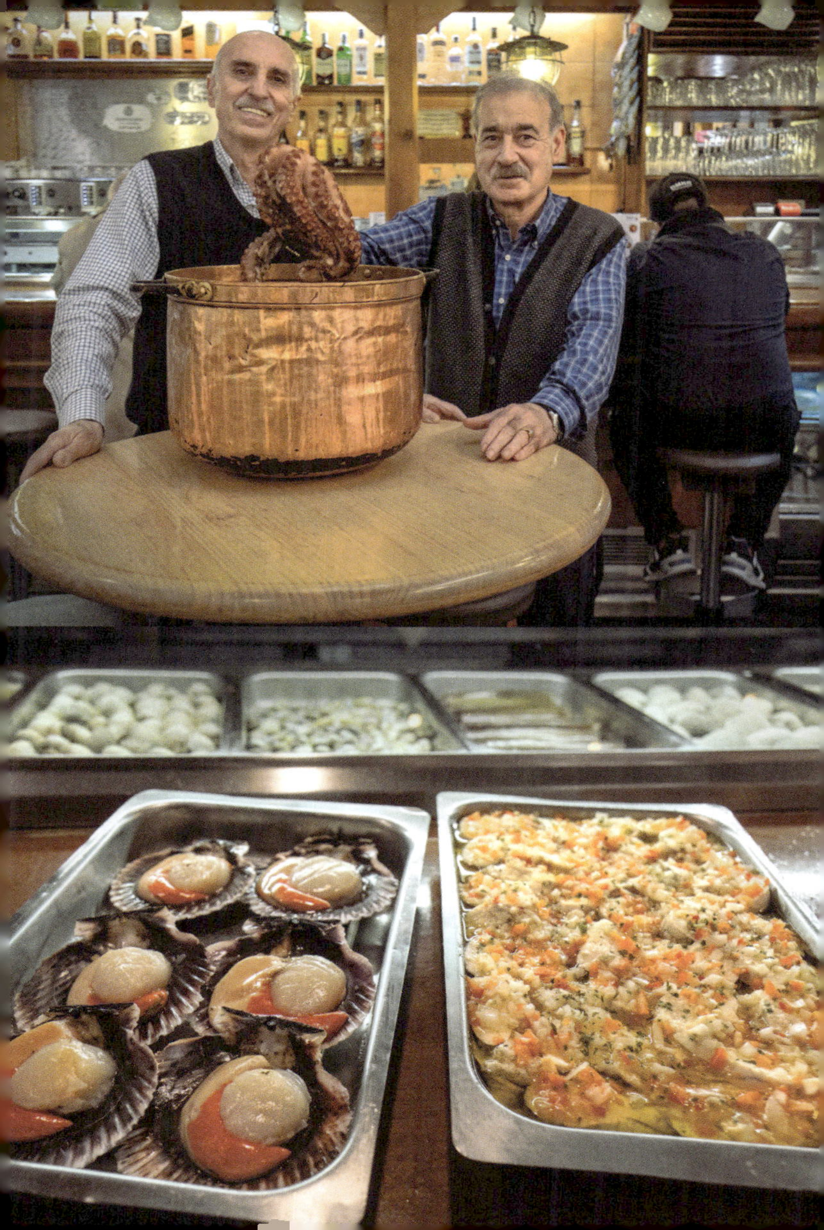

SENSE PRESSA

Address: Carrer Enric Granados 96, L'Eixample
Telephone: +34 93 218 1544 (reservations required)
Hours: 1:30pm-5pm & 8:30pm-11pm; closed Sunday & Monday

Stress-Free Dining

In 2005, José Luís Díaz was thinking about retiring after working for many years in great local restaurants. He wanted to leave behind the stress of big kitchens and get to cook the recipes that he loved with a different rhythm and with more time and care. And so he opened Sense Pressa (literally "Unhurried"), a cozy, modest eatery, along with his son and sommelier, Víctor, who runs their small wine shop around the corner.

Each night, José Luís and his team cook around 25 covers (by reservation only) in a single, leisurely seating for customers who come from all over the city to eat in Sense Pressa's comfortable, welcoming atmosphere. Here, the solicitous attention and the unhurried tempo are both important parts of the meal.

The cuisine is based in Spanish multiregional traditions, with that magic combination of simplicity and remarkable ingredients that follow the seasons. Lamb, pork, and Atlantic and Mediterranean fish and seafood from the best sources are given classic treatments that have been thoughtfully reconsidered to improve the dish and the experience. José Luís offers a fixed menu and also a roster of dishes that change daily and with the season.

The local favorite is the absolutely wonderful dish of chickpeas with a "broken" fried egg and *espardenyes*, a kind of sea cucumber. José Luís invented the dish, taking as inspiration another seafood-legume combination, the classic clams with beans. The chickpeas are profoundly luscious and creamy. The egg unifies all the ingredients but also allows their individual identities to shine. The sea cucumber has a much more intense flavor than that of clams, and so calls for a counterpart that can stand up to it – hence the chickpeas.

Among other great dishes we enjoyed recently at Sense Pressa was the succulent lobster salad, featuring shelled European lobster from the Cantabric. Surrounded by lettuce and cherry tomatoes, it comes dressed with a magic white truffle vinaigrette, made with Jerez and Modena vinegars and olive oil. José Luís manages to keep the dish refreshing and aromatic, delicately balancing the cloak of truffle. It's yet another reason to linger at the table.

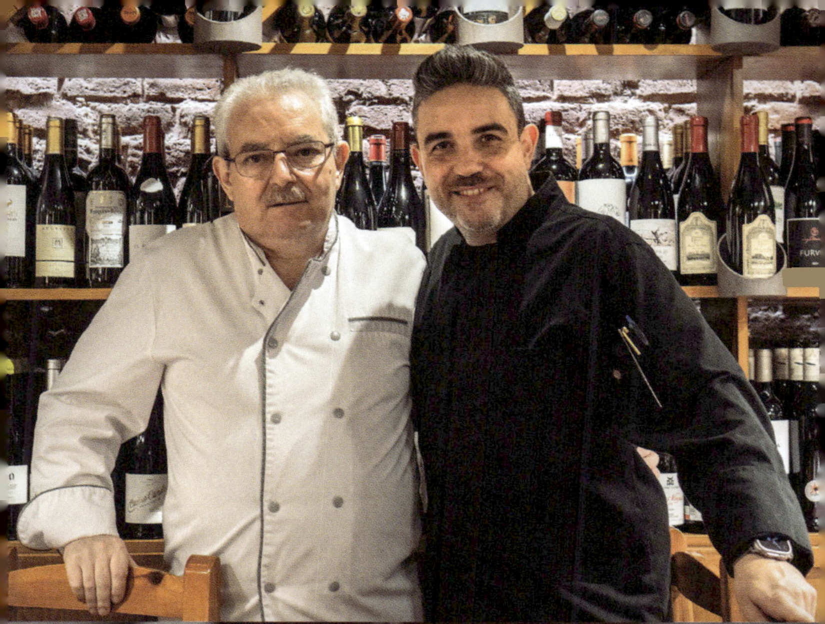

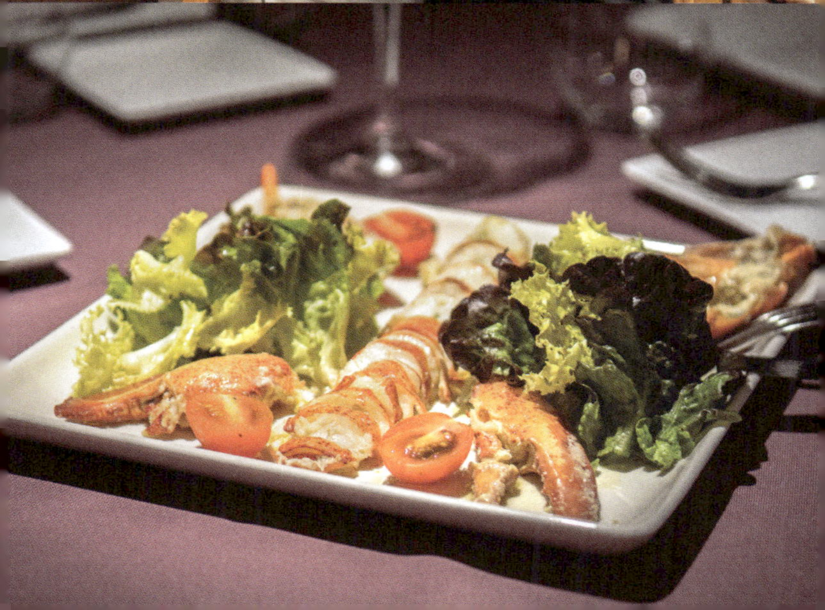

TAKTIKA BERRI

Address: Carrer de València 169, L'Eixample
Telephone: +34 93 453 4759
Hours: 1pm-4pm & 8:30pm-11pm; closed Sat. night & Sunday

Always a Party

Taktika Berri, a family-run Basque restaurant, specializes in *pintxos*, tapas affixed to a piece of bread with a toothpick and traditionally presented open-air, on plates spanning the length of the bar. Patrons are handed an empty plate and are free to help themselves. Once you have finished, simply mosey up to the register and the *camarero* will count the number of toothpicks, or pintxos consumed.

A pintxo crawl is a fine start to an evening, so order a Txakoli — a cloudy white Basque wine that pairs well with olives or anything from the ocean — and dive in.

With tumbler in hand, sidle up to the bar and try *la gilda*, the quintessential pintxo: anchovy, olive and guindilla pepper. Next, look for its cousin, featuring *boquerones*, roasted green pepper and egg, plus a dollop of mayonnaise, vinegar and herbs. The foie gras we tried was rich, buttery and smooth – in a word, excellent. The *tortilla de bacalao* was oily but tasted light; it was so popular, it flew off the plates. *Morcilla*, a thick black sausage made of pig's blood, rice, onions and spices, was served with a smoky salsa with a note of chipotle, a perfect complement. Though not our favorite, *xistorra*, a spicy Catalan sausage made with paprika, is a less-adventurous option for carnivores.

The bar is as important if not more so than the *comedor* in the back, which serves more filling dishes. Some of the *platos estrellas* from the restaurant include *tortilla de patatas / bacalao* (Spanish potato / cod omelet), *pochas* (white beans), *tronco / cogote de merluza* (hake) and *chuletón* (chops). Reservations are required, so call in advance. Eating at the bar is permitted during the day, but at night, service is restricted to pintxos. Get here early because, from the second the door opens at 8:30 each evening, the bar teems with locals anxious to bite into the best Basque tapas in town.

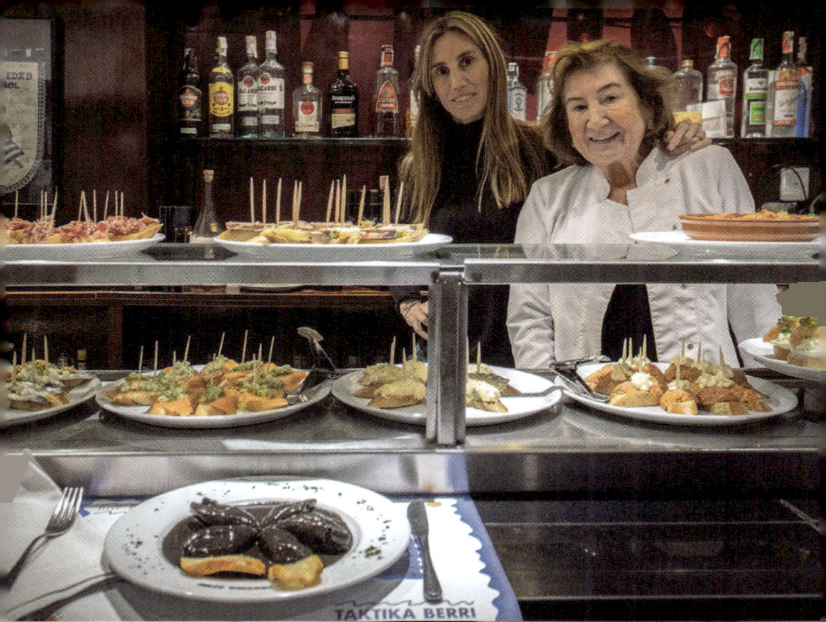
TAKTIKA BERRI

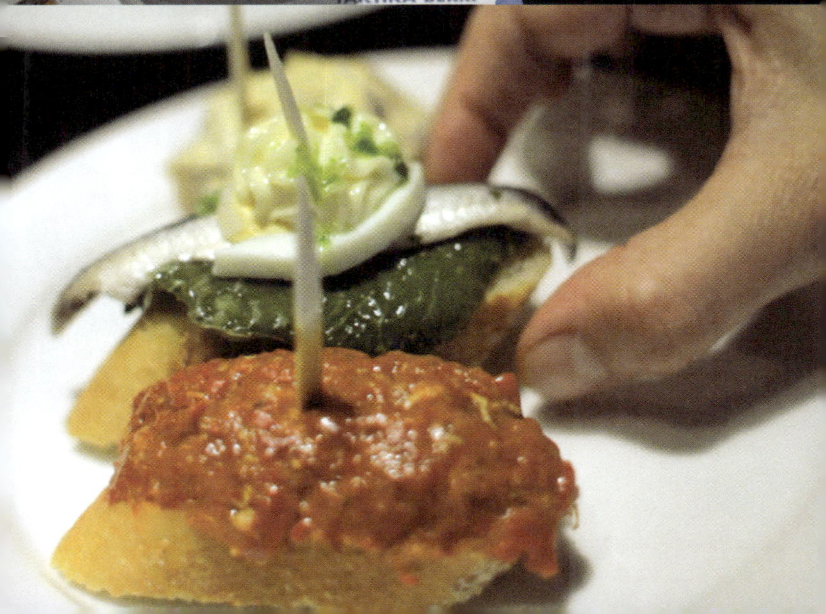

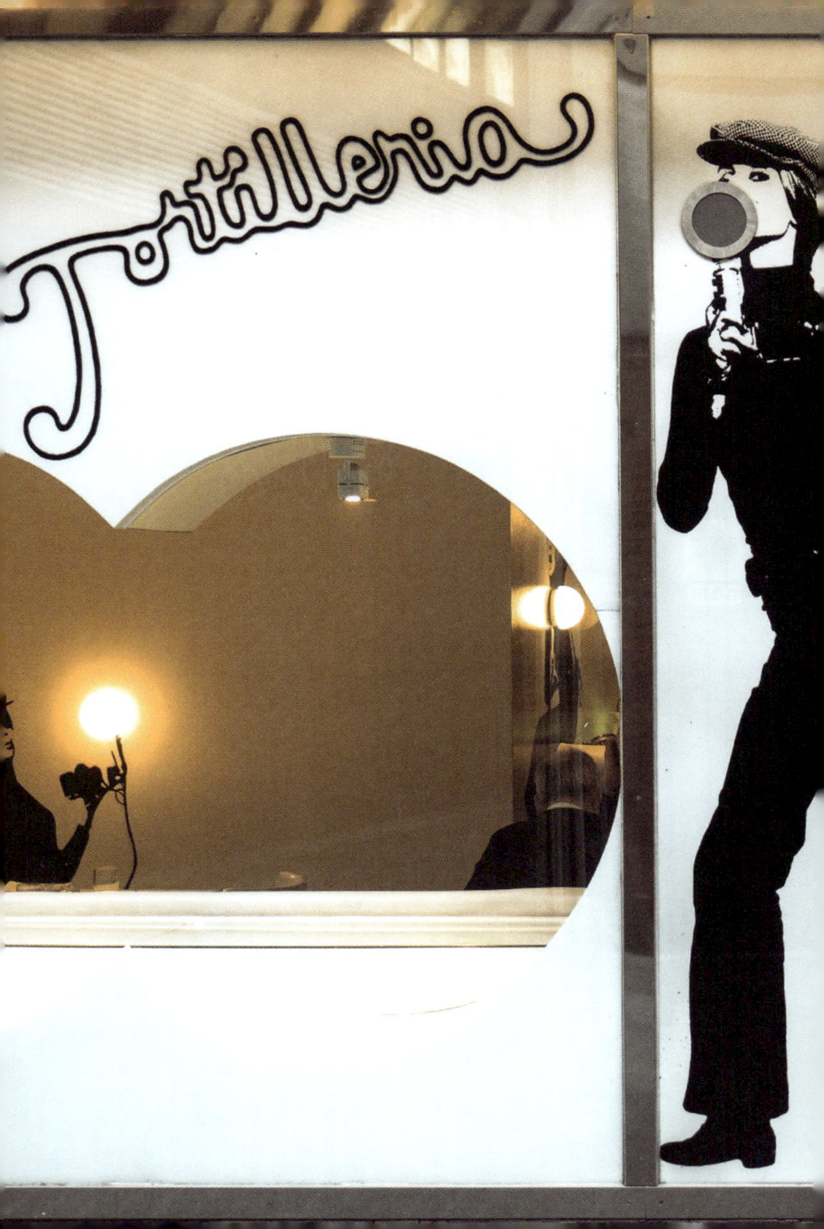
Tortilleria

GRÀCIA & UPPER BARCELONA

AGRESTE

Good Weed

Address: Carrer de Funoses-Llussà 2, El Coll
Telephone: +34 93 213 5005
Hours: Wed.-Sat. 1pm-3:30pm & 8pm-10:30pm;
Sun. 1pm-3:30pm;
closed Monday & Tuesday

Up in Barcelona's hills, in the El Coll neighborhood, where the city ends and the sky is cut by the spiky shapes of the pine trees in Collserola Park, Agreste de Fabio & Roser – formerly known as Mala Hierba, or "bad weed" – is sprouting up. Emphasizing sustainability and healthy eating, the restaurant crafts delicious dishes that merge Catalan and Italian traditions with contemporary flourishes.

Brought together on the Camino de Santiago, room manager Roser Asensi and her partner, chef Fabio Gambirasi, created this project in 2017 to immediate praise. Years later, we still hear words of admiration flying around the room over the course of our meal. The menu showcases a respect for ingredients on the part of Fabio, who once worked in a Michelin-starred kitchen in Milan. Though there are many appealing options, we settled on seasonal *calçots*, a special Catalan spring onion, for what we imagined would be a simple first course. However, it was a splendid reconceptualization of a traditional dish. Instead of fire-grilled, the calçots were cooked at a low temperature, the "grill flavor" evoked through smoked herring eggs. Romesco dipping sauce is subbed with a delicate *ajoblanco* ("white garlic") cream, a riff on the popular cold soup of the same name. It was all beautifully topped with *alliaria*, edible fresh flowers that Roser picks in the forest behind the restaurant. Here was the first of many elegantly executed concepts.

The meat main was truly spectacular, equal parts feral and elegant: beef marrow served inside the bone and covered with raw mince made from an organic T-bone steak. The bone sat on top of a piece of scorched cork and burning rosemary leaves, the heat slowly cooking the meat. For a perfect ending, the pure cocoa and paprika "ice cream" was unexpectedly light and barely sweet. After the meal, we made our way down the hill back to the city, feeling certain that Agreste will continue to grow like a weed, becoming even bigger and stronger on our next visit.

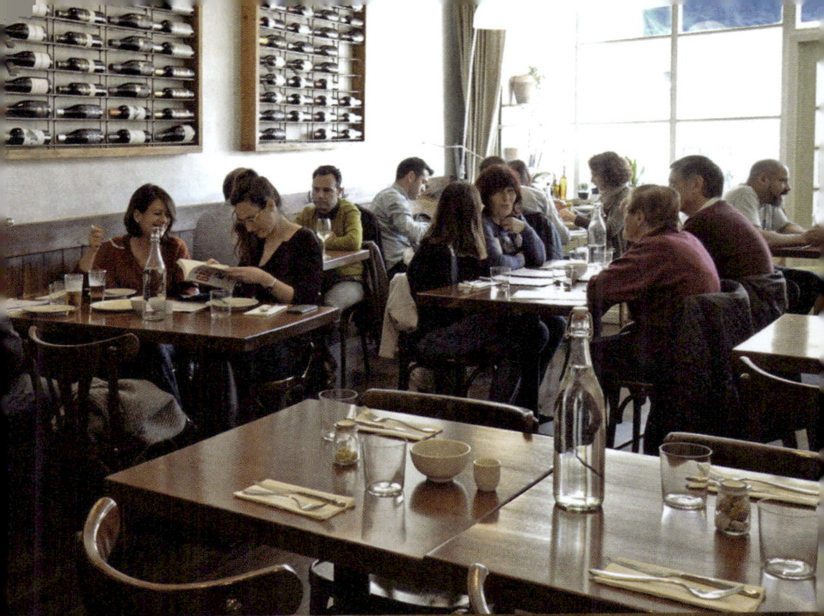
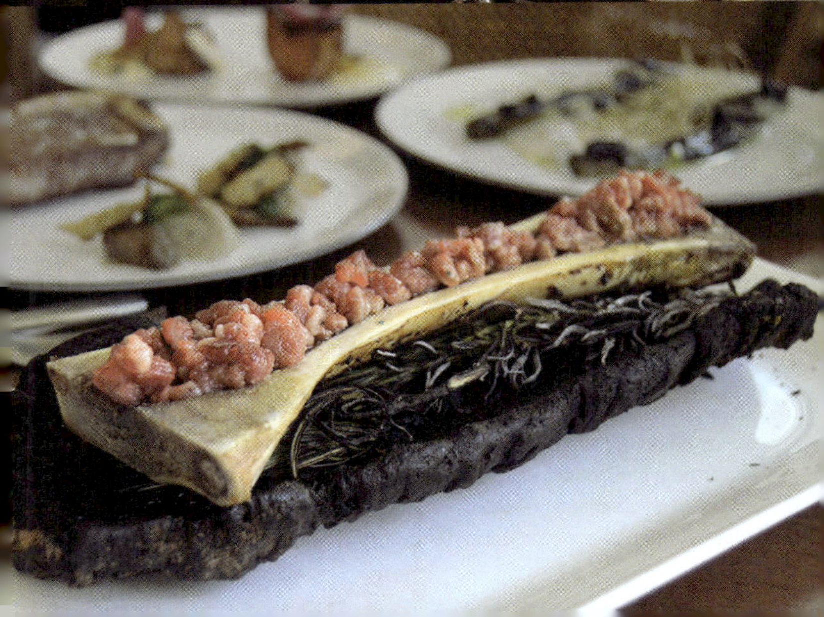

BERBENA

Back to Basics

Address: Carrer Minerva, 6, Gràcia
Telephone: +34 69 195 7797
(reservations recommended)
Hours: Mon.-Thurs. 7:30pm-midnight;
Fri. 2:30pm-4:30pm &
8pm-midnight;
closed Saturday & Sunday

Sure, all the ingredients in Berbena's kitchen are organic, but even the basic ingredients stand out: Water, coffee, beer, wine and, in particular, bread are the shining stars here, not just afterthoughts. Chef Carles Pérez de Rozas is serious about offering elevated versions of these essentials: "I think the basics should be reclaimed as the foundation of the meal pyramid... a wonderful bread or specialty coffee or craft beer [must be offered] on the menu."

After a long career in high-end kitchens, it was in Lima, Perú, that he decided to split off from haute cuisine to return to something "more elemental, more worldly." Carles came back home to Gràcia, the Barcelona neighborhood he grew up in, opening Berbena in a building close to his childhood home.

The specialty coffee at Berbena is provided by the magnificent SlowMov; the beers on tap are light and floral craft pale ales from two Catalan breweries; the wines are mostly natural, organic and biodynamic; the water is purified using a reverse osmosis system and offered for free, a rarity in Barcelona. As for bread, Berbena bakes two kinds with flours from the Cerecinos mill in Zamora.

The cuisine incorporates elements from Carles's varied career, with a Catalan base. The dishes – small plates made for sharing – are constructed according to criteria Carles learned from the masters. One-two-three: two ingredients and a third one to prop them up. For example, the exquisite thinly sliced *cecina* (dried and cured beef, one) is paired with fresh celeriac (two), with a final touch of grated lemon and black pepper (three). Another dish we loved for its evocative power is the Amish tomato and cucumber salad with grated *botarga* (cured fish roe), expressively decorated with nasturtium leaves. The aquatic vegetables soften the ocean taste of the botarga, resulting in a refreshing and succulent experience that is more freshwater than saltwater. Every visit to Berbena is a high class venture that is 100% grounded in the basics.

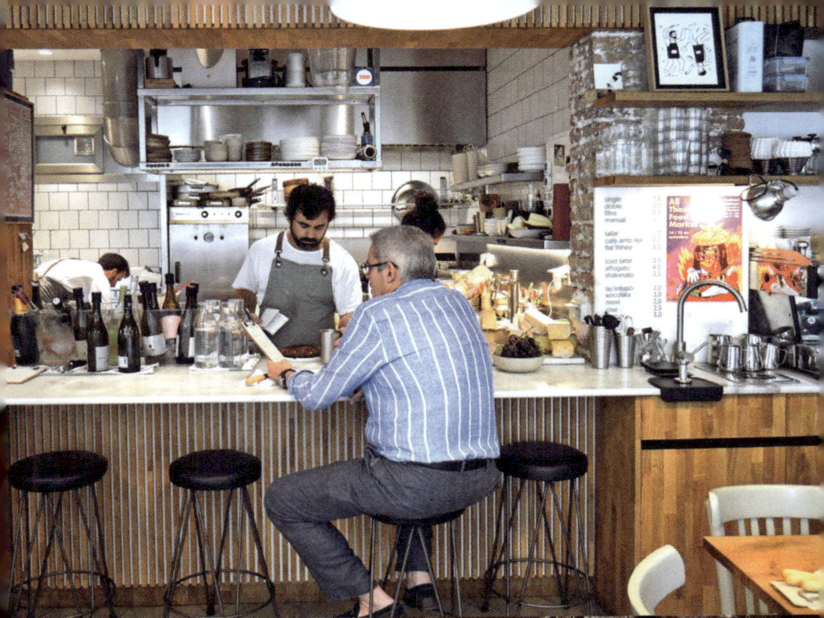
single
doble
filtre
manual
tallat
cafè amb llet
flat White
iced latte 3.5
affogato 4.0
shakerato 3.5
te/infusió 2.0
xocolata 3.0
most 2.0
All
Food

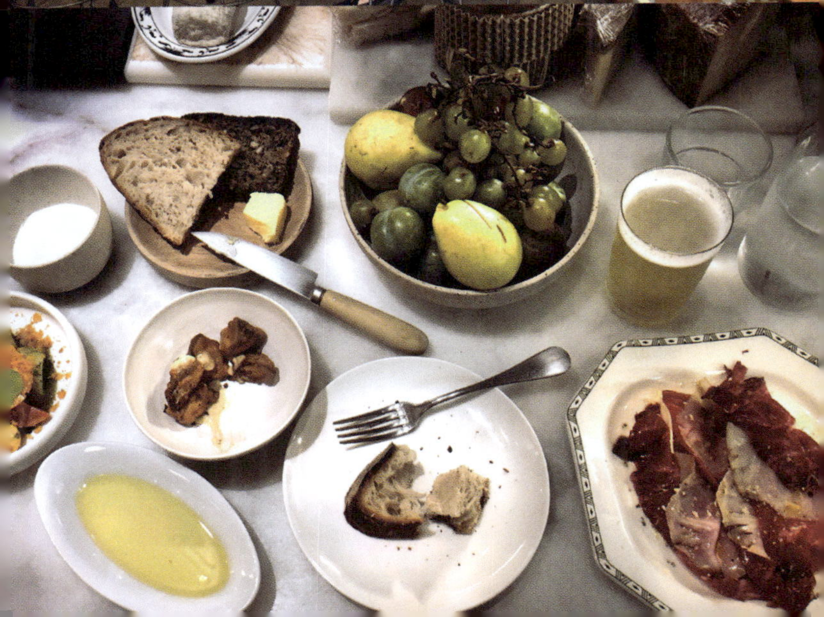

BODEGA MANOLO

Address: Torrent de les Flors 101,
Gràcia
Telephone: +34 93 284 4377
Hours: Tues.-Fri. 10am-5pm;
Sat. 1pm-5pm;
closed Sunday & Monday

More than Meets the Eye

At first glance, Bodega Manolo seems like the usual wine shop/tapas bar that Barcelona does so well: a solid place to replenish our wine stocks from the barrels, quench our thirst with a cold *caña* or satisfy our hunger pangs with a *vermut* and a tapa or two of oil-drenched anchovies. None of which sound too shabby. However, at dinnertime, the brilliant white tablecloths in the rear reveal the venue's greater ambitions.

Bodega Manolo is not for the fainthearted or the figure watcher. These are indulgent, rich, yet seriously delicious plates of food from the talented hand of owner Manolo, who learned his trade under Josep Lladonosa, head chef of iconic Barcelona restaurant 7 Portes, as well as during internships in other kitchens. He takes traditional, high-quality Catalan ingredients and serves them in gutsy, generous portions with a creative touch.

Who could resist ordering a plate of *patatas bravas*, here called "anarco bravas." Crispy, chunky-sliced fried potatoes with a moreishly pungent garlic and squid ink sauce are drizzled with parsley oil, tomato sauce and a further daub of briny ink on the plate to scrape the spuds through. A purée of potatoes livened up with a poached egg yolk and a pork trifecta – *jamón* topped with *morcilla* (paprika-infused black pudding) and crispy bacon – goes by the winking name "destroyer," perhaps for the potential effect it might have on the arteries. On a slightly lighter note, there's a dish of elegant, delicate white beans topped with meltingly tender octopus, peppery arugula leaves and more generous smears of that squid ink sauce which surprisingly never gets tiring.

Though vegetable dishes and accompaniments are few, the eggplants cooked on the *plancha* grill with a drizzle of honey and zesty piece of toasted goat's cheese are a delight. But it's the generous portion of pan-fried foie gras in a sweet and tangy sauce of port, braised apples and booze-soaked raisins that is really the showstopper.

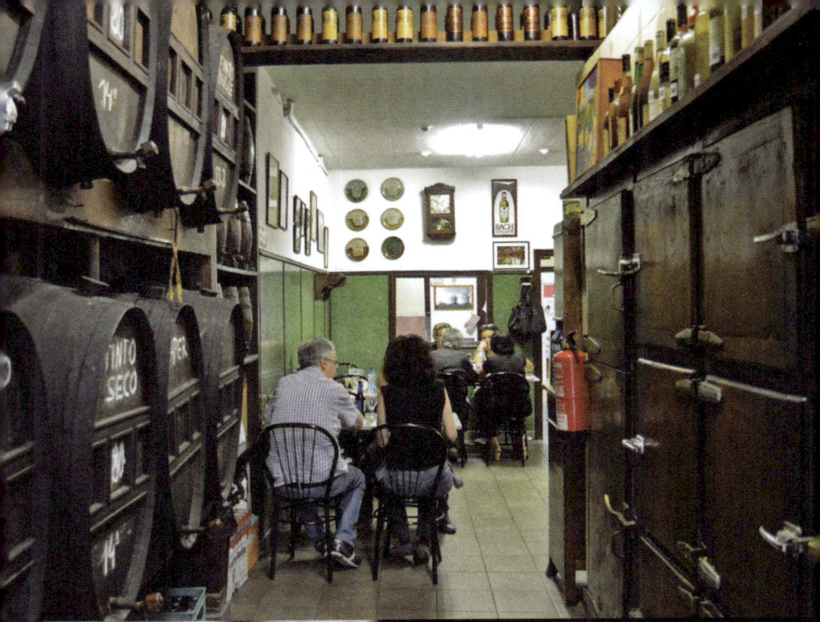
TINTO
SECO
BACH

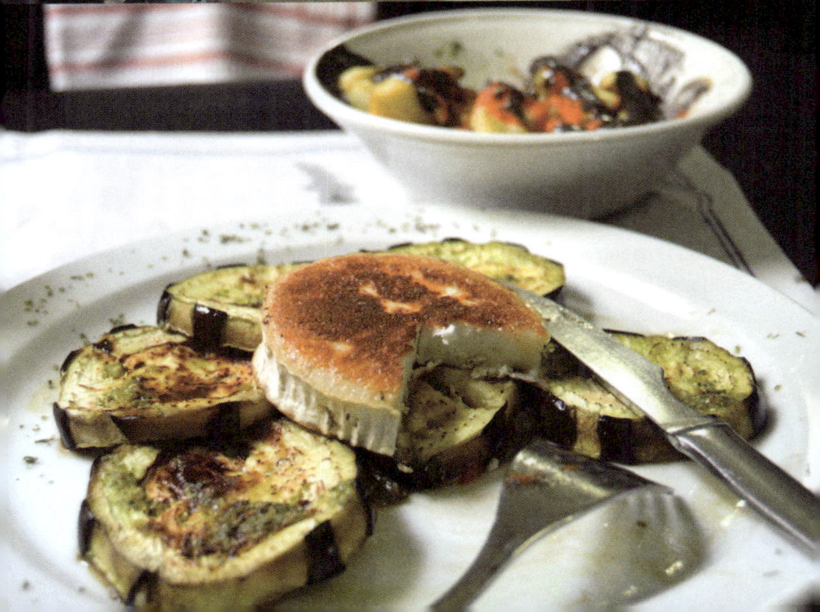

BODEGA PÀDUA

Antiques Roadshow

Address: Carrer de Pàdua, 92,
El Farró
Telephone: +34 932 12 3056
Hours: Mon. 8am-5pm;
Tues.-Sat. 8am-midnight;
closed Sunday

The classic neighborhood bodega in Barcelona is a place where customers feel at home. At Bodega Pàdua, an old bodega turned bar-restaurant in El Farró, this quintessential spirit – usually invisible to the eye – is, somewhat surprisingly, physically manifested on the walls. The long space, which extends to a patio in the back, is decorated with mementos from the community: old photos, antique objects, a claviharp, written tributes to local musicians and house pets, and even pieces of the old iconic SEAT 600 car, which still has lots of fans in Spain.

Most of these objects are the personal belongings of Bodega Pàdua's clients, creating a community spot that is as welcoming as it is appealing. "Neighbors love to come here with friends and say, look, that radio or this photo is mine," says owner Jordi Ratón Sánchez.

The restaurant, like many former bodegas in Barcelona, was originally a bulk wine shop. Jordi's father used to work there before buying the place in 1979. When Jordi took over the business in the 90s, he decided to revive the culinary offerings that were popular when his mom was working in the kitchen. Jordi offers daily specials on weekdays, serving dinner until midnight. The menu also features a variety of traditional dishes like homestyle paella, beef entrecote, *cap i pota*, candied duck or pig feet, plus tapas, salads and *cocas* (Catalan-style flatbreads), drinks and the house *vermut*.

When Moritz, a local beer brand, heard about the vintage city car pieces decorating Bodega Pàdua, they outfitted the bar with a tap made from a SEAT 600 motor. Soon enough, the bodega became the headquarters of Club 600 de Catalunya, a fan club for the iconic car, which was the Spanish version of the Fiat 600. Once a year they celebrate the SEAT 600 with a street party, inviting clients and neighbors to drink beers poured from the car-motor tap.

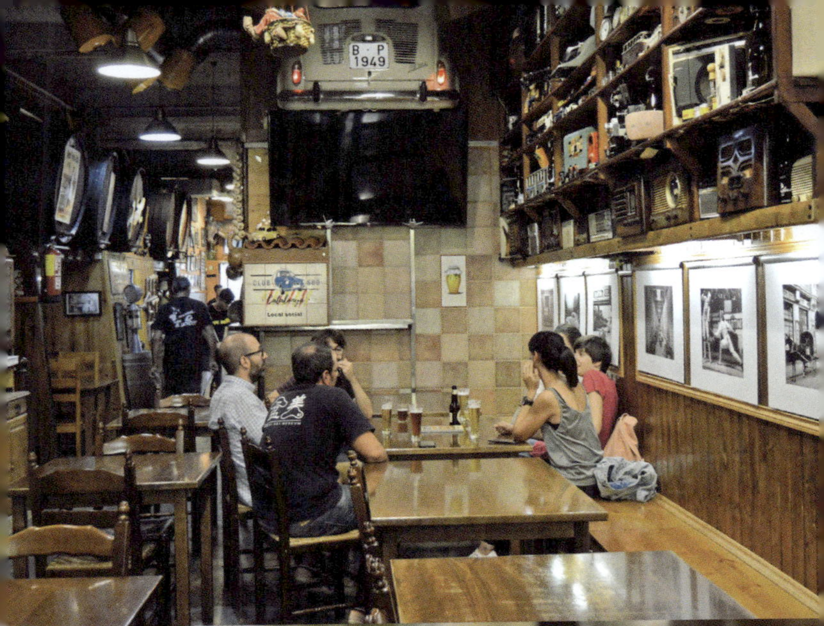
B P
1949
CLUB 600
Local social

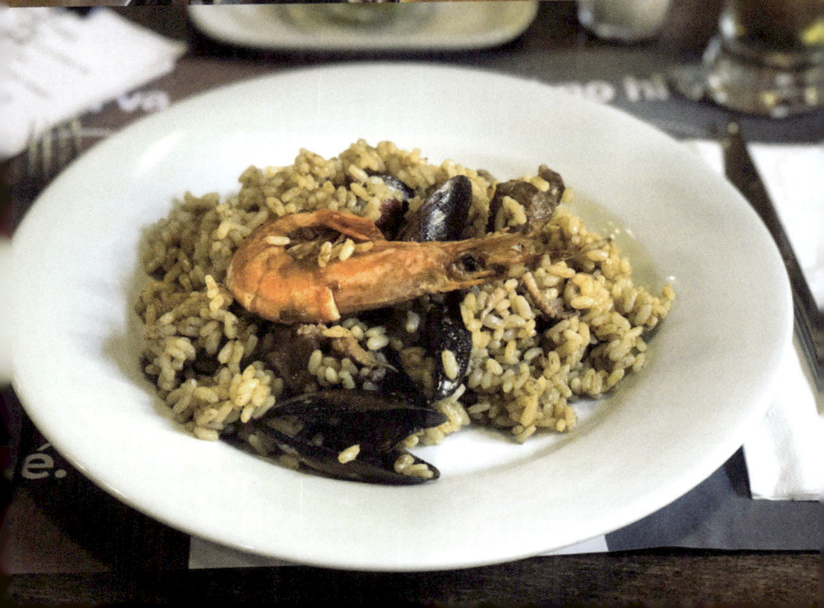

BODEGA QUIMET

Address: Carrer de Vic 23, Gràcia
Telephone: +34 93 218 4189
Hours: 11am-4pm & 6pm-11pm; closed Sun. & Mon. evenings

Same As It Ever Was

De toda la vida is a Spanish expression that basically means "It's been around forever," and it's a sure thing that the locals in Barcelona's Gràcia neighborhood will utter those words if you ask them about Bodega Quimet.

After brothers Carlos and David Montero bought the bodega from the Quimet family in 2010, they made the somewhat unusual decision to keep everything, from the low prices to the décor, pretty much the same as it always had been. In the early afternoon, you'll see many an *abuelo* (grandpa) popping in for a quick apéritif accompanied by the traditional *banderilla*, a variety of olives, artichoke hearts, *piquillo* peppers and sardines impaled on a long stick.

In the evening, the crowd is younger, filling the small space with the loud chatter of good friends sharing stories while sipping drinks and munching tapas. The venue is well known for their high-quality *embutidos* (sausages) and tinned foods, particularly seafood. *Conservas* are a huge part of the culinary culture in Spain and, even in regions where fresh seafood is widely available, they form a significant part of the menu in any self-respecting tapas bar.

We ordered the "Variado Vermut del Quimet," an array of tuna, cockles, razor clams, anchovies and olives accompanied by a basket of *pan con tomate*, or peasant bread rubbed with tomato. Everything on the plate was excellent but the *atún* (tuna) in particular was high-quality stuff – certainly no "chicken of the sea." We also tried some tasty *papas arrugás* ("wrinkled potatoes"), a traditional dish from the Canary Islands that was served with a sumptuous *mojo* sauce made from olive oil, garlic, paprika and vinegar.

It may be a bit early to wonder if there are any little Monteros being groomed for the next generation, but we can't help but hope so. Like everyone else in Gràcia, we fully expect Quimet to always be *de toda la vida*.

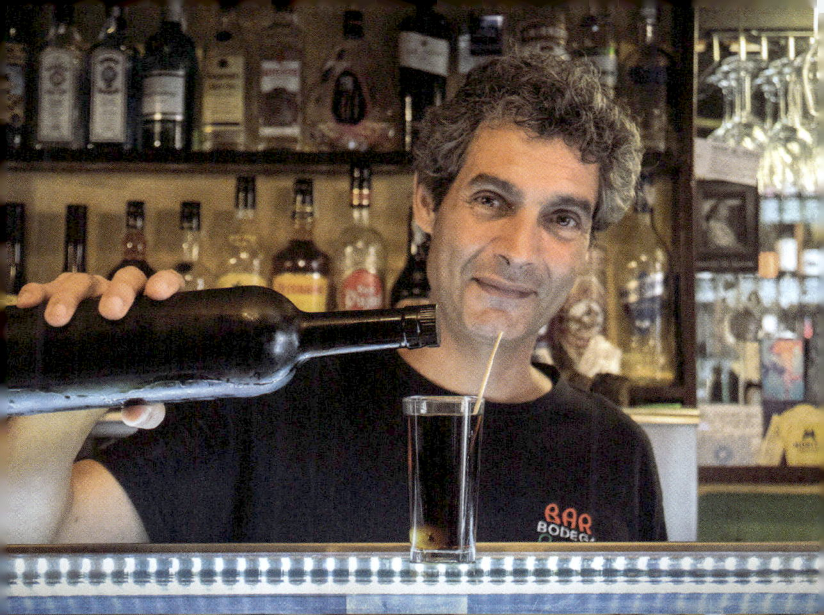
BAR
BODEGA
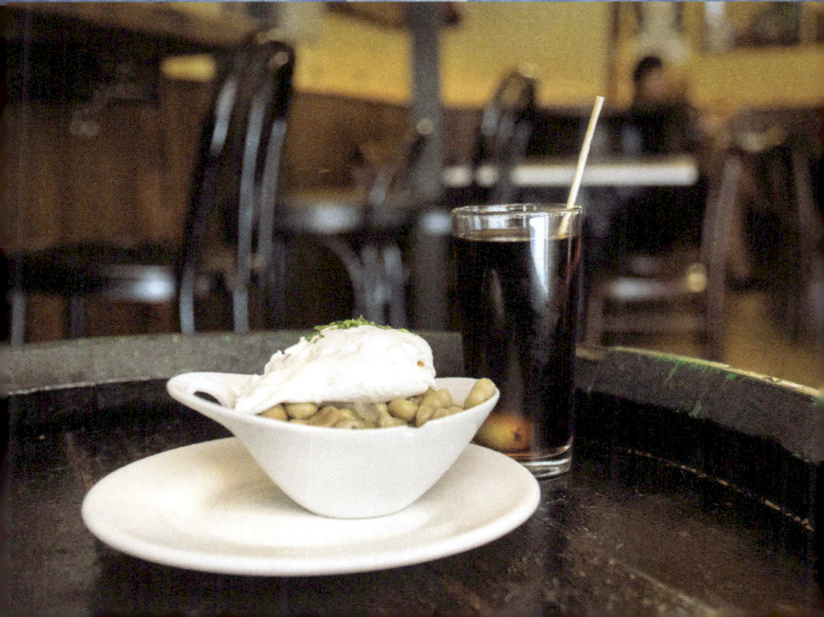

CASA JORDI

Address: Passatge de Marimon 18,
Sant Gervasi
Telephone: +34 93 200 1118
Hours: 1pm-4pm & 8:30pm-11:30pm
closed Sunday

Friendly Takeover

A fine example of a classic 20th-century Barcelona restaurant, Casa Jordi is decorated in the old *masía* (traditional Catalan farmhouse) style over two floors but adapted to urban dimensions. The food, market-to-table cuisine with a seasonal menu and daily specials, is rooted in traditional Catalan cooking. Here, Barcelona's classic dishes blend the popular and rustic, simple and refined. One can see and taste as well the French influences that have been present in the city over the last couple of centuries and that have become integral to local traditions, as well as fundamentally Spanish preparations and ingredients – such as exquisite Basque *kokotxas* (cheeks) of hake or Iberian ham from Extremadura or Huelva.

The formula here remains the same as when the restaurant first opened in 1968: no pretensions, just highly enjoyable, straightforward and excellent cooking in an old-school place with white tablecloths and warm, professional service.

The recipes and presentation, likewise, are virtually the same as they were when Casa Jordi opened, with a few minor differences (a teriyaki sauce, a basket to serve croquettes, a Kobe beef hamburger). Among the essential dishes on the menu are *esqueixada* (shredded salt cod with tomatoes, onions, olive oil and vinegar), the roasted vegetable dish known as *escalivada*, rustic *cargols a la llauna* (snails grilled in a tin casserole), sole and prawns *al cava*, duck *magret à l'orange* with honey and rosemary and *tournedó* with Café de París sauce.

The kitchen delivers on all these and more with a refined hand. The local artichokes were meaty within their light, crisp tempura coat and we loved the grilled squid, which were perfectly tender and flavorful with just a touch of garlic and parsley – a prime example of how lovely simplicity can be.

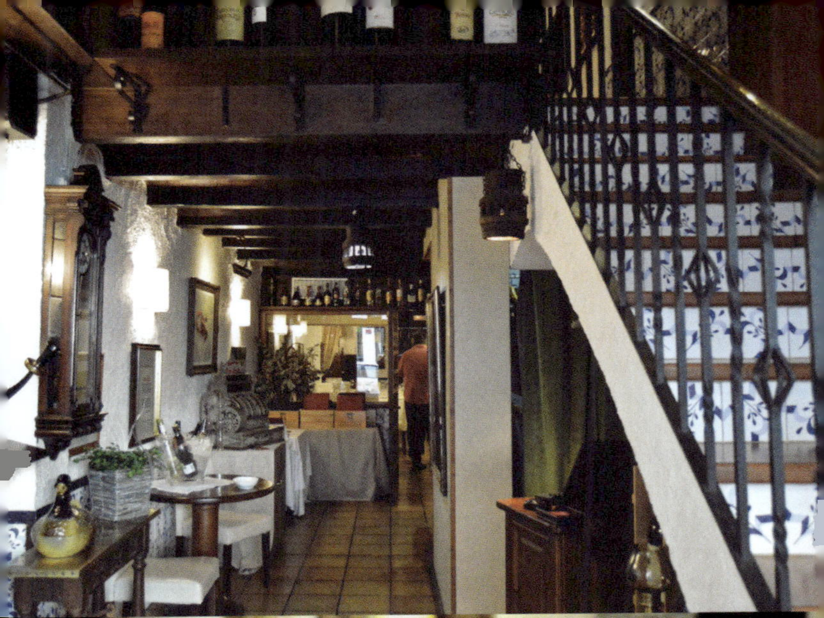

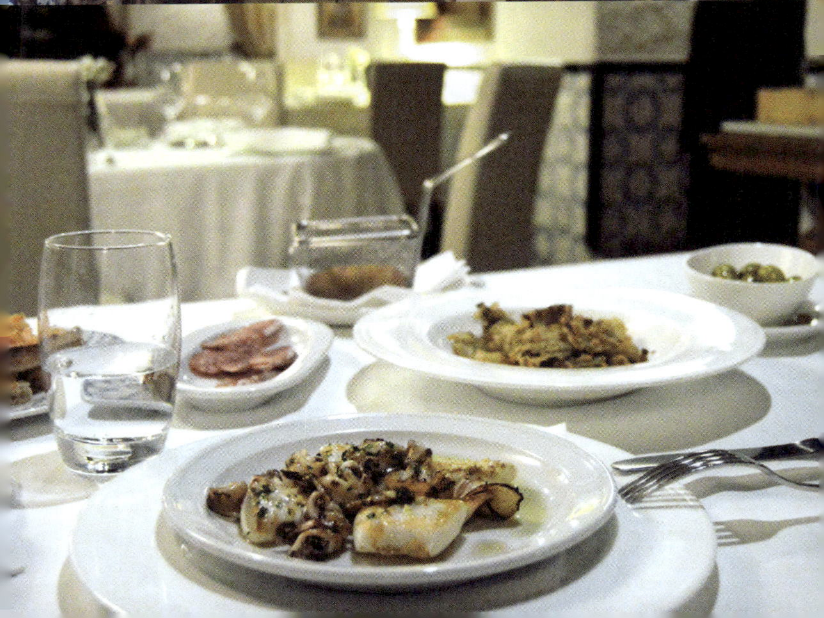

EL RACÓ DEL PEIX

Address: Carrer Tajo 8, Horta
Telephone: +34 93 760 7311
Hours: Sun.-Mon. 1pm-5pm;
Tues.-Sat. 1pm-5pm & 8:30pm-midnight

Market Marisquería

When the neighborhood of Horta (meaning "vegetable garden") was still just a village, it was known for its abundant streams and the bountiful vegetable farms that drank from those waters. A climb up Collserola Natural Park offers some of our favorite sea views, and there's no need to head to water level to find great fish and seafood dishes. The former village's authentic fish corner, El Racó del Peix, is the neighborhood go-to for fresh seafood straight from the market.

The restaurant is like owners Arturo Garzón's and María José Millán's fourth child. With a family history of working in Barcelona's markets, the two understand how any business impacts its community, and they strive to serve their neighbors in Horta. Run out of an old farmhouse – built in 1908 alongside the village's now-disappeared creek bed – the Mediterranean-style *marisquería* is flanked by two terraces ideal for the warm days of spring and fall. Inside the old house there is a rustic charm, every stone, every chip in the paint authentic to the historic neighborhood.

Arturo and María José work with suppliers from all over the Iberian peninsula to source their array of offerings: prawns, lobster and squid from the east; juicy cockles, marinara soaked clams and grilled razor clams from the Atlantic; or the fantastic wild turbot and monkfish from the north. But the real specialty are the rice dishes, from the classic seafood paella or black rice to the *Arròs del Senyoret* ("Little Lord's Rice," made with peeled langoustines).

A must-try that is always present on the menu is the brothy rice with blue crab. The secret of this dish is the powerful flavor of the blue crab fumet, a concentrated stock spotted with onion, tomato, red pepper and cuttlefish. Hunks of crab are nestled into the bomba rice, pairing perfectly with cava or a local white with some body. While Horta may no longer be a rural vegetable patch, we're happy to dine on the fruits of the sea out here.

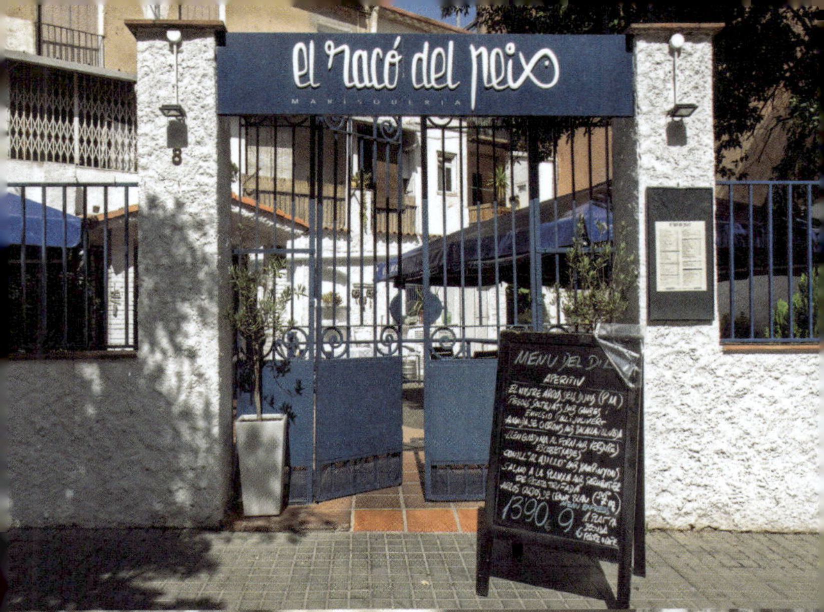
el racó del peix

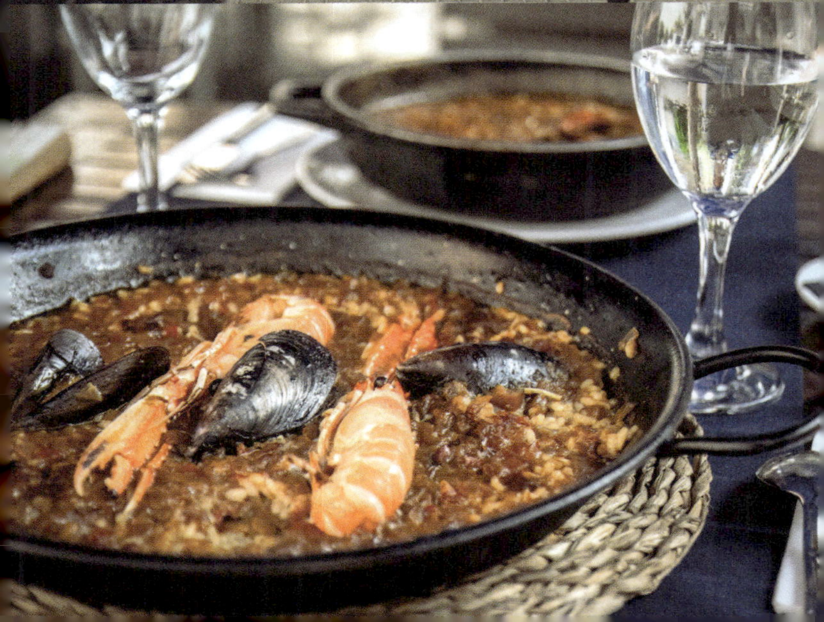

FONDA PEPA

Viva La Kitchen

Address: Carrer de Tordera 58, Gràcia
Tel. +34 932 07 2253
Hours: Tues.-Sat. 1pm-4pm & 8pm-11pm; closed Sunday & Monday

Back in the day, weary travelers in Spain could make a stop at a village *fonda*, a type of inn or tavern, for a hearty meal and a place to rest their heads. Today, in Latin America, fonda has a more contemporary meaning: cantina. Both rely on down-home, no-frills fare. But at Fonda Pepa in Gràcia, Catalan Pedro Baño and Mexican Paco Benítez have taken this concept to new gastronomic heights. The restaurant has the easygoing vibe of a village canteen, with the flavors of a royal kitchen.

The pair of chefs had spent years working in some of the greatest European kitchens – including Barcelona's own Caelis and Lluçanes, as well as Noma in Denmark, all restaurants under the glow of Michelin stars. They've brought that shine down to earth in the long, narrow Fonda Pepa, with its old-school marble tables, lovely back patio and open kitchen.

More than the merging of the chefs' names (Pe and Pa), "Pepa" is a colloquial moniker given to the first Spanish constitution. Like that constitution, Fonda Pepa has a populist touch: its recipes – seasonal, traditional Catalan dishes with Mexican influences – are prepared with premium local ingredients.

Their cooking is well showcased on a short menu of basics. The *patatas bravas* make an impression with a remarkable hint of chipotle in the sauce. Other notable essentials include the ham and roast beef *croquets*, cod *bunyols* (fritters), a rice dish *à la presse* with prawns, and crispy piglet. Not to be missed are the seasonal off-menu specials, which are some of the fonda's most interesting. The flagship dish is their rich *cap i pota* (cow's head and leg) with octopus, served in a compact and gelatinous terrine with splashes of a delicious aioli and poured over with bouillabaisse. For those in the Gràcia neighborhood, the cry of ¡Viva la Pepa! has taken on new meaning.

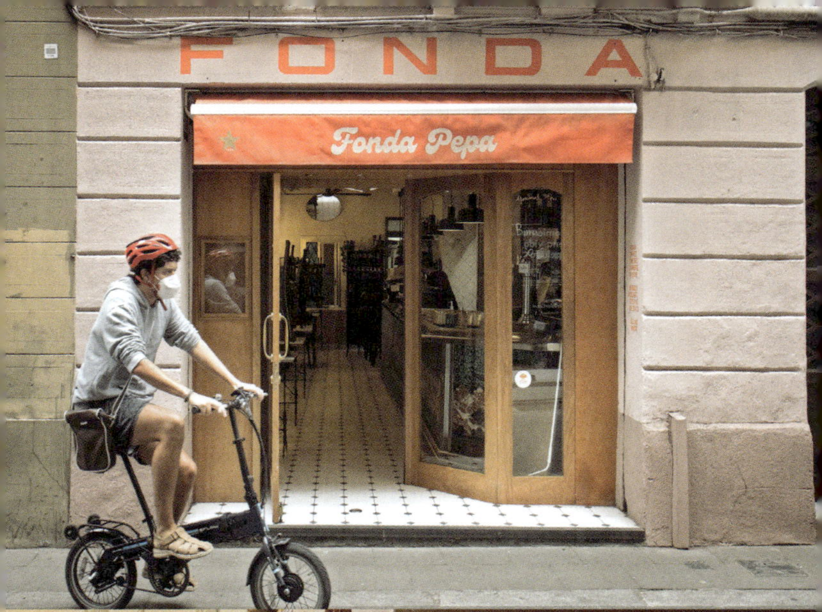
FONDA
Fonda Pepa

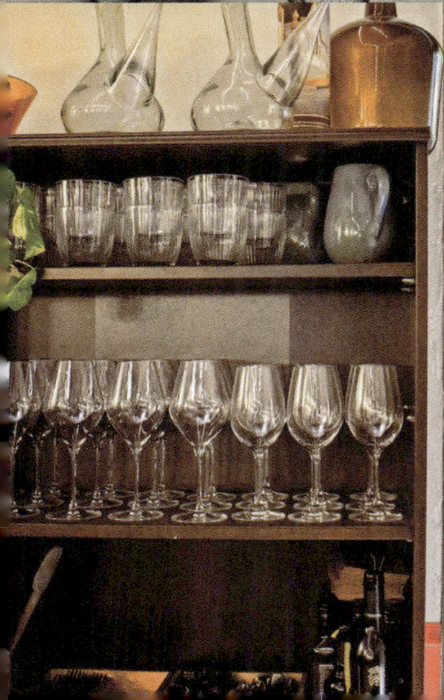

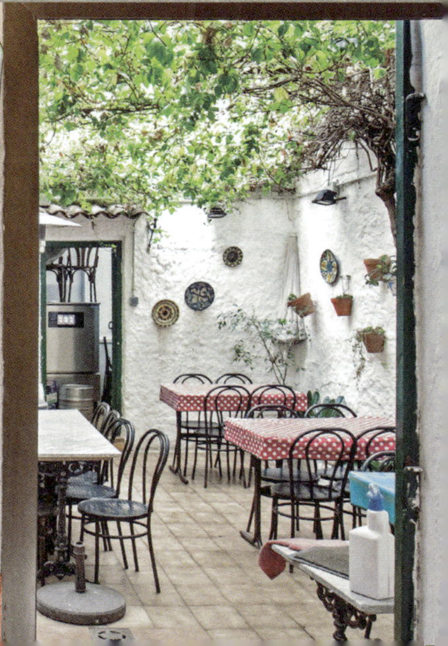

HERMÓS BAR DE PEIX

Address: Mercat de la Llibertat,
Plaça de la Llibertat, Gràcia
Hours: Tues.-Fri. noon-5pm;
Sat. noon-3pm;
closed Sunday & Monday

A Fishy Beauty

The protagonist of the book *El Quadern Gris* (The Grey Notebook), Hermós is a homely, humble fisherman with an ironic name ("beautiful" in Catalan) and a love for *suquets de peix*. This fish stew is Hermós's only relief from the pain of life on the northern coast, a story famously written by Catalan journalist and food writer Josep Pla. Owner of our longtime Gràcia favorite La Pubilla (p. 70), Alexis Peñalver seems to understand Hermós well. So well, he opened Hermós Bar de Peix as a tribute to the magnificence of the Catalan fishing tradition. This is all celebrated with fire, stews, casseroles and bottles of wine in a little bar inside La Llibertat market, right next to its fishmonger.

This market bar used to be an old haunt of ours, before the owner retired post-pandemic. After some consideration, Alexis – whose restaurant is located just outside the market – decided to take over the business and extend the La Pubilla family. In this open space, customers sit on stools around the counter, with a direct view of all the action. We can see orders fly like harpoons from one side to the other. Alexis himself stands at the ready to cut and mix the cold dishes, Carlos manages the grill and Sara expertly selects the wine with one eye on local authenticity and the other on finding something special for each guest.

The majority of the products come from the market itself and Alexis builds daily specials from what is available. Don't miss out on the *suquet de llotja*, fish market stew. The seared razor clams, mussels with lime and grilled red prawns (a wonder from the south of the Iberian peninsula) coexist with more complex (and equally excellent) rice dishes, seafood stews and hot mains. Close your eyes, and the aroma from the grill evokes a Mediterranean fisherman's seaside cottage, where once upon a time the catch of the day was grilled fresh each evening.

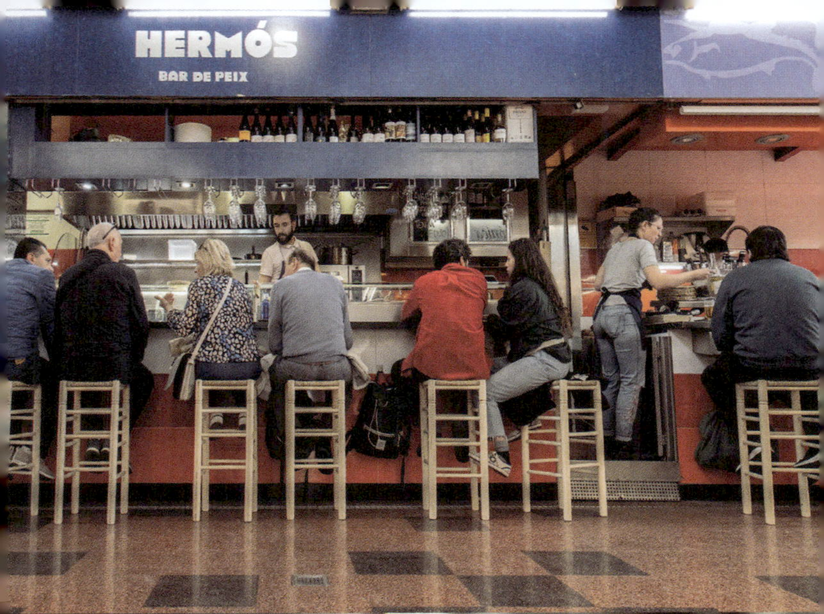
HERMÓS
BAR DE PEIX
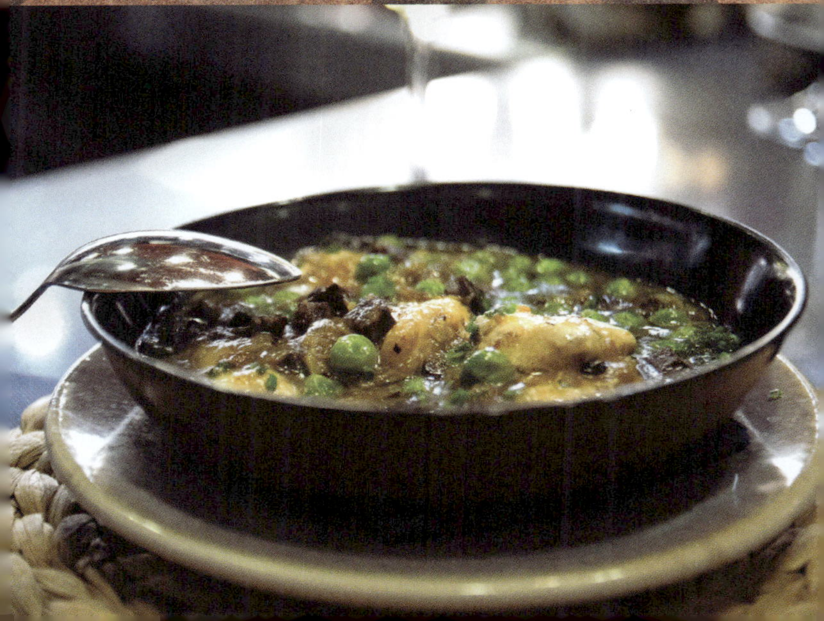

LA ESQUINICA

Little Shop of Tapas

Address: Passeig de Fabra i Puig 29
Nou Barris
Telephone: +34 933 58 2519
Hours: Tues.-Sat. 8am-midnight;
Sun. 8am-4pm;
closed Monday

Despite its name, La Esquinica ("little corner") is no longer on a corner, nor is it little by any measure. But the spirit Jose María Utrillas and his brother-in-law, Paco, brought to it in the 70s is still alive: great tapas, good prices, personable waiters and a familiar neighborhood feeling

The spacious interior is decorated with traditional objects from Aragon, Jose María's homeland, and features an open kitchen. The large street terrace is dotted with umbrellas. The menu is long, with more than 30 tapas plus some seasonal or daily specials ranging from oysters to green asparagus. And even with all that indoor and outdoor space, it is still possible for lines to form on the weekends.

Their specialties cover the spectrum of Spanish classics, from Galician-style octopus to Andalusian *chipirones* (fried baby squid) and Cantabrian anchovies. Of course, there are several Aragones specialties like the celebrated Teruel cured ham, *longaniza* (chorizo) and *morcilla* (blood sausage). Some of our favorites are the more Mediterranean tapas, like *chirlas* or *rosillonas* (small saltwater clams) and *tallarinas* (also known as coquinas clams).

The tapas are cured, fried – like the *boquerones* (fresh anchovies) or the Padrón peppers – or, more commonly, grilled with a classic touch of parsley and garlic, like the mushrooms, the cuttlefish and the razor clams. Only a few require more elaborate preparations, such as the *callos* (tripe stew), the potato omelet, the bombas and croquettes. But Esquinica is famous in all of Barcelona for its *patatas bravas*, preparing around 1,000 kg of potatoes per week. Cut into squares, fried and served with an *allioli* (aioli) and a combination of sweet and spicy paprika, there are no secrets, just quality.

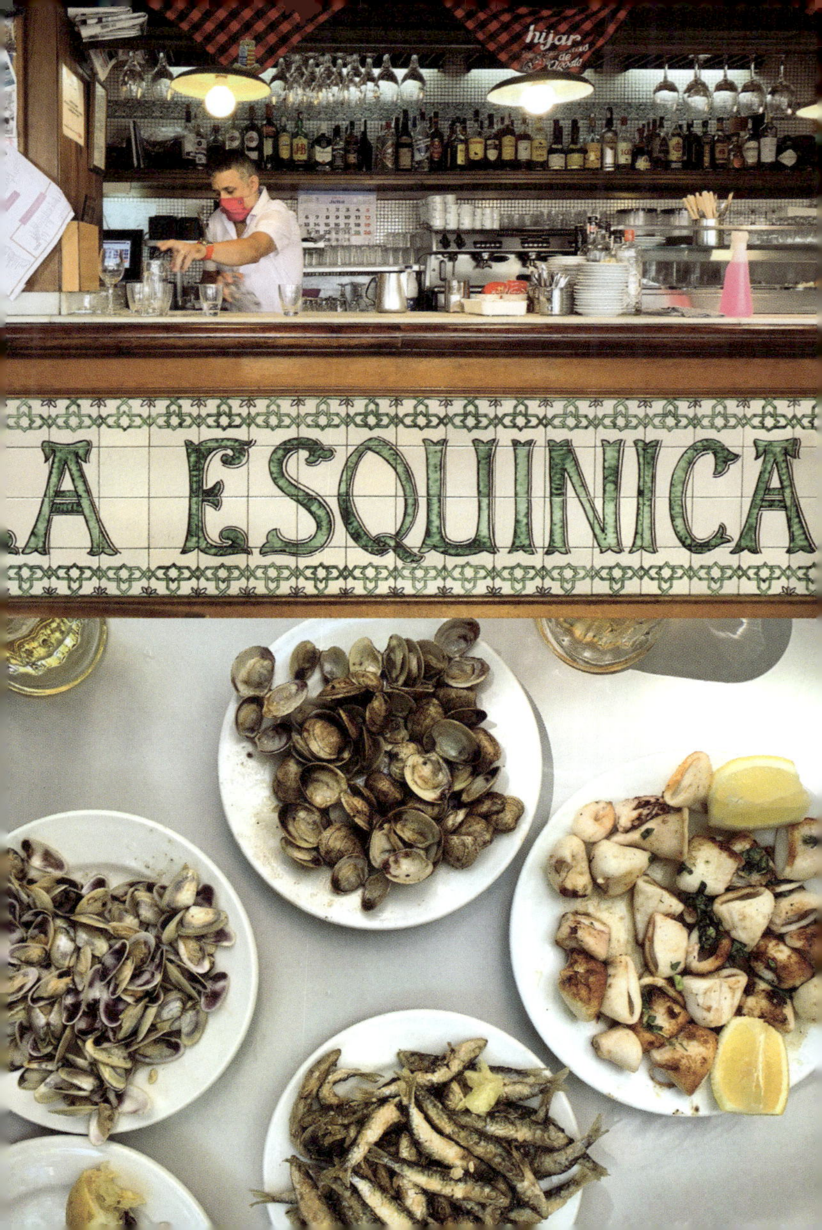
hijar
A ESQUINICA

LA PANXA DEL BISBE

Address: Carrer del Torrent de les Flors 158, Gràcia
Telephone: +34 93 213 7049
Hours: Tues.-Sat. 1:30pm-3:30pm & 8pm-11pm; closed Sunday and Monday

Mountain Man

The Bishop's Belly, La Panxa del Bisbe, is not the midsection of a Catalan priest, but both a restaurant and a mountain. The latter is one of the peaks of the sacred Catalan mountain of Montserrat, so-called because its shape evokes a small head over a rotund, pronounced belly. Chef Xavi Codina loves the mountain so much, he named his restaurant in honor of the peak.

At La Panxa, Xavi has created a menu of almost 30 tapas or *platillos* (small dishes) and four desserts, combining traditional Catalan cuisine with international influences. Much of the menu changes according to season and customers' tastes, but there are a few perennial favorites, such as the homey croquettes, with their generous quantity of chicken and carrots; duck liver with pears and wine; and the *cap i pota*, a traditional dish made from pork trotters and head that Xavi varies all through the year.

La Panxa's seafood specialties are some of our favorites. Xavi respects the unique flavors of his ingredients, coaxing out a delightful intensity in each – especially for such wonderful specimens as the Galician clams. He cooks these with El Prat artichoke hearts and very delicate, almost creamy *mongetes de Santa Pau* (a type of tiny white beans) and dresses the dish with a typical sauce from southern Catalonia, *picada* ("minced"), made with ground almonds and bread. The rockfish soup with clams and mussels is another highlight, a soul-comforting *cuenquecillo*, or "small bowl," enough to have an individual good dose of broth made from rockfish and pieces of monkfish, with a couple of bread slices luxuriating within.

When we're more interested in meat, we might order *picanya* (the Argentinian beef chop) with potato threads and *béarnaise* sauce or the succulent lamb neck with potato and red pepper *escalivado* (meaning "roasted" or "baked"), served with a *pensamiento* (literally "thought" but also the word for pansy), a pastoral touch that harkens back to the restaurant's mountain roots.

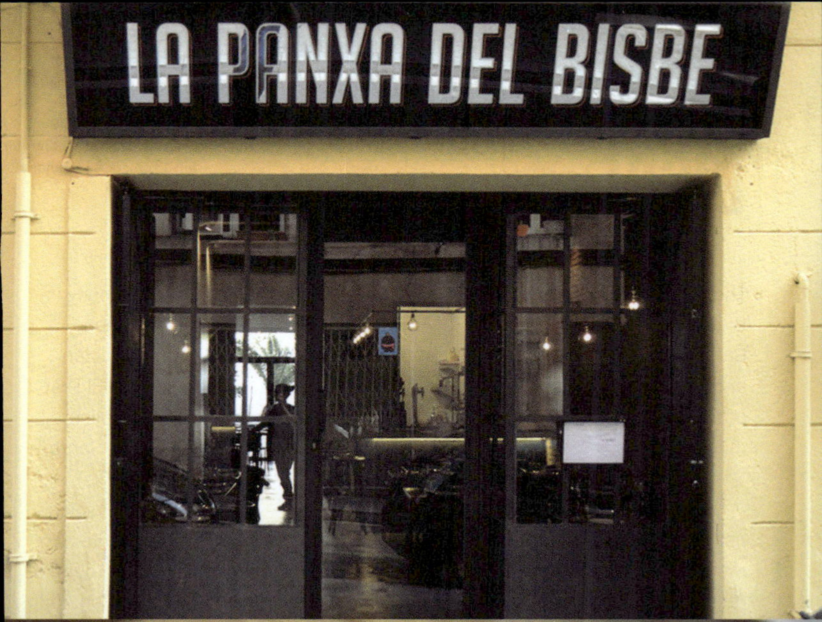
LA PANXA DEL BISBE

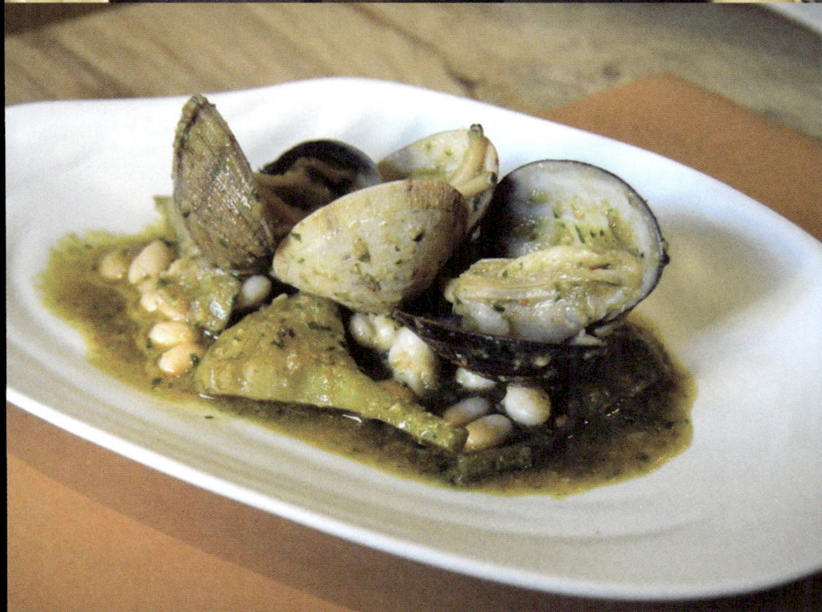

LA PUBILLA

Address: Plaça de la Llibertat 23, Gràcia
Telephone: +34 93 218 2994
Hours: 9am-4pm & 7pm-midnight; closed Sunday & Monday

Destined for Greatness

When chef Alexis Peñalver was looking for a location for his restaurant, he found this gem adjacent to the Mercat de la Llibertat in Gràcia and decided to keep the name of the original establishment. *Pubilla* is a bygone word in Catalan for the eldest daughter destined to receive the family inheritance if there were no male heirs. Nowadays, a pubilla (the prettiest girl in town) is named *reina de la fiesta* at many festivals in Catalonia.

Here you won't find a menu in Spanish or English, only Catalan. This was by design, not only to facilitate seating and ordering, but also to encourage patrons to have a tableside dialogue with the affable staff, commandeered by Dídac Pellicer. He used to work with Alexis at Casa Juliana, where they first met. They decided to open a restaurant together whose focus would be authentic Catalan market cuisine.

Lunch at La Pubilla begins with Arbequina olives, hinting at more local ingredients to come. On one visit, we had *saltat de coliflor amb ibèric i alls tendres*, cauliflower delicately sautéed with bite-sized pieces of *jamón ibérico*, garlic and green onions – a dish that confirms that Alexis is a master at preparing and proportioning ingredients. Raise your hand if you like meat dripping off the bone: *¡Si, señor!* Our second course, *galta de porc amb patates enmascarades*, was a simple yet spectacular combination of perfectly cooked pork cheek and potatoes. For dessert, we grinned ear-to-ear while spooning a homemade *compota de poma i codony*, apple compote and quince jelly. Lunch reservations are required during the week. On Saturday, the format changes from *menú* to *à la carte*, the atmosphere is more relaxed and the pace is slower. And in August, when many businesses shut down for extended vacation, La Pubilla is thankfully one that keeps its doors open.

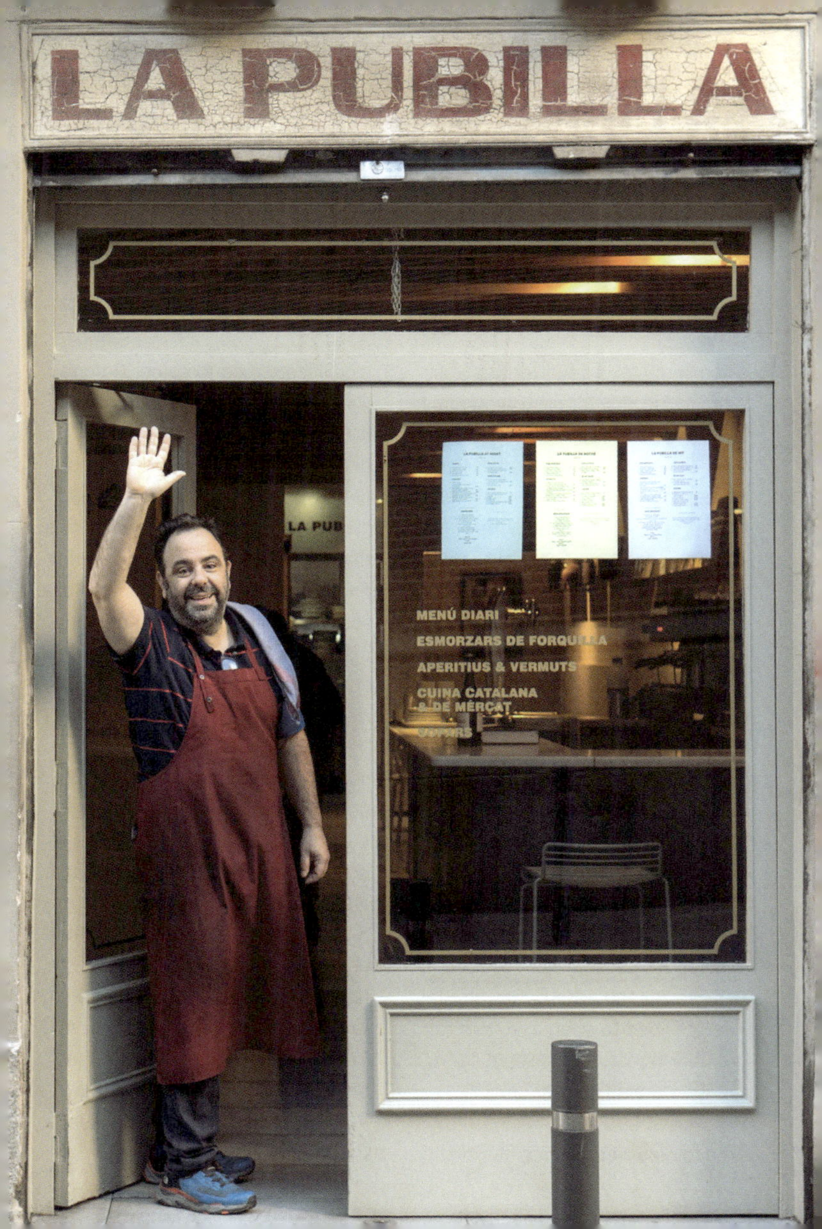
LA PUBILLA
MENÚ DIARI
ESMORZARS DE FORQUILLA
APERITIUS & VERMUTS
CUINA CATALANA
& DE MERCAT

LAS DELICIAS

Tapas with a View

Address: Carretera del Carmel, Carrer de Mühlberg 1, El Carmel
Telephone: +34 93 429 2202
Hours: Tues.-Sat. 10am-4pm & 7pm-10:30pm; Sun. 10am-4pm; closed Monday

Manolo, the protagonist of Juan Marsé's 1965 novel, *Last Evenings with Teresa*, possibly the saddest Spanish romance ever written, spends a great deal of his time drinking and playing cards with the local elders at Las Delicias.

The bar was founded in the mid-1920s using a natural cave that was turned into a bomb shelter during the Spanish Civil War. El Carmel, a working-class neighborhood on Rovira Hill with spectacular views over the city, was home to the Andalusian, Galician, Aragonese, Castilian and Extremaduran immigrants who moved to Barcelona looking for brighter futures during the postwar years. Las Delicias soon became their favorite local eatery, as portions were larger than usual.

Decades later, portions are still very generous, the bar is still a neighborhood institution and the menu still reflects the origins of those who once settled down here. There are Andalusian specialties such as *calamares a la andaluza* (deep-fried squid), *morcilla de Jaén* (pork blood sausage) and *pincho moruno* (marinated chicken on a skewer); Galician specialties like *lacón con cachelos* (boiled pork shank) and *pulpo a la gallega* (boiled octopus); Aragonese *longaniza* (pork sausage) and Castilian *callos* (beef tripe stew).

But if there is a tapa that makes it worth the trek – El Carmel is renowned for its steep streets and the lack of access to public transport – it's the *patatas suizas*. Fried potatoes served warm with spicy romesco (instead of tomato sauce) and a less garlicky aioli, the result is milder than the classic brava sauce but equally yummy.

A good way to burn off the calories inevitably gained with Las Delicias's tapas is to go for a stroll to the El Carmel bunkers, which offer arguably the best viewpoint in Barcelona and are little known to tourists.

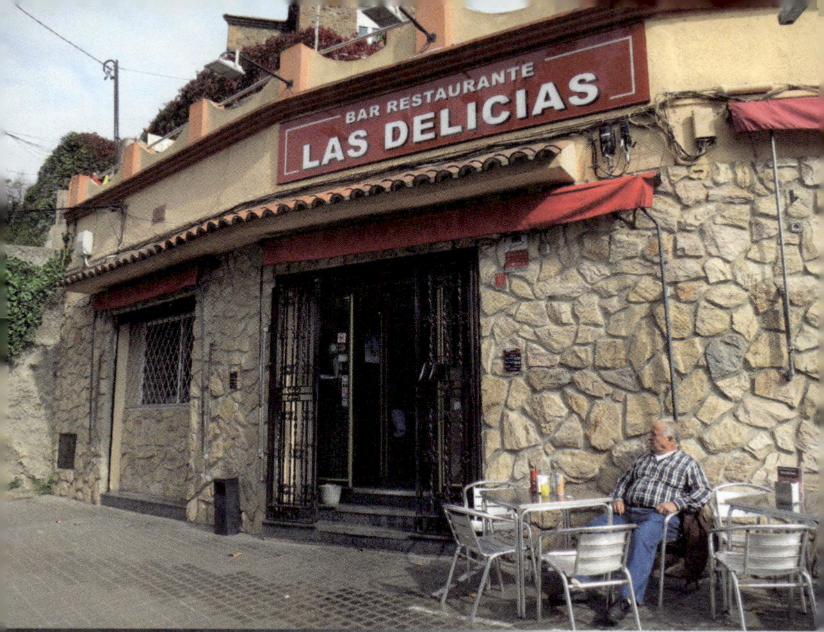
BAR RESTAURANTE
LAS DELICIAS

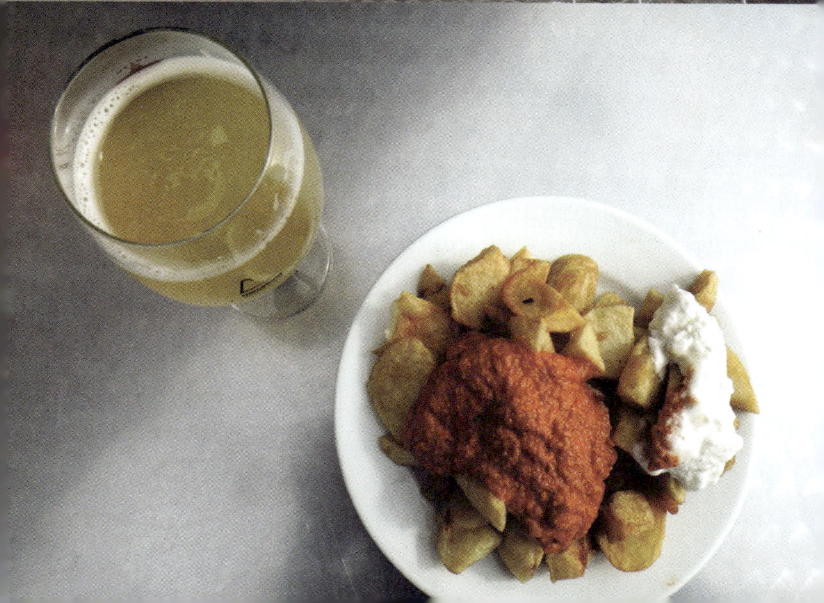

LATA BERNA

Address: Carrer Torrent de les Flors 53, Gràcia
Telephone +34 93 193 0288
Hours: 1pm-4pm & 7:30pm-midnigh

The Tin Man

The name of this appealing Gràcia eatery is a play on words, an amalgam of *la taberna*, or "tavern," and *lata,* or "tin." Owner and head chef Juanjo Martínez has dedicated his restaurant to the culture of canned food and other uncanned treasures that are linked to traditional Spanish *tapeo* and rituals like *vermut* hour, which always include preserved foods.

The concept here is la lata y la tapa. *Conservas*, canned foods, are intimately connected with the vermut tradition and the spirit of the traditional taverns – and thus a part of the Spanish culinary soul and nostalgia. At the same time, these products have a rising gourmet status. To consolidate this link, Juanjo began working with one of the most beloved local brands of high-quality canned specialties, Espinaler. Using high-quality fresh ingredients, he created a repertoire of amazing hot and cold tapas that are often served in an evocative tin container.

His cooking style draws from many Spanish regional culinary traditions and is inflected with modern international influences and a little insouciant punk attitude to free the mind and palate. Among his many innovations are the *tortita de camarones de Triana*, a typical crispy Andalusian pancake of shrimp with an atypical Thai vinaigrette, and the delicate, delicious scallop ceviche with passion fruit caviar. We love the *patatas bravas encabronadas*, in which the "mischievous" potatoes are served in a tin with two bold sauces, a garlicky white and a spicy red one. Another favorite is the creamy, savory mini *caneloni* (a traditional Catalan preparation with some Italian influence) of roasted meat or spinach, also served in a tin, with dried tomatoes and a hint of basil. But best of all is the soft-shell crab in black tempura (made with squid ink) with tartar sauce and yucca chips. It may look like a crustacean-shaped lump of coal, but the combination of flavors and textures is beyond brilliant.

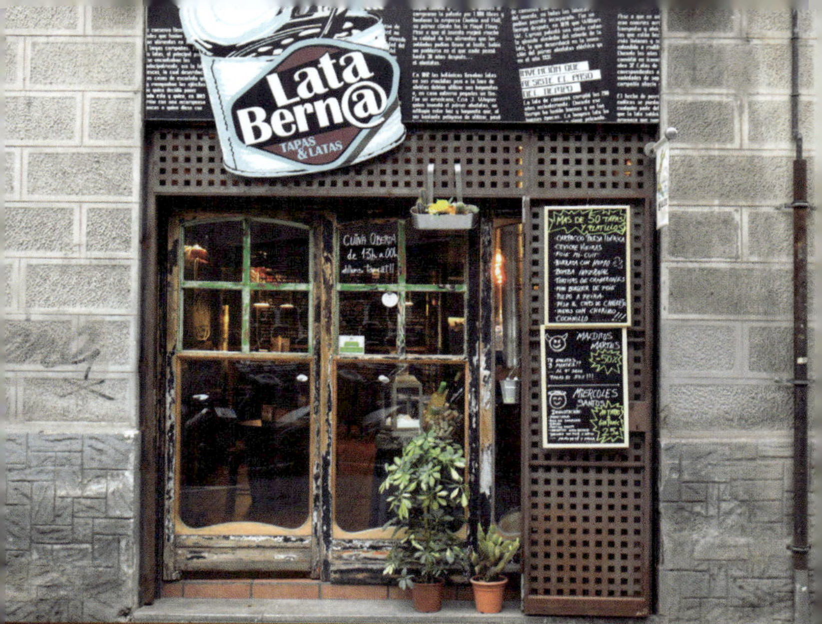
Lata
Bern@
TAPAS & LATAS
INVENCION QUE RESISTE EL PASO DEL TIEMPO

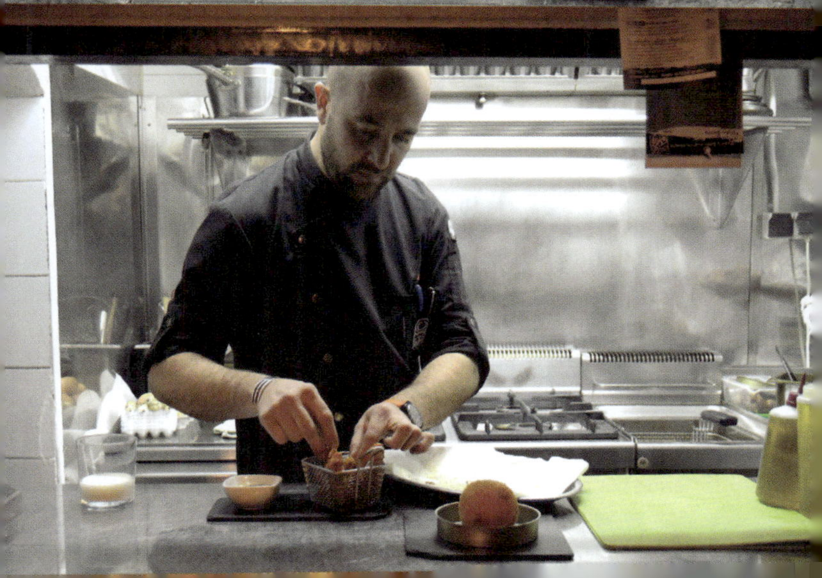

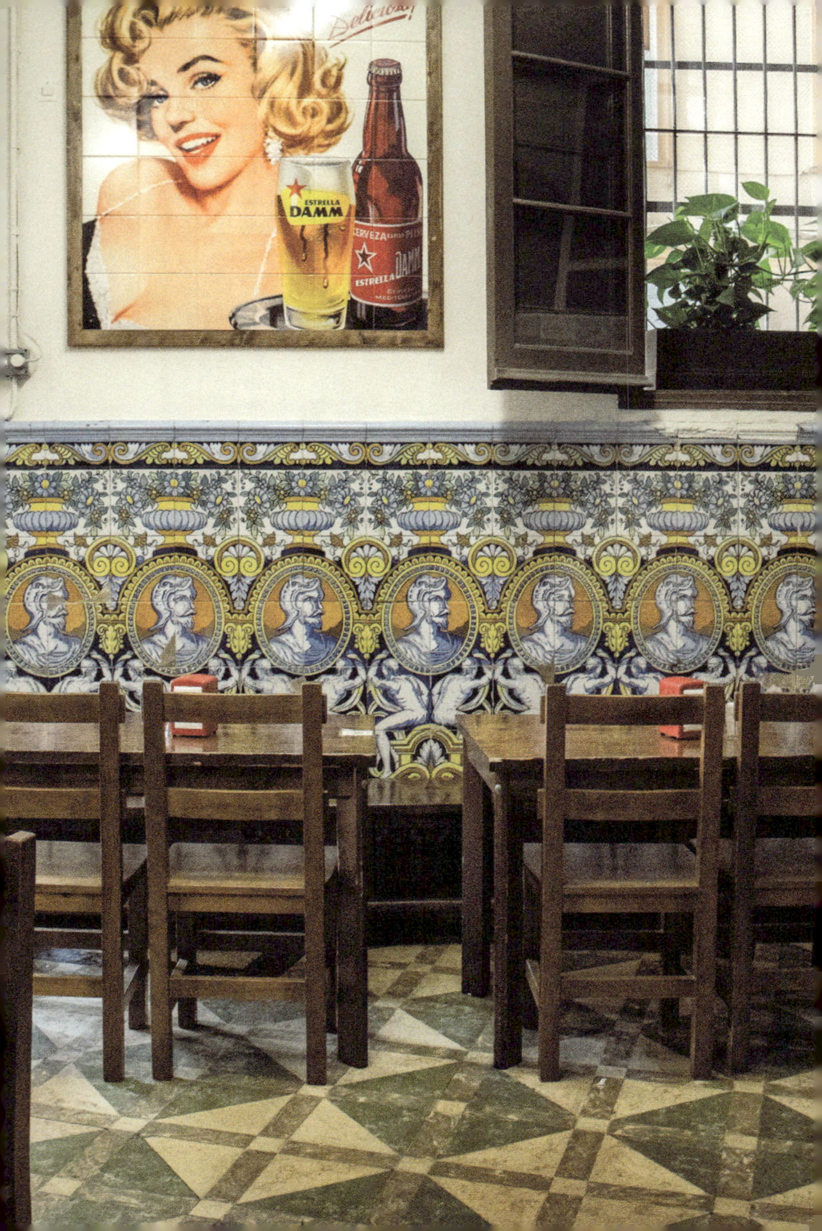
ESTRELLA
DAMM

SANTS-MONTJUÏC

BAR BODEGA SALVAT

Address: Carrer d'Andalusía 2,
(corner Carrer Sagunt),
Sants-Montjuïc
Telephone: +34 93 011 4622
Hours: Mon.-Sat. 9am-10pm;
Sun. 9am-4pm

Home Sweet Bar

Some sociologists say that Spanish society and culture can't be properly understood without spending time in its bars. In Barcelona, there are as many bars as taxis and 10 times more bars than bookshops. Bar Bodega Salvat in the *barrio* of La Bordeta is a perfect example of a local spot that's not just a bar, but a second home for its loyal clientele.

Depending on the time of day, you might spot housewives sipping coffee before visiting the local food market, workers reading the paper during their break, seniors playing dominos, students doing their homework or Barça football fans watching a live match. On Sundays, the pavement outside the bar is the most crowded in the neighborhood.

However, it's Bodega Salvat's famous anchovy dish that attracts people from all over the city. The tasty and fleshy fish, straight from the Cantabrian Sea, is seasoned with a homemade sauce of wine vinegar, black pepper and paprika. Legend has it that in the 1950s, three of Club Barcelona's most famous football players, the Hungarians Kubala, Kocsis and Csibor – the Messi, Neymar and Suárez of their time – used to go to Bodega Salvat after training for anchovies and alcohol.

With the recent shift in management back to the bodega's original owners (the Salvat Vidal family), the menu remains short but well-balanced. There's a variety of vegetarian, seafood and meat tapas. Grilled artichokes and onions as well as *piparras* (green pickled chilies) are good vegetarian options. Meat tapas highlights include *torreznos* (strips of crispy fried bacon), chorizo and *cecina de León* (cured beef). Drinking options vary from lager to dark beer on tap and house wine from Priorat, but it's the house vermouth from Reus that matches perfectly with a plate of anchovies.

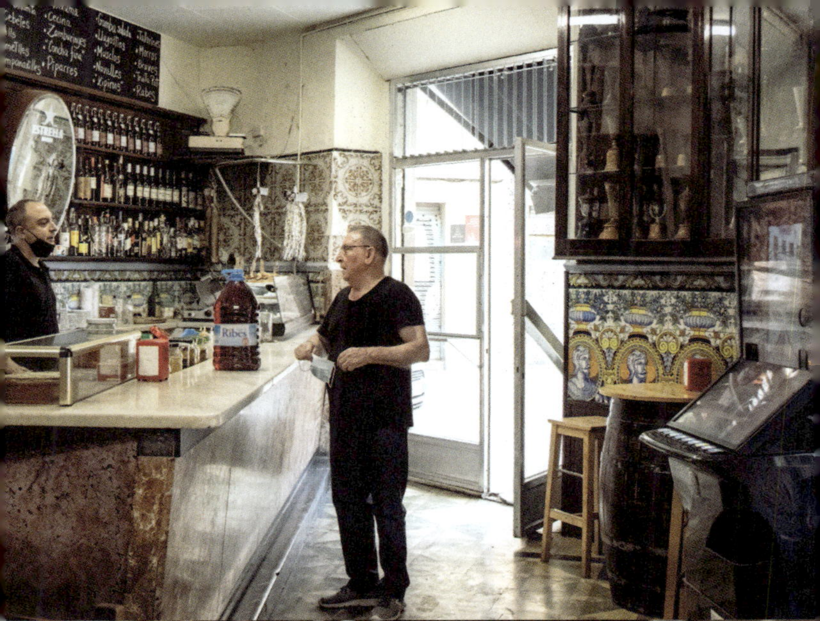
Ribes

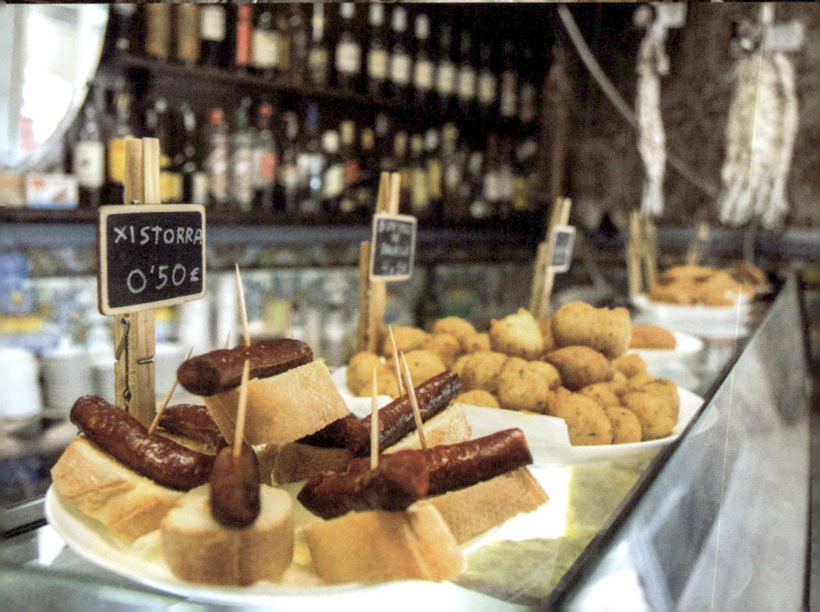
XISTORRA
0'50€

GRANJA ELENA

Address: Passeig Zona Franca 228, Sants-Montjuïc
Telephone: +34 93 332 0241
Hours: Mon.-Fri. 7am-3:45pm; Sat. 7am-1pm; closed Sunday

From Farm to 'Farm'

Granja Elena, a family business now run by its third generation in the same barrio in which it was founded in 1974, was originally a small *granja*. A kind of typical Catalan shop-bar, one can eat breakfast and supper at a granja, as well as buy farm products like milk, cold cuts for *bocadillos*, coffee and hot chocolate. Significant change really came to Granja Elena with the mother of the sibling trio who now own the place: She started cooking dishes at home to sell at the shop, a move that was such a success that the family decided to put in a new kitchen so that these traditional dishes could be prepared in the shop itself.

Today, Granja Elena serves meals in the Catalan-Spanish tradition, but with a bit of sophistication. These include *cap i pota amb samfaina* (beef head and leg stew with ratatouille) and a delicious and potent *callos* (spiced tripe stew with chorizo and blood sausage, often also with beef leg and sometimes also with chickpeas), which is tender but substantial and served in a thick marble bowl.

One seasonal specialty we enjoyed recently was a great first course of red mullet cured in salt and marinated in Kalamata olive oil, served with chive and dill in a granite dish. Each bite evoked a Mediterranean forest – a bit of surf and turf that transported us, if only for a moment, far from the concrete and asphalt just outside the restaurant. Another such taste came from a bowl of tuna and egg yolk with soy sauce and Galician sea urchin. The salmon eggs on top offered a little splash of the sea as they popped in our mouth.

Best of all, however, was the roasted tuna *galete* (jowl) with piquillo peppers. The galete was like butter, pleasantly gelatinous and refined, and the pepper purée complemented it with a subtle, earthy sweetness.

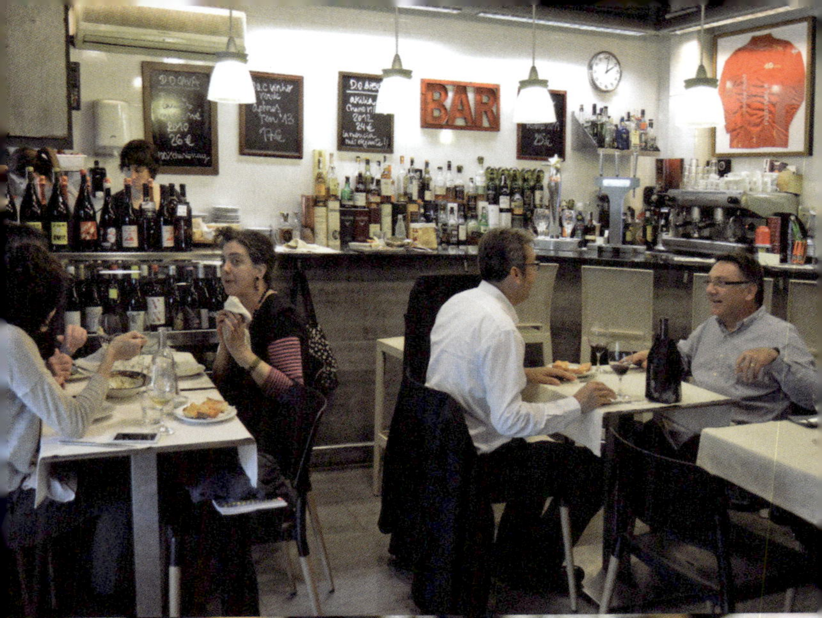
BAR

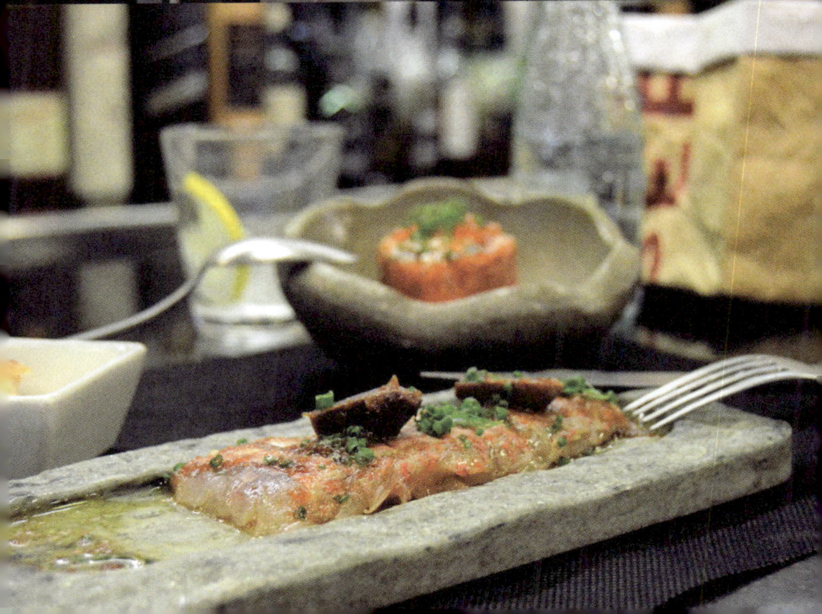

LA CHANA

Address: Carrer del Poeta Cabanyes 8
Sants-Montjuïc
Telephone: +34 93 016 1843
Hours: Wed.-Fri. 7pm-11pm;
Sat. 12:30pm-11pm;
Sun. 12:30pm-5:30pm;
closed Monday & Tuesday

Andalusian Flavors, Hold the Flamenco

Owner Natalia García, who grew up in Cádiz, has made her tiny bar La Chana into a gastronomic community center of sorts. This is especially true for other *Gaditanos* and *Sevillanos* living in Barcelona who long for a taste of authentic southern specialties. She and her small staff serve up dishes rarely found in this part of Spain, as well as a variety of cheeses, sausages, cured meats and wines from Spain's southwest.

In Andalusia – and most other parts of Spain – fried food is a way of life, so we began in typical fashion with an assortment of crispy bites of seafood. The *chocos* (cuttlefish), *boquerones* (fried anchovies), *cazón en adobo* (fried dogfish marinated in vinegar) and *ortiguillas* (sea anemone) were all fresh and tasty, served on small plates with a little pile of breadsticks as accompaniment. While the fried dishes are good, La Chana's truly special offering is its list of imported products from the south. This section of the menu, *De Barbate al Poble Sec,* is chock-full of unique, delectable treasures.

Barbate, a fishing village located an hour south of Cádiz at the mouth of the Strait of Gibraltar, is world-famous for its tuna, mostly eaten domestically in the form of salt-cured tuna, or *mojama de Barbate*. Good mojama isn't dry and tough like jerky, but supple and delicate, with a slight, iron-rich tuna flavor. Sliced thin and dressed with olive oil (and perhaps scattered with a few Marcona almonds as garnish), this is a must-try at La Chana.

Along with the mojama, we passed around a dish of *hueva de maruca*, the bright orange salted and pressed roe sack of the ling fish, which had an interesting, slightly waxy texture and bold flavor. We absolutely loved the *chicharrones de Chiclana*, rich pork belly that had been slowly cooked in pork fat and spices, then sliced thin and served at room temperature with a sprinkling of black pepper.

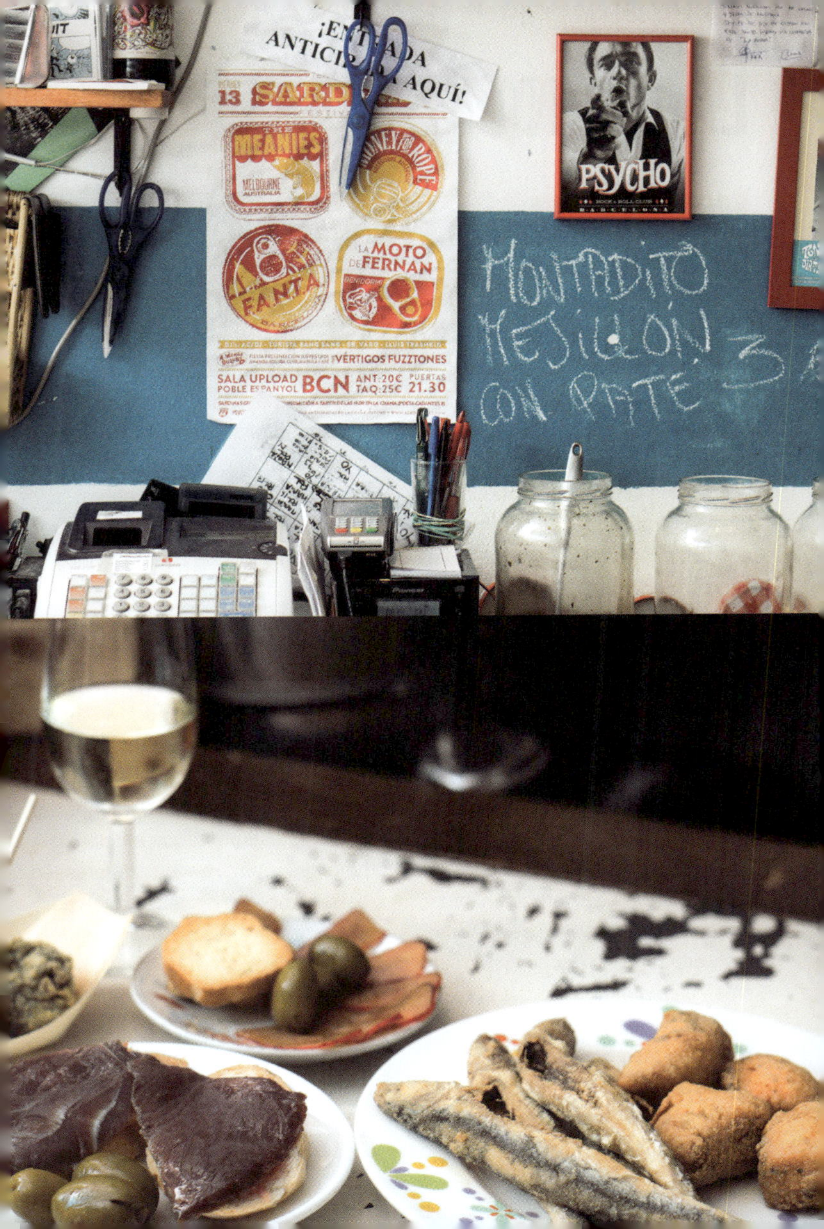
AQUÍ!
13
THE MEANIES
MELBOURNE AUSTRALIA
FANTA
LA MOTO DE FERNAN
VÉRTIGOS FUZZTONES
SALA UPLOAD
POBLE ESPANYOL
BCN
ANT:20€
TAQ:25€
PUERTAS
21.30
PSYCHO
MONTADITO
MEJILLÓN
CON PATÉ
3

LA MUNDANA

Vermut Culture 2.0

Address: Carrer del Vallespir 93,
Sants
Telephone: +34 93 408 8023
(reservations required,
reserves@lamundana.cat)
Hours: 1pm-3:30pm & 8pm-10:30pm

Although shaped by a diverse set of international influences, the working-class Sants neighborhood's now-sophisticated culinary scene is tied together by something more local: *vermut* culture. Vermut has long been central to the Catalan identity, although it fell out of favor in the late 20th century. The last decade has seen its resurgence in Barcelona, and La Mundana is one of the best places to indulge.

Opened by Catalan chefs Alain Guiard and Marc Martín in 2015, La Mundana is a "gastronomic *vermutería*," a small bar with a few tables, a patio area and bar stools positioned at a countertop in front of the kitchen. Naturally, there are 14 kinds of vermut on offer, as well as wine, cava and other alcoholic drinks; the small plates that come out of the kitchen are just as diverse.

Perhaps the bar's most famous tapa is the fried potato brick that is *bravas de la Mundana*, their take on the traditional *patatas bravas*. On top of each crunchy potato slab, there are alternating dollops of an *allioli* made with smoked black garlic and a spicy paprika *brava* (wild) sauce.

But no vermut tasting would be complete without a pickled treat. La Mundana's *banderilla* (a skewer of succulent olives, *piparra* chile, sun-dried tomato, artichoke and a tiny boiled quail egg) fits the bill. The vermutería also has unexpected smoked ingredients sprinkled throughout the menu, such as smoked oysters, bread and butter. Stronger yet is the smoked sardine, which is chopped and served with *scarmoza* cheese sauce and cherry tomatoes.

While the kitchen at La Mundana pays homage to Barcelona's culinary past, its dishes are very much a product of the present. In that way, it mirrors Sants, the neighborhood it's nestled in – the former industrial zone may be reshaped and made over, but its history is always proudly on display.

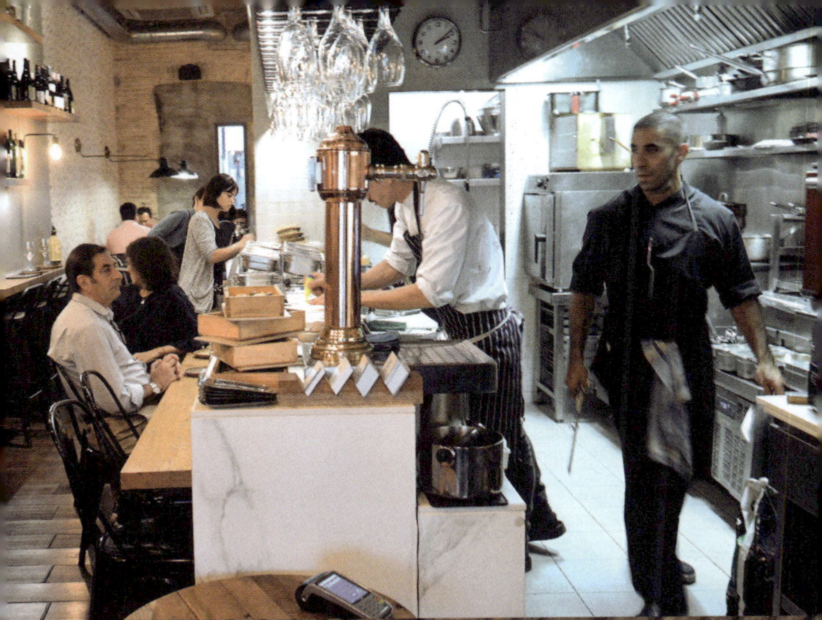

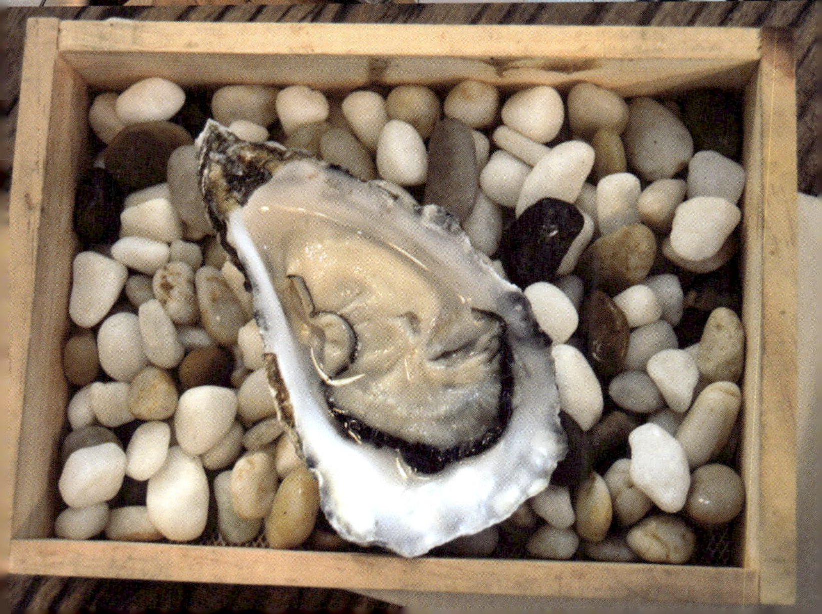

O MEU LAR

Galician Surf y Turf

Address: Carrer Margarit 24,
Sants-Montjuïc
Telephone: +34 93 329 7074
Hours: Wed.-Mon. 1:15pm-4:45pm &
8:15pm-midnight ;
closed Sun. & Wed. nights
and on Tuesday

Galicia, the autonomous region in northwest Spain, is famous for its extraordinary beef and an abundance of spectacular seafood. Like many Galicians, chef Antonio Rodríguez has a strong culinary connection with his homeland, and this serves as the foundation of his *brasería* (restaurant-grill) in Poble Sec.

Almost all the ingredients Antonio uses at O Meu Lar – its name means "my home" in Galician – are Galician, potatoes included. Here, you can get a *tapa* or half tapa of Padrón peppers (during the two months they're in season) as well as great Galician *tetilla* (cheese that looks like its name, "teat"). We love their mouthwateringly fragrant sautéed clams with smashed garlic, parsley, lemon and white wine – they're so tasty that we're compelled to mop up every last drop with bread.

O Meu Lar's specialty is Galician beef grilled over coals, known as *ternera Gallega*. The highly aromatic, tender beef needs special care in cooking in order for its best qualities to shine. Antonio offers several cuts, such as a 400-gram *entrecôte* or an enormous *chuletón*, or chop, weighing in at nearly 1 kilo – perfect for sharing – which is served in a smoking-hot clay dish so that the meat finishes cooking at the table.

O Meu Lar's bevy of seafood options also includes barnacles, crab, razor clams, cockles and scallops. We like the *polbo á feira,* or "festival-style" octopus, in which the cephalopod is cooked, sliced, dressed with paprika and served with some boiled potatoes, as was traditionally done at fairs in rural Galician villages.

We like to cap off our feast with Galician digestifs or a top-notch black coffee with a few drops of orujo, Galician white grappa. And whenever we go, we note that this is the kind of place where the owner makes the rounds to tables full of friends and regulars – all of whom undoubtedly call O Meu Lar their home away from home.

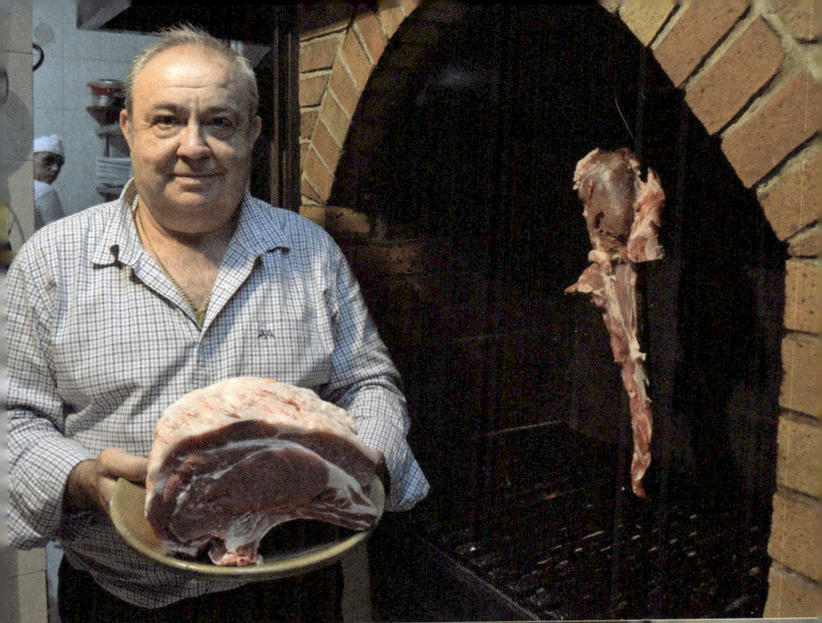
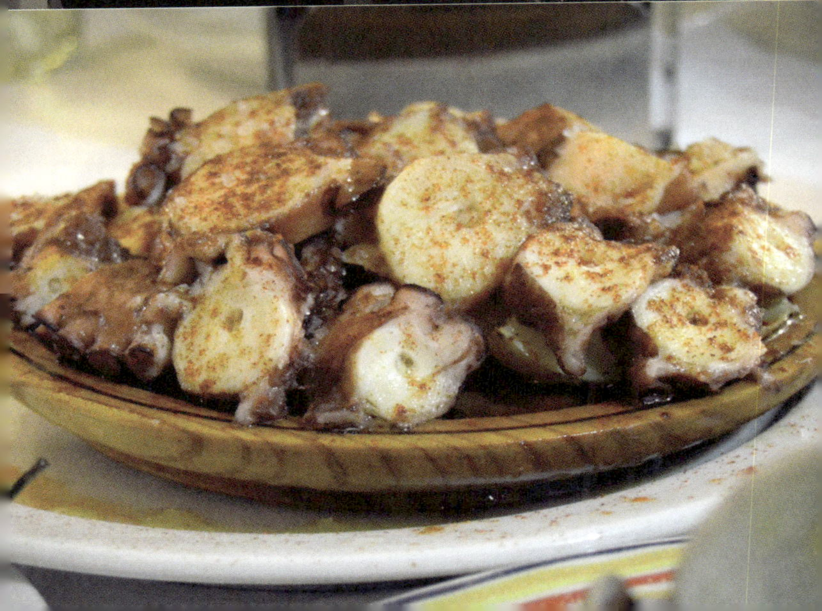

OLIVOS COMIDAS Y VINOS

Address: Carrer de Galileu 159, Sants
Telephone: +34 931 45 3715
Hours: Tues.-Sun. 1pm-5pm;
Fri. 8pm-11pm;
closed Monday

Showtime in Sants

Olivos Comida y Vinos is like an independent movie playing at a small cinema on a quiet street in Sants, a neighborhood just outside of Barcelona's center. It leaves you with the impression of having had an unexpected, intimate connection with something personal and precious. They don't have customers – they have fans.

The architects of this vision are chef Ezequiel Devoto, born in Argentina to Italian parents, and his wife, María Escobar, who hails from Spain's Andalusia region. The Slow Food cuisine is Catalan at heart, including reinterpretations of traditional dishes like *bacallá a l'all cremat*, a baked codfish with potato mousseline, tomato and roasted garlic. But Italian touches and recipes from Ezequiel's personal stash are spread here and there, like the gnocchi that his grandmother used to make (very light, without egg) or the tiramisu from his mother (a delicate take, flat and creamy, served in a dish with a thin layer of biscuit and chocolate chips).

From María's side, the menu inherits treasures from Málaga, like the Iberian pork specialty *zurrapa* (made from frayed pork meat and fat, similar to French rillettes, which you spread on bread), the sweet Málaga wine or the rustic peasant egg cookie. Despite the constant seasonal flexibility of the menu, a few dishes are sacred cows for the fans. There's the *arroz de pages*, a succulent rice dish cooked al dente and served with mushrooms, capers and squid in its ink. Another must includes the *croquets*, made with oxtail and an umami-rich sauce. And we can't forget the vinos on offer, a mix of natural and organic wines as well as more conventional reds, whites and rosés – something for every taste and every plate.

In Barcelona, where mainstream culinary trends, big hospitality groups and huge investments in interiors and PR are frequently the rule that moves the masses, the independent, honest spirit at Olivos is a treasure.

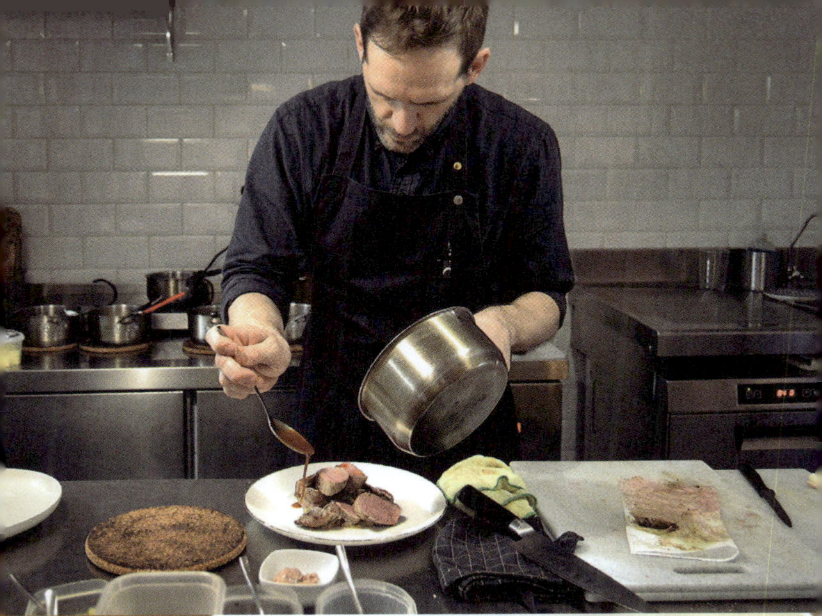

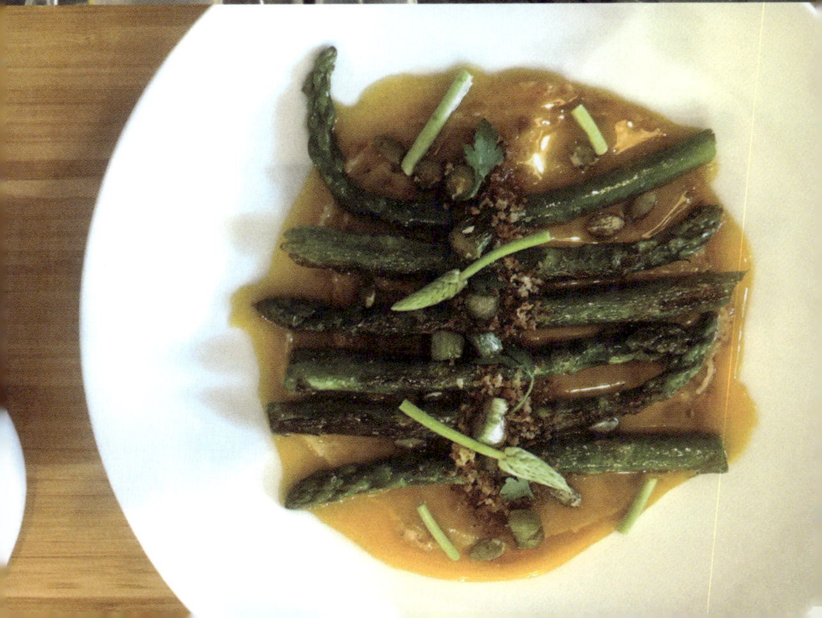

TABERNA NOROESTE

Address: Carrer de Radas 67,
Poble Sec
Telephone: +34 931 15 0911
Hours: Mon. 2pm-4pm & 8pm-10pm
Thurs.-Fri. 8pm-midnight;
Sat. 2pm-4pm & 8pm-midnight
Sun. 2pm-4pm;
closed Tuesday & Wednesday

Travel by Tapas

Born right before the Covid-19 storm, Taberna Noroeste opened its doors in February 2020, mere weeks before the pandemic hit Spain. Even with the series of closures, this project from the chefs Javier San Vicente and David López has grown healthy and strong, and is known across the city for elevating the popular cuisines of Galicia and western Spain's Castile and León – while incorporating Catalan touches.

Playing with a wide variety of ingredients and representing their respective hometowns, the two chefs work together to translate and polish these popular cuisines into a modern language – one that's more sophisticated and with less buzzy subjects than typically seen in Barcelona.

They have a small yet powerful menu of 15 tapas. Some carry the common thread of smoke from their Robata grill, which is fueled with *sarmiento* (vine branches). This includes their open *empanada* (a typical Galician dish) of *calçots* and romesco (classic Catalan ingredients), and the hearty surf-and-turf combo of *mar i muntanya* (stingray) and pig ear in a delicious stew of chickpeas. Another powerful tapa is their celebrated crispy croquette-bomb of *cocido* (a classic stew), which features a creamy and intense interior balanced by the addition of pickles served on top.

We didn't miss the opportunity to taste Maresme peas, a delicacy that's only offered for a short time, right at the start of their season. In this case, the tender, tiny and sweet peas were grown by the sea, making them sweeter than usual. They were delicately served with sea urchin roe (uni) and fennel. One of our favorites was the seafood salad, a small bowl of clams, razor clams, mussels and the venerated *percebes*, or goose barnacles, a distinctive symbol of the Iberian Atlantic coast. Every bite is an immersive trip.

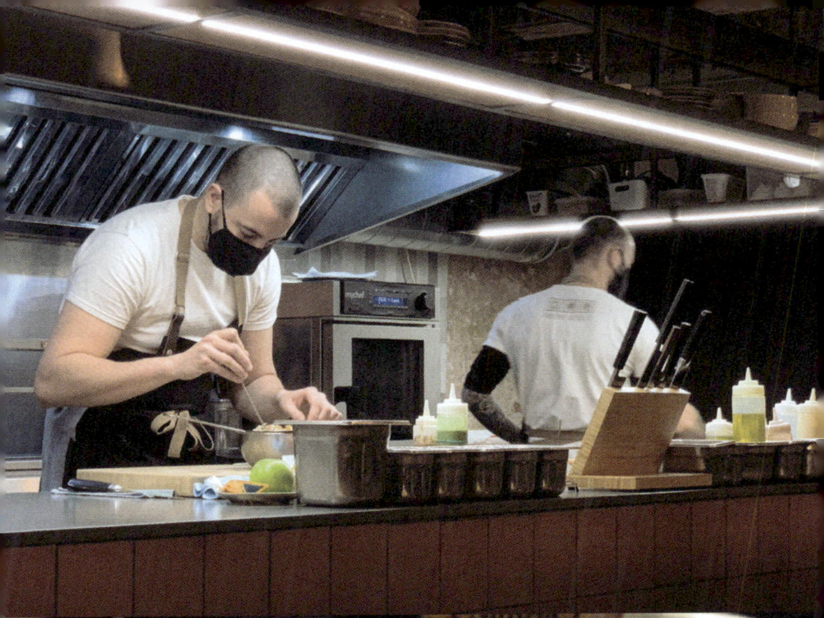

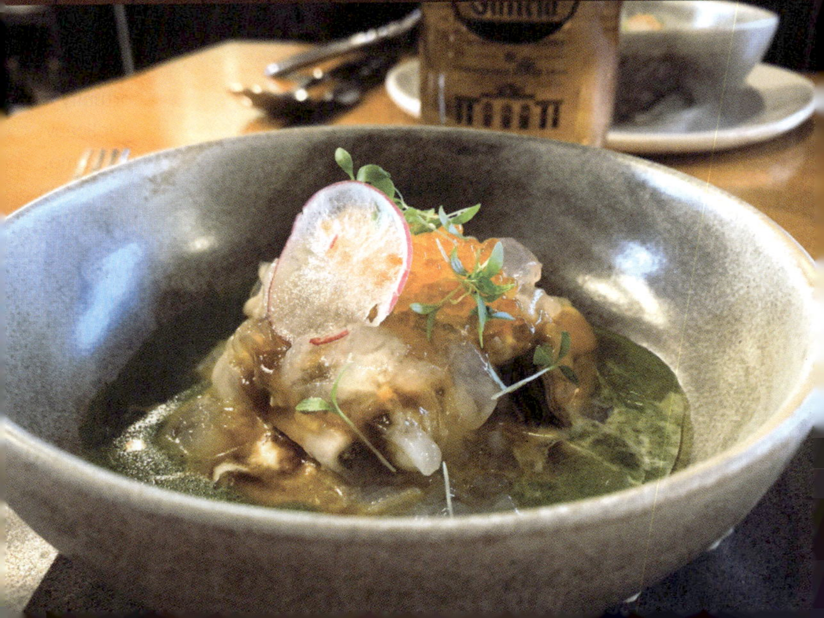

TERRA D'ESCUDELLA

Address: Carrer Premià 20,
Sants-Montjuïc
Telephone: +34 93 422 1613
Hours: Mon.-Wed. 9am-5pm;
Thurs.-Fri. 9am-midnight;
Sat. 1pm-midnight;
closed Sunday

Homage to Catalonia

In *Homage to Catalonia*, his diary of fighting for a leftist militia during the Spanish Civil War, George Orwell wrote about craving food at the front. But if he had come to Catalonia in peace-time with no food shortage, he may still have eaten at a politically minded place like Terra d'Escudella.

Located in Sants, a district with a historically very strong working-class identity, Terra d'Escudella's traditional, seasonal Catalan cooking is made with only fresh, local ingredients, at very affordable prices. The set lunch menu changes daily and offers the kind of old-school dishes that Catalan grand-mothers used to make: meatballs with cuttlefish, assorted sausages, cod with romesco sauce.

There's also a highly recommended evening tapas menu with platters of artisanal *charcutería* and cheese, *patatas bravas* with aioli sauce and homemade croquettes among other old-style dishes. A list of sandwiches with traditional cured meats such as *donja* (pork sausage) is also available.

Desserts are not an afterthought here: *crema catalana* foam, Marcona toasted almonds covered with caramel, hazelnuts with white chocolate and a shot of ratafia, honey and the ricotta-like *brossat* cheese, sheep's milk yogurt, curd pudding with almond cookies and nougat ice cream are just a few examples.

Wines come from all over the Catalan-speaking areas, and the list changes monthly. Each week, the restaurant highlights a different wine sold by the glass. Catalan craft beers such as the celebrated Cervesa del Montseny have an important presence here too. Even the soft drinks and distilled spirits are Catalan.

In short, Terra d'Escudella is a gastronomical homage to Catalonia, an ode to Catalan popular cuisine and a little trip back to the 19th-century *fondes dels sisos* (humble inns frequented by workers, artisans and travelers). The restaurant's walls are covered with posters that resemble old Anarcho-syndicalist, Bolshevik, feminist and labor union propaganda – Orwell's politics would have been right at home here too.

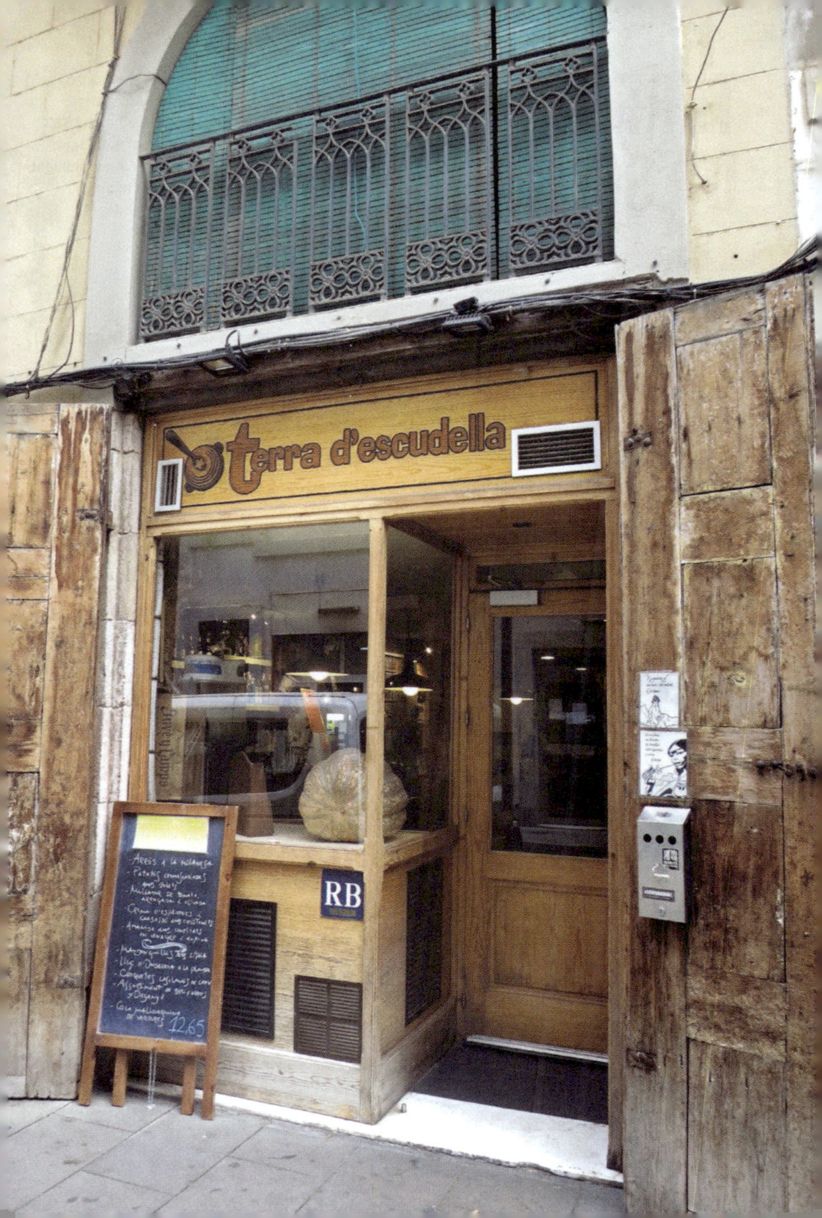
terra d'escudella
RB
12,65

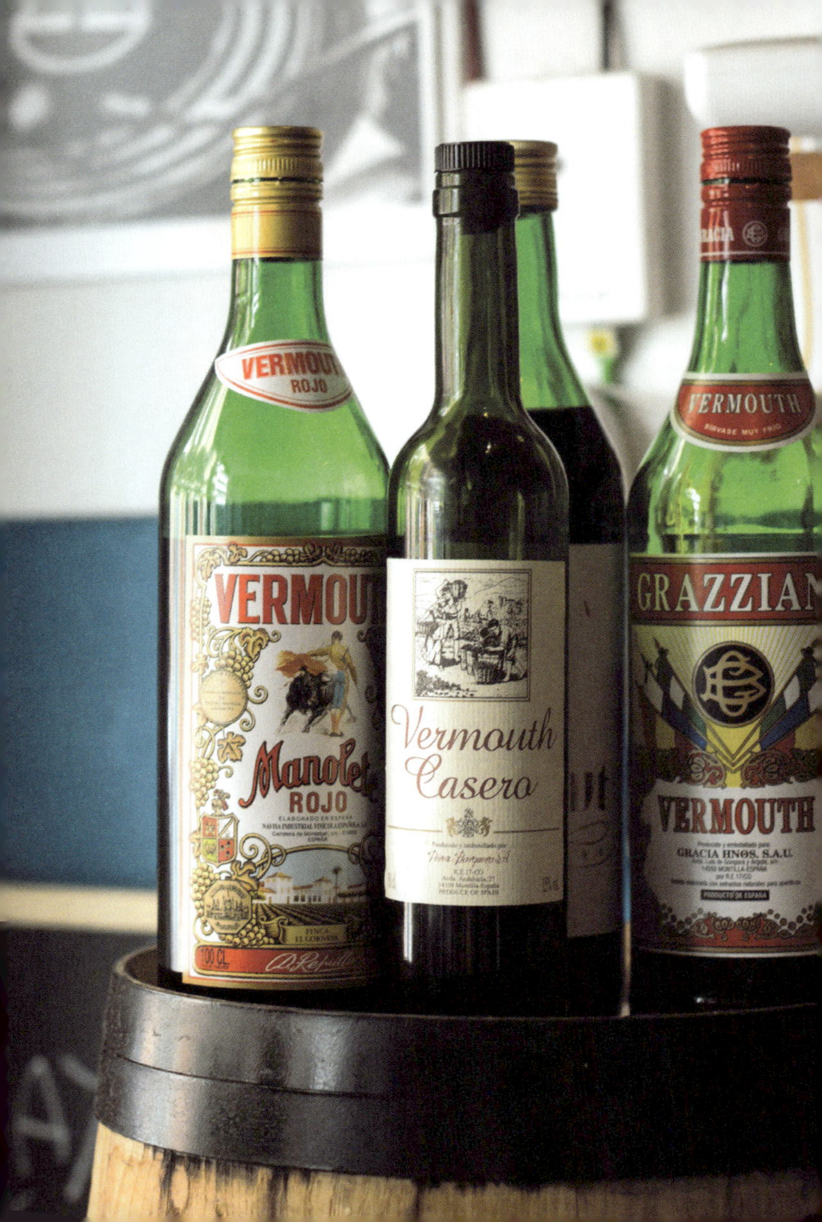
ROJO
ROJO
ELABORADO EN ESPAÑA
100 CL
Vermouth
Casero
PRODUCE OF SPAIN
VERMOUTH
SIRVASE MUY FRIO
VERMOUTH
GRACIA HNOS. S.A.U.
PRODUCTO DE ESPAÑA

SANT MARTÍ & SANT ANDREU

CAN PINEDA

A Workers' Canteen Grows Up

Address: Carrer de Sant Joan de Malta 55, Sant Martí
Telephone: +34 61 707 3897
Hours: Tues.-Thurs. 1pm-3:45pm & 8:30pm-10:45pm; Fri.-Sat. 8:30pm-11:30pm; closed Sunday, Monday & holidays

The rustic family favorite Can Pineda has been holding down this corner of Barcelona's El Clot neighborhood since 1904. It was not a restaurant originally, but a typical wine shop and canteen, where local factory workers would come for a glass of wine to go with a simple meal or to drink while warming up their lunch boxes.

A family business since the 1970s, dish by dish, Can Pineda has gone from simple bar to a more ambitious restaurant, turning excellent seasonal and local ingredients into carefully prepared dishes with a Catalan foundation and Spanish, French and Italian influences. The sardine *coca* (a traditional flatbread) highlights the deeply savory qualities of the fish with caramelized onion, tomato and *olivada* (tapenade). It offers a delightful contrast to the fleshy fish. We also like the homey meatballs (pork and beef), which are paired with delicious *xipirons*, or baby squid, in a satisfyingly earthy Catalan rendition of surf and turf.

In winter, the stew of artichokes and *mongetas del ganxet* (Catalan white beans) also combines flavors from land and sea with a few big, briny clams from Carril, a village on the Atlantic coast. The white truffles from Italy's Piedmont region bring their beguiling perfume to a few of the restaurant's Italo-French dishes, like the creamy, delicate fresh pasta or the *pochè* eggs with foie.

Our favorite of all, however, is the *guisantes lágrima*, sweet, tender and juicy peas, cooked with bits of ham and bacon, garlic and mint leaves, which imbue the dish with a subtle yet thoroughly enticing aroma.

We always make sure to save room for dessert – perhaps the praline biscuit with broiled yolk or the Roquefort cheese with pear and pepper. But most likely, we'll ask for the house specialty: *bombetas*, small bites of crispy phyllo that gush forth warm cream or chocolate when bitten into.

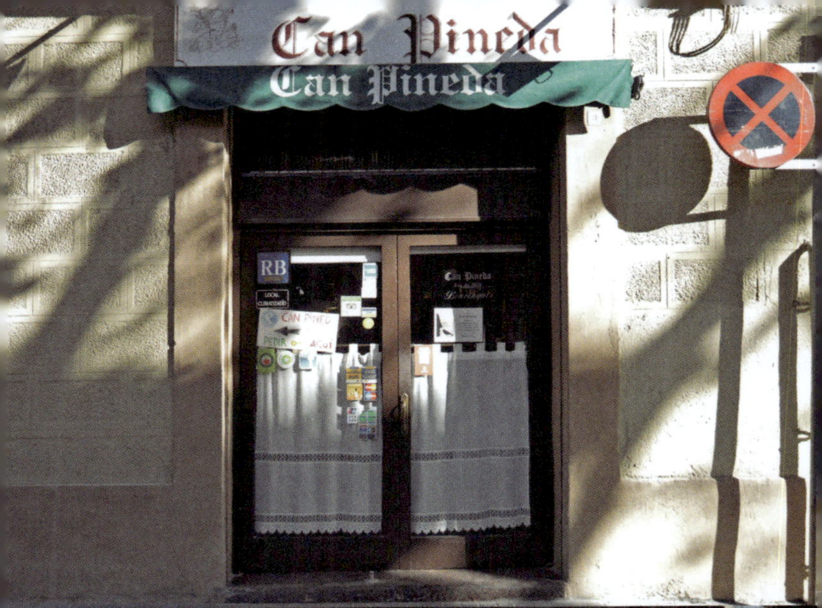
Can Pineda
Can Pineda
RB
Can Pineda
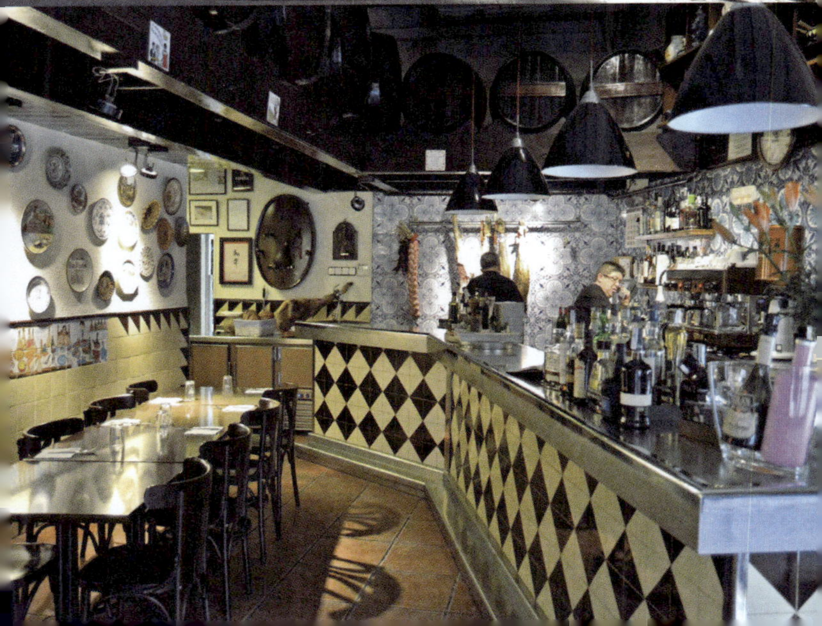

EL RACÓ DEL MARINER

Address: Port Fórum, Carrer Port Esportiu, Local 1, Sant Adrià de Besòs
Telephone: +34 64 559 3096
Hours: Tues.-Sat. 8:30am-6pm; Fri.-Sat. 8:30am-7:30pm (no dinner service); closed Sunday & Monday

Sole Survivor

At El Racó del Mariner (The Sailor's Corner), everything and nothing has changed. For 40 years, the beloved seafood restaurant catered to fishermen, port workers and, later, the public at the old fishermen's dock in the port of La Barceloneta. But in 2016, during the final stages of the port's transformation into a marina for luxury yachts, El Racó del Mariner was forced to move.

Despite its new address in the modern Port Fórum area, there's still a sense of continuity. Inside, you can see the same faces – waiters Samba and Mamen and owner Jenifer Santana – stationed near the wooden boat-like bar, as if they were at the helm of a brand new ship amidst a sea of tables. Much of the décor from the previous location has been relocated to the restaurant's new home, such as the ship's wheel, the fishing nets and photos of boats.

But, of course, it's the food that provides the real constant here. There are the iconic grilled and fried fisherman's tapas of prawns, langoustines, clams, razor clams, squid, octopus, sardines and anchovies. Perhaps the most classic dish is the *morralla*, or fried fish, but the most in-demand are their great fish and seafood stews; soups; seafood casseroles of lobster, hake or monkfish; and the exquisite rice dishes. All continue to be made with the same impeccably fresh raw materials, mostly local (some even sourced by Jenifer's husband, a fisherman), and the same traditional preparations as before. Many of the habitués of the old venue come to the new location, six or seven kilometers up the road, because the food is just that good – it's worth the trip.

Like many others, undoubtedly, we are thrilled that El Racó del Mariner has managed to hold on to its authenticity and excellent cuisine. It's a tribute to themselves and a gift to the rest of us. And if the new location requires us to walk a little bit more, then all the better for us to arrive a little hungrier.

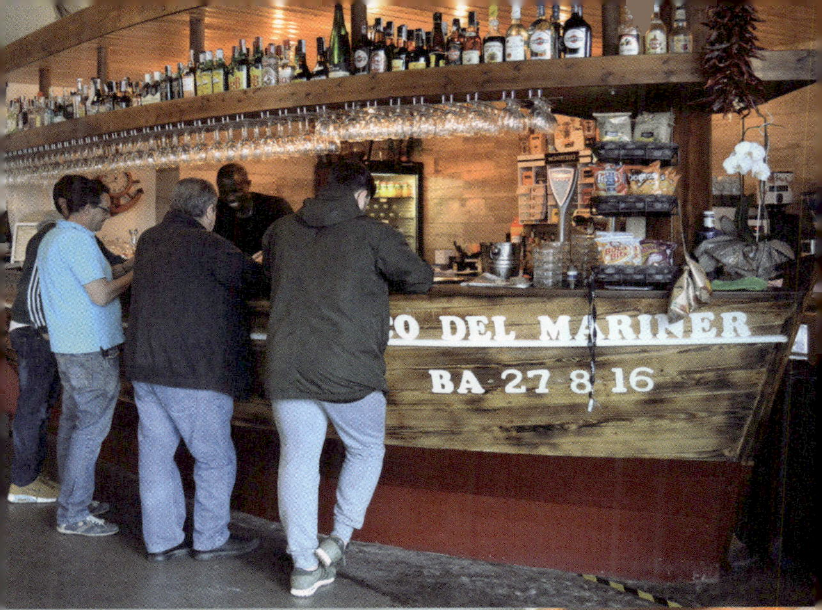
DEL MARINER
BA 27 8 16

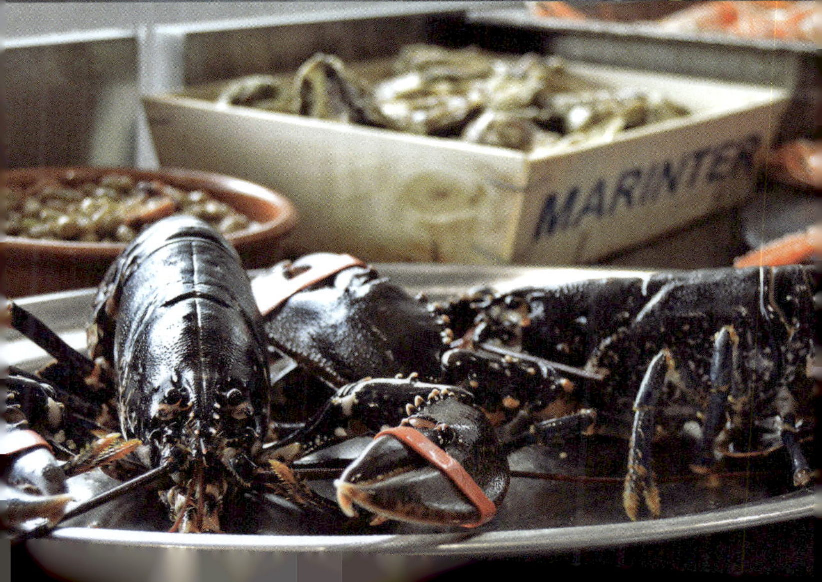

ELS PESCADORS

Address: Plaça de Prim 1, El Poblenou
Telephone: +34 93 225 2018
Hours: 1pm-3:30pm & 8pm-10:30pm

A Fine Kettle of Fish

Anchoring one end of Poblenou's quiet and lovely Prim Square, Els Pescadors sits surrounded by the white houses that once belonged to the fishermen for which it's named. The old tavern opened in 1848, and through the 19th century, it was frequented by those fishermen, as well as workers from the numerous textile factories in the area.

Current owners Josep María Maulini and his wife, Toia Durán, created the restaurant as it is today, complete with an elegant, expansive terrace. They serve traditional Catalan seafood dishes, with all the Andalusian, Basque and Galician influences inherent in that cuisine. (Many fishermen came – and still come – from those coastal areas to work in Catalonia.) Everything is made with the utmost care, with a clean, direct and unembellished cooking style – the better to let the ingredients speak for themselves.

On a recent visit, we ate some *caixetas* ("little boxes"), local shellfish that are like something in between mussels and barnacles. They were full-flavored and very firm, a bit sweeter than expected and perfect just as they were, served warm and unadorned. We also enjoyed the Basque delicacy of *kokotxas,* soft, creamy and very juicy cod cheeks, which came with some green beans and chopped leeks enrobed in a foamy *pil pil* sauce. But our favorite may very well have been the *suquet*, a Catalan fish soup traditionally served in taverns or on boats as a communal meal. Fish heads and bones are used to make the broth, to which are added meatier chunks of fish, as in French *bouillabaisse.* This restaurant's exquisite version of *suquet* included Catalan *buffet negre* potatoes and a concentrated soup of fish and vegetables with a succulent piece of *escórpora,* red scorpion fish.

Els Pescadors has seen many changes through the years, but we like to think that the fishermen who once lived in those white houses around this tavern would feel very much at home here today. We certainly do.

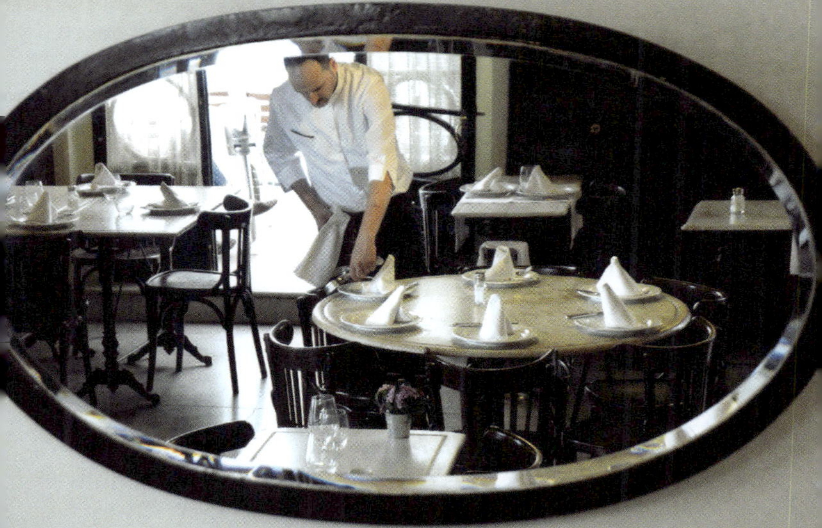

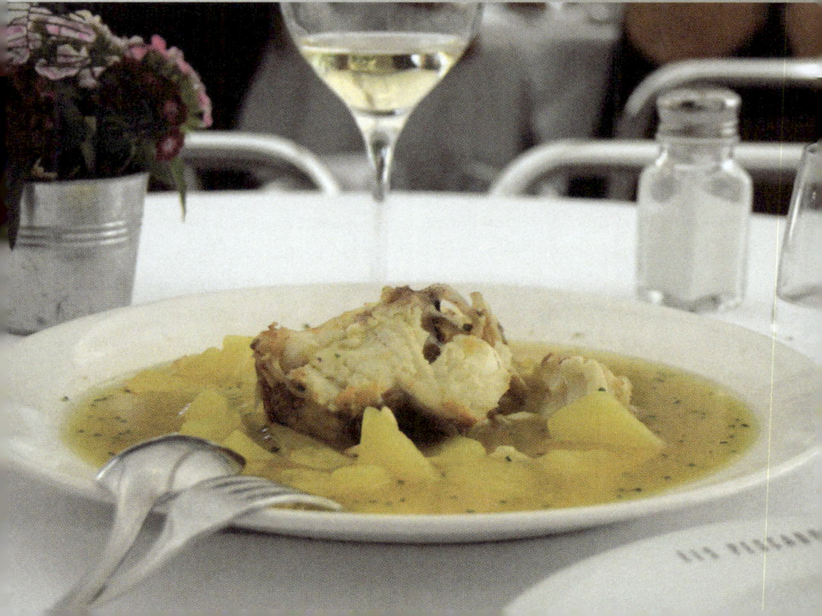

TOCATECA

Gastronomic Unicorn

Address: Carrer Garcilaso 172, El Congrés, Sant Andreu
Telephone: +34 93 408 6288
Hours: Tues.-Thurs. & Sat. 1pm-4pm & 8pm-11pm; closed Sunday, Monday & Friday

A quiet residential area that feels caught between its Catalan village roots and industrial past, the Sant Andreu district is seeing factories transformed into creative arts complexes and parks, and a former *canódromo* (dog-racing track) that is now an "innovation center." Though the El Congrés neighborhood is not a part of town that's considered a dining destination, it has had its own gastronomic unicorn since 2012: TocaTeca. A unique establishment of its kind in the area – for now, at least – the restaurant is a gourmet endeavor sustained by a couple of professional chefs, Maria Cots and Guillem Carulla.

The quality is clear – from the fish they serve down to the flour used in the kitchen, a special variety for batters that comes from Jerez de la Frontera in Andalusia. As a result, the fried *sonsos* (Mediterranean sand eel) and squid are delightfully crispy (not oily at all), as are the must-order cod fritters that are served with a generous and delicious side of honey for dipping.

Obligatory eats include the *rabo de toro* (oxtail). They cook about 18 kilos of this dish per week. Cooked for more than six hours with red wine, glazed in the oven and served in sauce with a sprinkle of onion, it's a refined, small dish that packs a high concentration of succulence and flavor.

But perhaps our favorite at TocaTeca is the scallops a la carbonara. A wonderful dish drizzled with an Italian influence, it was originally created in a smaller size for a neighborhood tapas contest, De Tapes per Sant Andreu 2017. The larger portion now comes as three perfectly grilled scallops smothered in a light carbonara sauce and sparkling with crispy pancetta pieces. It's a fantastic and complementary union of flavor and textures. As we've come to discover, at TocaTeca nothing disappoints – and unicorns do exist, at least in Sant Andreu.

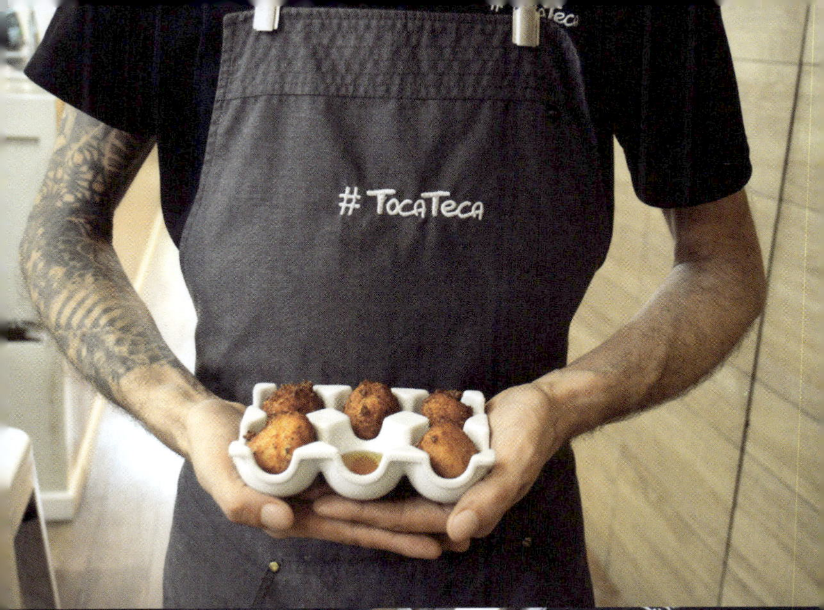
#TocaTeca

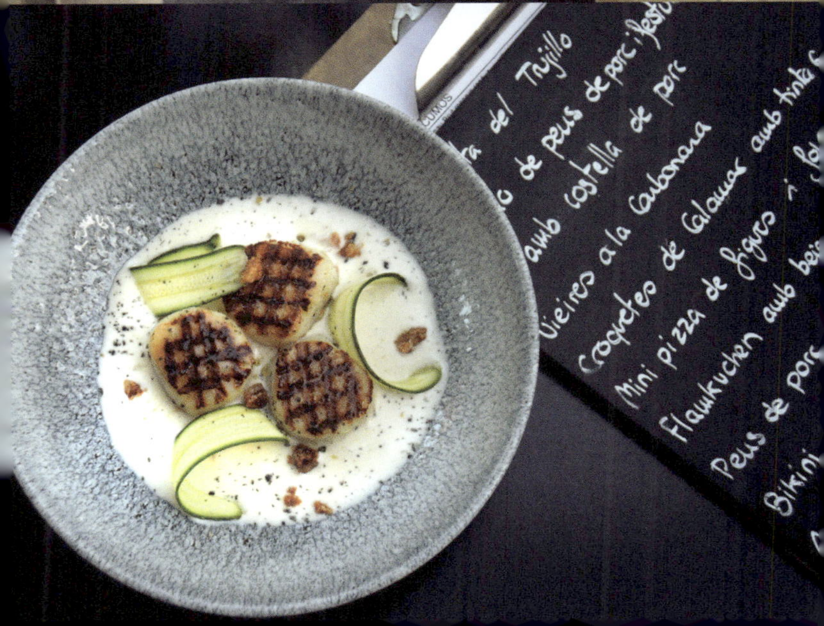
del Trujillo
de peus de porc i
amb costella de porc
Vieires a la Carbonara
Croquetes de Calamars amb tinta
Mini pizza de figues i
Flamkuchen amb
Peus de porc
Bikini

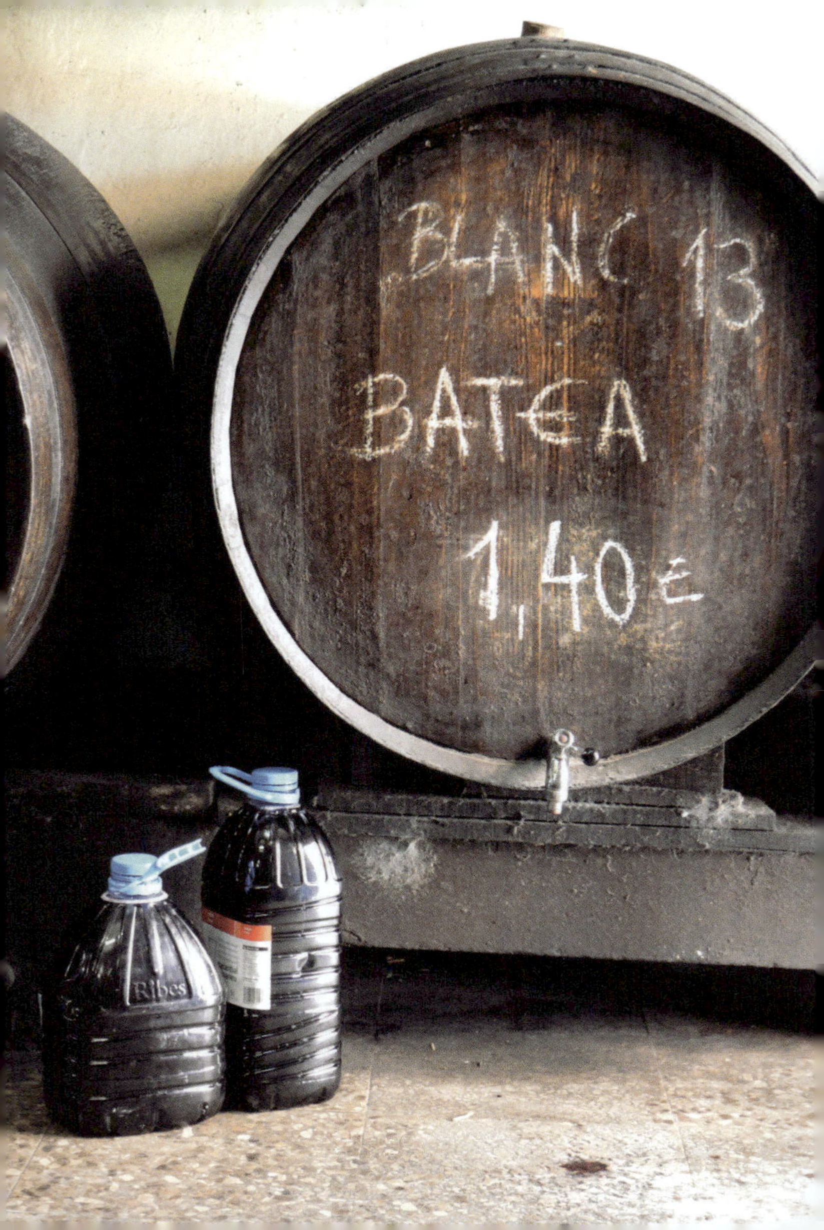
BLANC 13
BATEA
1,40€
Ribes

THE URBAN WINE ROUTE

THE RED & THE WHITE

Understanding Catalonia's Wine Regions

Wine has a long history in Barcelona, and many of the bodegas dotting each neighborhood are keepers of that past. Walk into one of these old bars and you'll see the large barrels from which wine was once (or still) poured, back when they were bulk wine shops.

Catalonia has the greatest number of protected wine appellations, called *denominaciones de origen* (D.O.), in Spain. There are 12 appellations pertaining to Catalonia: 11 are specific regions and one is an umbrella appellation encompassing Catalan wines outside those geographies, simply called "D.O. Catalunya." These 12 D.O.s encompass about 35 different grape varieties in total, and the four most significant subregions, in terms of quantity, are Penedès, Costers del Segre, Priorat and Montsant. Although Catalonia is renowned for its cavas (p. 110) and white wines, some of Spain's best reds are made here as well. All Catalan D.O.s produce good reds, but the most compelling and critically acclaimed wines come from Priorat, which is further distinguished by a Qualified D.O., or D.O.Q., and its younger brother Montsant.

Encircled by the Serra de Montsant mountains, Priorat has a sunny Mediterranean climate, with hot, dry summers and steep hillsides covered in poor volcanic soil composed mostly of slate. Stands of centuries-old vines yield a small quantity of excellent wine with a great deal of power and concentration. Some locals believe that the Romans constructed the oldest stone terraces on the craggy hillsides 2,000 years ago. But the old vines and terraces are just a part of the greater viticulture in the region that flourished until the 19th century, when phylloxera, an aphid that destroyed much of Europe's wine production, and political crisis interrupted production.

In the 1980s, a group of passionate winemakers led by René Barbier and Álvaro Palacios began the difficult task of cultivating the old grenache and carignan vines, as

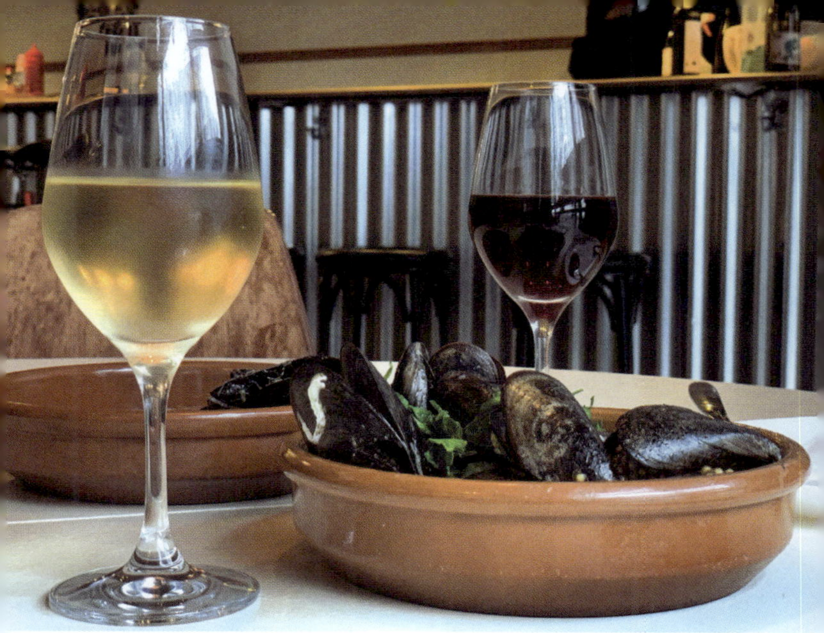

well as introducing such international varieties as cabernet sauvignon and syrah. These producers became known for making intense, structured, big-bodied wines that are also remarkably fresh, elegant and somehow both jammy and mineral in flavor. Two of the best-known wineries of the region are Clos Erasmus and Palacios's L'Ermita.

The wines of Montsant come from vineyards adjacent to Priorat, and while the grape varieties and terroir are similar, Montsant is known more for its new vines, new concepts, younger winemakers and high quality at lower prices. Montsant wines, with their more integrated tannins, are largely less structured and more rounded and delicate than Priorats.

When we think of white wine in Catalonia, we think of its seemingly endless possibilities. Production of whites here has a 2,000-year-old history. The wide-ranging diversity in the climate and calcareous soils, from the mountains to the sea, and the combination of old grape varieties and newly introduced "foreigners" with traditional and experimental methods of production make for innumerable styles and no taboos.

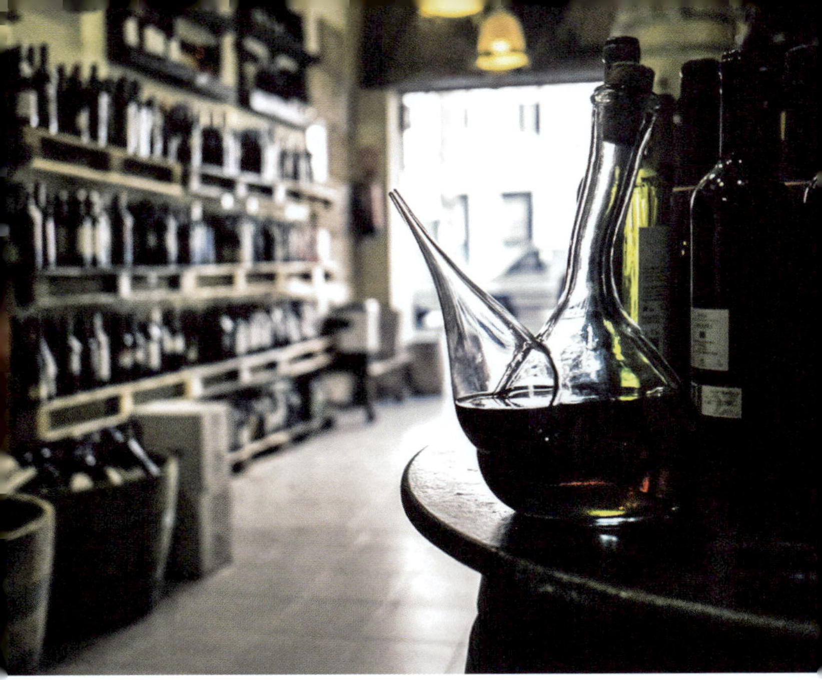

The traditional Catalan grape varieties used to make white wine are mainly macabeo, xarel-lo, parellada and garnatxa blanca, but this area has the largest number of white grapes included in all of Spain's D.O.s. Where other Spanish D.O.s usually are defined by one or a few varieties, in the Catalunya D.O. there are more than 16 whites (and 19 reds). In fact, this umbrella appellation, which covers wines that do not fall under the official subregions (Montsant, Penedès, etc.), was created to allow the use of all the grapes of the other Catalan designations in the entire area.

Penedès is the largest area in Catalonia specializing in white wine, in no small part because of all the juice from there that's destined for cava. Although producers can vinify all the varieties included in the D.O. (and such international varieties as chardonnay, sauvignon blanc and riesling), the main varieties grown and used are still the traditional macabeo, parellada and xarel-lo. Xarel-lo in particular is winning more and more fans as a varietal wine.

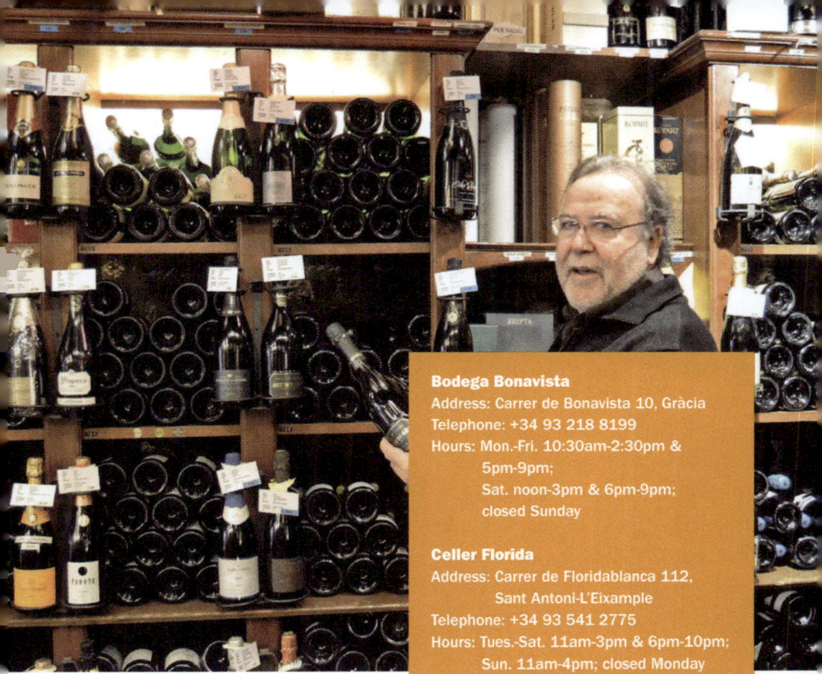

Bodega Bonavista
Address: Carrer de Bonavista 10, Gràcia
Telephone: +34 93 218 8199
Hours: Mon.-Fri. 10:30am-2:30pm & 5pm-9pm; Sat. noon-3pm & 6pm-9pm; closed Sunday

Celler Florida
Address: Carrer de Floridablanca 112, Sant Antoni-L'Eixample
Telephone: +34 93 541 2775
Hours: Tues.-Sat. 11am-3pm & 6pm-10pm; Sun. 11am-4pm; closed Monday

La Vinya del Senyor
Address: Plaça Santa Maria del Mar 5, El Born
Telephone: +34 93 310 3379
Hours: Sun.-Mon. noon-midnight; Fri.-Sat. noon-1am

This extraordinarily delicate grape possesses aromas with tropical notes and has just a touch of minerality in the glass.

In contrast, the Terra Alta D.O. specializes in garnatxa blanca, a Catalan variety that makes a full-bodied, structured wine, perfect for combining with strong-flavored, oily fish, white meat and even powerful sauces. Terra Alta also produces blends of garnatxa blanca with a small percentage of other Catalan varieties, such as macabeo or vinyater.

For a taste of the full range of Catalan wine, we recommend the shops listed above, all of which have friendly staff who are happy to help you navigate the D.O.s and D.O.Q.s. **La Vinya del Senyor** is a proper wine bar and **Bodega Bonavista** has a few tables to taste wine, cheese and charcuterie.

CAVA

Spain's All-Day Sparkler

While cava is produced in many areas of Spain, most production takes place in Catalonia, and especially Penedès, an area of historical importance for this type of wine. The word "cava," in fact, means "cellar" or "cave" in Catalan. In the 18th century, Catalonians began learning about sparkling wine when they became the cork suppliers to the first French wineries that were making champagne. In fact, cava is produced using the same *méthode traditionnelle* that is used for champagne: After the base wine is fermented from the pressing, it's bottled, usually with a mixture of sugar and yeast, to undergo a second fermentation to produce that festive fizz. The typical white grape varieties of xarel-lo, parellada and macabeo produce sparkling wines with fresh citrus flavors and bright notes of fruit and white flowers.

There are several types of cava available in wine shops: the classic white, the enigmatic *blanc de noirs*, with a base white wine made from red grapes, and the glamorous rosé. Levels of aging are identified with specific stamps on the top of the bottle: white guarantees a minimum of nine months of fermentation inside the bottle, green indicates a minimum 15 months for Cava Reserva and black, denoting a minimum of 30 months, is for Cava Gran Reserva. The last two designations can offer especially interesting, complex aromas of toast, nuts and vanilla.

The wines are also categorized by sweetness level, from Dulce, the sweetest, containing at least 50 grams of sugar per liter, to Semiseco, with 35 to 50 grams, all the way down to Brut (3 to 12 grams), Extra Brut (under 3 grams of sugar) and Brut Nature, which has no added sugar and reveals perhaps the most of the original wine's character.

Cava goes particularly well with a traditional hearty Catalan breakfast, but it can also be enjoyed as a light apéritif with some salad, olives or

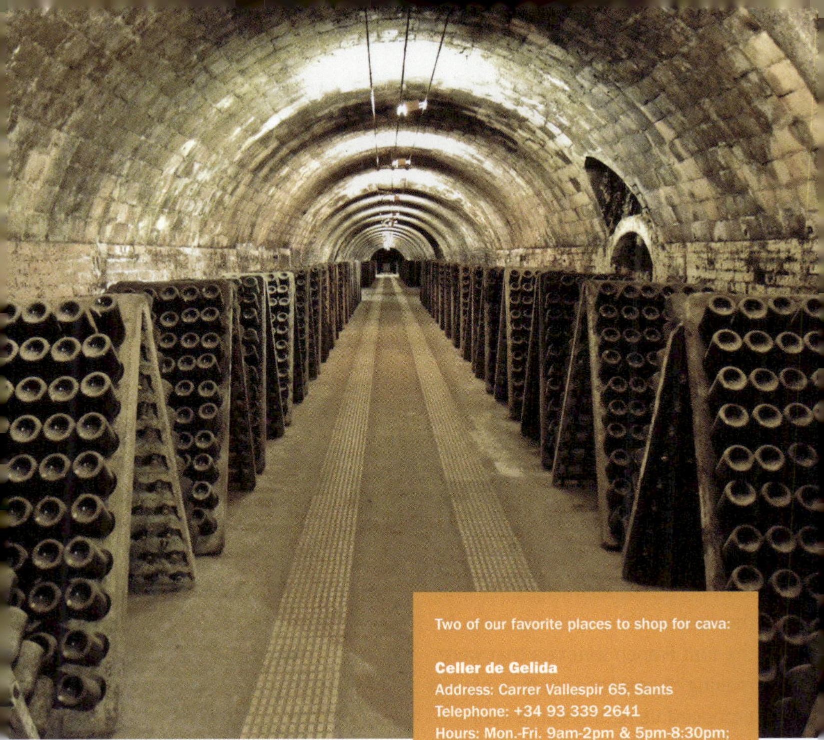

Two of our favorite places to shop for cava:

Celler de Gelida
Address: Carrer Vallespir 65, Sants
Telephone: +34 93 339 2641
Hours: Mon.-Fri. 9am-2pm & 5pm-8:30pm; Sat. 9:30am-2:30pm & 5pm-8:30pm; closed Sunday, holidays, August and Sat. afternoons in July & Sept.

La Teca de Vila Viniteca
Address: Carrer Agullers 9, La Ribera-El Born
Telephone: +34 93 777 7017
Hours: 8:30am-8:30pm (Sat. 8:30am-2:30pm in July & August); closed Sunday

pickles. We love it with a typical Sunday lunch of roast chicken and with every kind of cured or cooked meat. Cava has enough body to stand up to these kinds of dishes, while its bubbles and touch of acidity cut through the fat. It's also refreshing paired with paella at a *chiringuito* (snack bar) on the beach and is a natural accompaniment to birthday cake. In the Catalan workplace, it's common practice to keep a bottle at the ready in the fridge to celebrate an accomplishment – or to soften the blow of a setback. Whatever the occasion, the bottle should be kept cold, preferably around 6°C (43°F).

NATURAL WINE

A New Movement Takes Root

Naked, free, wild, raw, true, clean... natural wine has many names, except its most obvious one, just plain ol' wine. There's no makeup or camouflage, nor is there any sort of artificial interference – chemical fertilizers or industrial yeasts, to name a few – in the vineyards or during the vinification process. Some consider this wine to be a passing fashion, but it has more than a solid foothold in its homelands – France, Georgia and, to a lesser extent, Italy – and continues to conquer palates in new countries, like Spain.

Here, natural wine is proving to be a popular alternative to industrial vino, which must adhere to regulations set by the Denominaciones de Origen (D.O., the organizations that oversee the mainstream wine regions in Spain). While D.O. Catalan wines are delicious in their own right, compared to natural wines they have a limited and fixed personality, often based on artificial yeasts and interventions.

Barcelona is natural wine's flagship city in Spain, with an increasing number of specialized bars and restaurants joining the movement. At **L'Anima Del Vi**, French oenologist and Barcelona resident Benoît Valee has pioneered natural wine in Spain. What began as a little shop in Gràcia has grown into an attractive and welcoming bar in Born. Also in the neighborhood is **Can Cisa/ Bar Brutal**, an old bodega established in 1949, bought in 2013 and transformed into one of Barcelona's best spots for natural wine. This bar-restaurant-shop stocks hundreds of natural wines from all over the world, a list that is constantly being updated. Many are available by the glass, and in the company of excellent Mediterranean food that draws inspiration from both Catalonia and Italy.

It's not easy to find a place that blends quality and fair prices, tradition and modernity, identity and open vision into one easy-going

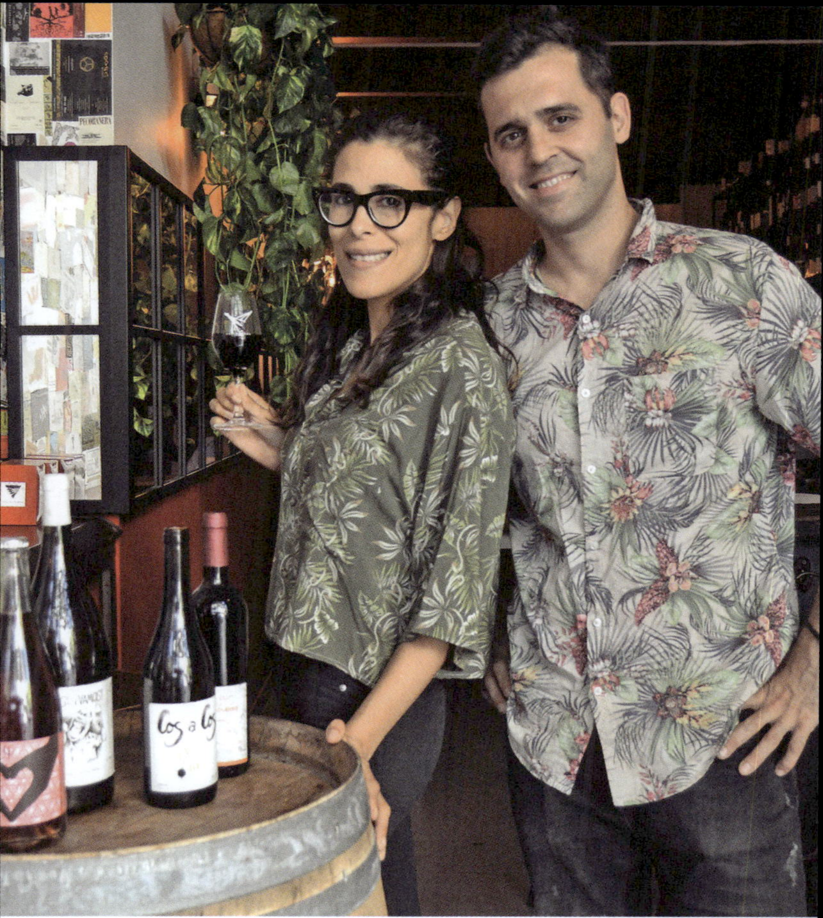

style. **Denassus**, in Poble Sec, has this touch. Here, you can find a range of plates, from traditional tapas to well-crafted, hearty meals, and a wine menu with 150 names. Of these, 70% are dedicated to biodynamic and natural wines, and the house wine is one made by the owners, in collaboration with partner wineries around Catalonia. **Garage Beer Co**'s bar over in Sant Antoni also sources its natural wine (despite its name) from a wide range of distributors, as well as directly from producers.

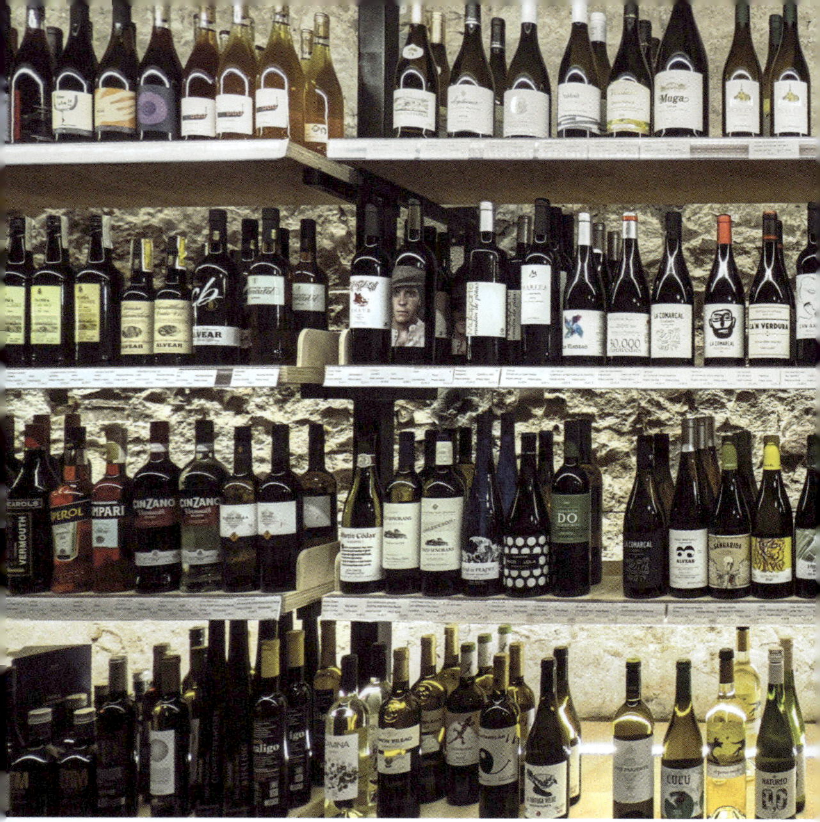

Finally, walking into **Vins Per Tu** in Clot feels like walking into a friend's home – a friend who spends all their money on wine. Here, generic, mass-produced bodega wine is replaced with carefully selected boutique natural wine, and instead of the standard tapas menu, you'll find innovative dishes, all for fair barrio prices. There is no wine menu. Instead, Willy, the owner, will open a few different bottles every evening to choose from, depending on the season, the weather, or simply what he's feeling that day.

That's all in the spirit of savoring natural wine. Can Cisa's sommelier Víctor Martín offers some advice to enjoy the dynamic, ever-changing complexity of natural wines: "It is a

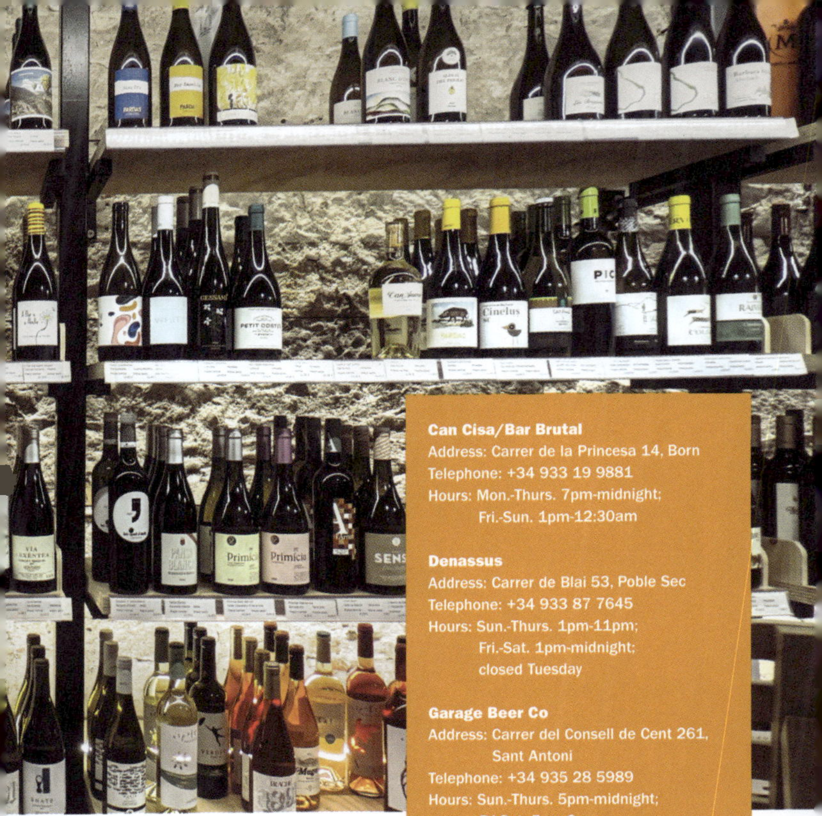

matter of energy. It is about how this wine makes you feel. It is a vibe that in other wines is not so present." Wine should be "alive," the product of dynamic vineyards. As with all living organisms, change is the name of the game: Natural wine evolves as you drink it, and the natural wine movement is changing our wine culture as we know it.

Can Cisa/Bar Brutal
Address: Carrer de la Princesa 14, Born
Telephone: +34 933 19 9881
Hours: Mon.-Thurs. 7pm-midnight;
Fri.-Sun. 1pm-12:30am

Denassus
Address: Carrer de Blai 53, Poble Sec
Telephone: +34 933 87 7645
Hours: Sun.-Thurs. 1pm-11pm;
Fri.-Sat. 1pm-midnight;
closed Tuesday

Garage Beer Co
Address: Carrer del Consell de Cent 261, Sant Antoni
Telephone: +34 935 28 5989
Hours: Sun.-Thurs. 5pm-midnight;
Fri-Sat. 5pm-3am

L'Anima Del Vi
Address: Carrer dels Vigatans 8, Born
Telephone: +34 933 68 3612
Hours: Wed.-Sat. 7pm-midnight;
closed Sunday (and for summer)

Vins Per Tu
Address: Carrer del Clot 39, Tienda 2, Clot
Telephone: +34 93 663 8074
Hours: Mon.-Sat. 6pm-11pm plus
Tues. & Sat. 11:30am-1pm;
closed Sunday

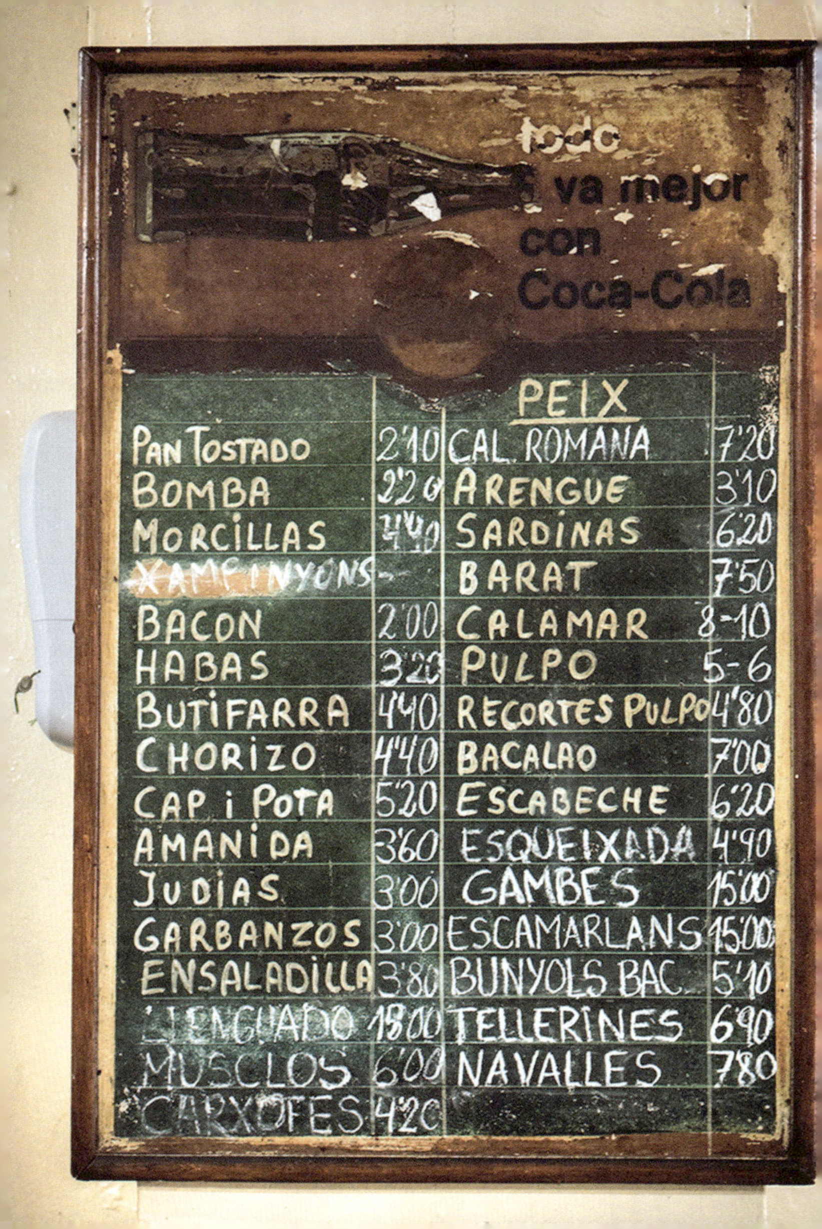
todo
va mejor
con
Coca-Cola
PEIX
PAN TOSTADO 2'10
BOMBA 2'20
MORCILLAS 4'40
XAMPINYONS
BACON 2'00
HABAS 3'20
BUTIFARRA 4'40
CHORIZO 4'40
CAP i POTA 5'20
AMANIDA 3'60
JUDIAS 3'00
GARBANZOS 3'00
ENSALADILLA 3'80
LLENGUADO 18'00
MUSCLOS 6'00
CARXOFES 4'20
CAL. ROMANA 7'20
ARENGUE 3'10
SARDINAS 6'20
BARAT 7'50
CALAMAR 8-10
PULPO 5-6
RECORTES PULPO 4'80
BACALAO 7'00
ESCABECHE 6'20
ESQUEIXADA 4'90
GAMBES 15'00
ESCAMARLANS 15'00
BUNYOLS BAC. 5'10
TELLERINES 6'90
NAVALLES 7'80

SPECIALS

CALÇOTS

Not Your Average Onion

We don't mind winter in Catalonia because it means the return of *calçots*, our beloved spring onions, and *calçotadas*, the wonderful celebrations that bring people together to eat them. As the legend goes, a 19th-century Catalan farmer was out experimenting in his fields when he came up with a new kind of longer, juicier green onion, the *calçot*. In creating the onion, the farmer also paved the way for the rise of a distinctly Catalan cultural event.

Why are people in Barcelona so crazy about getting together and eating calçots, which are really nothing more than scorched green onions? Because they are a good excuse to meet up with friends; because eating calçots requires a certain skill, and people love showing off; because it's funny how you end up with dirty hands and reeking of onions; and, last but not least, because they're delicious. When it comes to calçots, you always want to eat just one more.

The most popular way to cook calçots is to grill them over an open barbecue. Rather than fully cleaning the onions, it's best to leave some soil on their surface, which protects their outer skin. The calçots are grilled directly over the flames until they become completely burnt on the outside. (Don't worry: the best part – the inside – will be perfectly cooked.) They are typically served wrapped in newspaper to keep them warm and eaten off curved terracotta roof tiles. Calçots must be eaten directly with the fingers; the trick is to hold them by the green leaves with one hand and pull off the burned and blackened outer layer of skin with the other hand. The tender and juicy inner bulb is then dipped in *salsa romesco*, a special sauce made from dried red peppers, nuts, garlic, vinegar and olive oil that is typical of Tarragona.

Calçotadas typically take place between January and March in public barbecues in the countryside, known as *merenderos*; at rural Catalan restaurants called *masías*; or in peoples' homes. In Barcelona, many restaurants offering grilled dishes

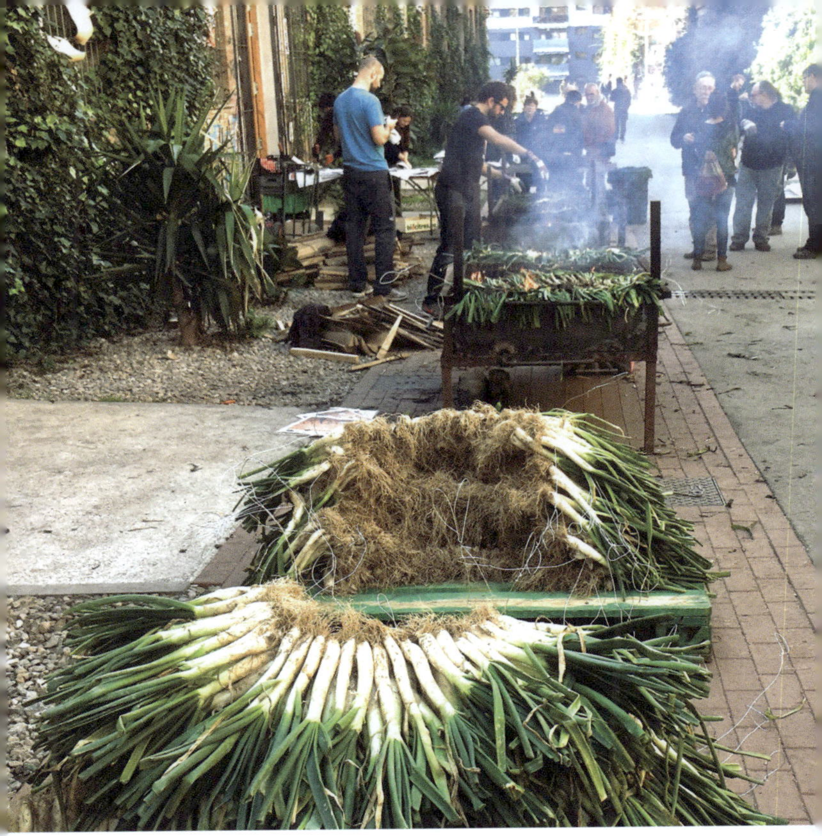

include calçots in their menus during the season. If you want to taste prized calçots from the Valls region, **Can Xurradas** in L'Eixample, a more upscale grill spot known for its meats, is a great option. For a *masía* experience inside the city, **Can Travi Nou** located in a beautiful and rustic 17th-century house – offers two special calçotada menus.

Can Travi Nou
Address: Calle Jorge Manrique s/n, Horta
Telephone: +34 93 428 0301
Hours: Tues.-Sat. 1pm-4pm & 8pm-11pm; Sun. 1-4pm

Can Xurrades
Address: Carrer de Casanova 212, L'Eixample
Telephone: +34 93 218 7370
Hours: Mon.-Sat. 1pm-4pm & 8pm-midnight; Sun. 1pm-4pm

CATALAN CHEESE

From Old Traditions to New Wave

Catalonia produces the greatest variety of artisan cheeses of all the regions in Spain, with more than 250 kinds at last count, many of them made by small producers or in milk cooperatives in the mountains using both pasteurized and raw milk from cows, sheep or goats.

The oldest documented Catalan cheeses are *mató, serrat* and the singular *tupí*. Soft, spreadable, ricotta-like mató is easy to make and is usually made from cow's milk, and somtimes also goat's milk. In medieval times, it was served with honey in a dessert called *mel i mató,* and this combo is still commonly offered today in cheese shops and traditional restaurants throughout Catalonia.

Serrat is an intensely flavored, round, compact (its name derives from the word *cerrado*, or "closed," for its structure), washed-rind sheep's milk cheese with an exterior that is traditionally decorated with various drawings and shapes. It's aged like Manchego and is similar in taste and texture, but smaller.

The pungent, spicy and creamy tupí has origins as old as those of serrat and was made by the same shepherds and farmers in the Pyrenees mountains. They put leftover and overly mature bits of serrat in a clay vessel known as a tupí and mixed them with a strong liquor like *orujo* (grappa), *anis* or *ratafía*.

Catalan cheesemaking in the 21st century has flourished dramatically, with a new generation of cheesemakers who are internationally influenced, yet also grounded in local traditions and interested in improving the national market with new cheeses.

Biologist Paula Fonollà manages cheese production at Mas Reixagó, whose raw cow's milk Sant Ignasi has a soft rind and paste, with an almost liquid center, intense barnyard flavor, grassy notes and a lengthy finish. Mas Reixagó is also known for Blau de Jutglar, a creamy, spicy blue cheese also made from raw cow's milk.

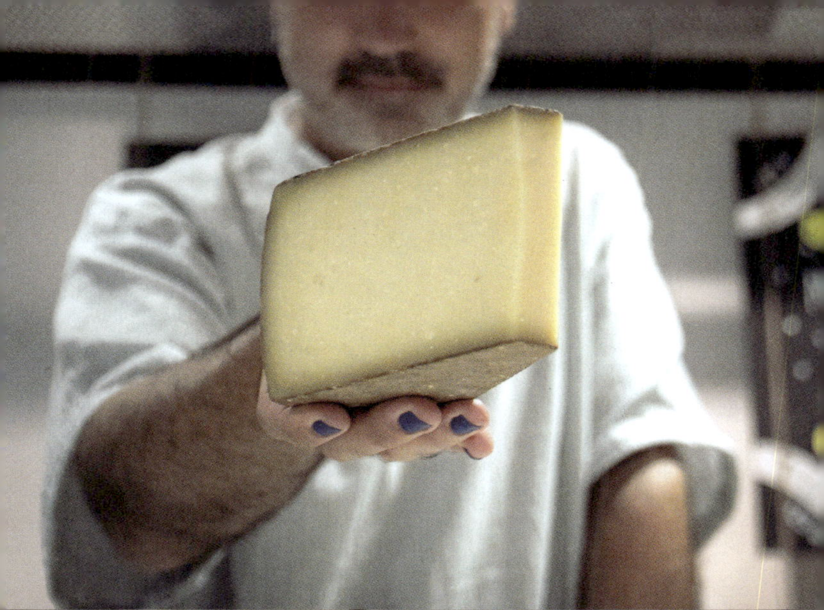

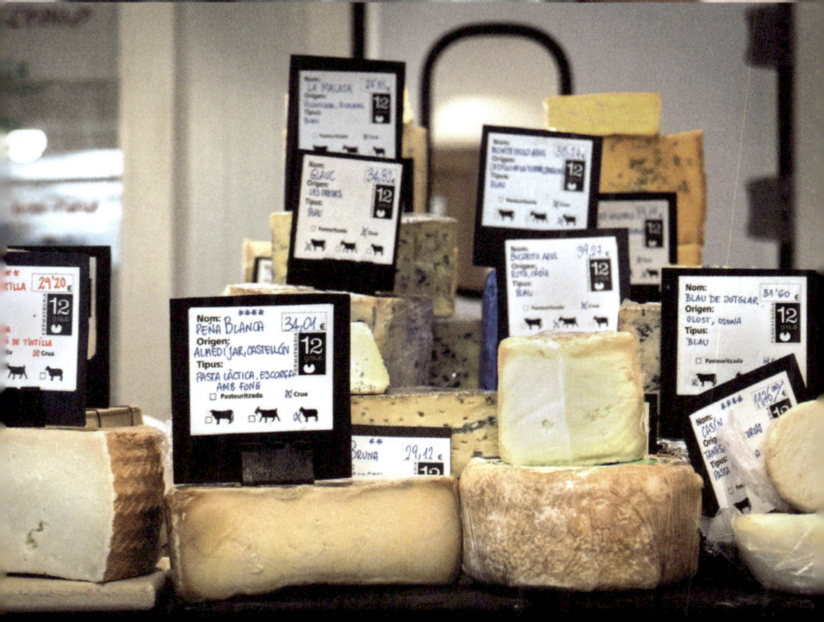

Nom:
PEÑA BLANCA
34,01 €
Origen:
ALMEDIJAR, CASTELLÓN
Tipus:
PASTA LÀCTICA, ESCORÇA AMB FONG
Pasteuritzada
Crua
12
Nom:
BLAU DE JUTGLAR
31'60 €
Origen:
OLOST, OSONA
Tipus:
BLAU
Pasteuritzada
12
Nom:
GLAUC
34,82 €
Origen:
Tipus:
BLAU
Crua
BRUNA
29,12 €
29'20 €
Crua

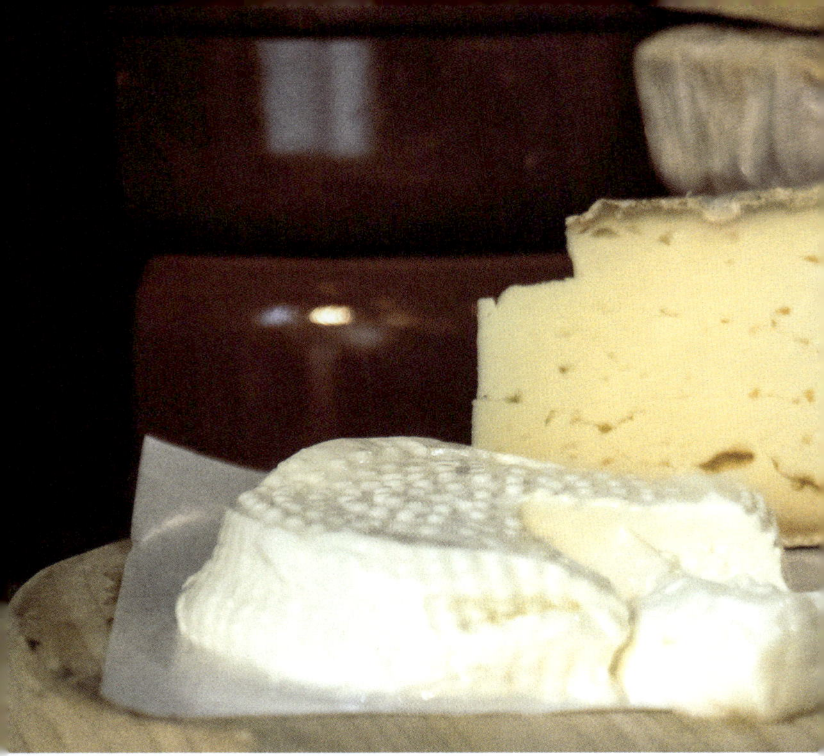

Former agronomic engineer Salvador Maura I Rajó of Mas d'Eroles makes the wonderful raw cow's milk Castellot, which has a brushed rind, compact interior and gentle persistence. We especially love his Brisat, also made from raw cow's milk, whose grape pomace-covered rind lends it a subtle hint of wine and fruit.

Pablo García of La Balda turns fresh milk from his neighbors in and around Sant Martin de Llémena into a simple soft cheese, Fermió, that is elegant, full-bodied and delicious.

The raw cow's milk Puigpedrós from Molí de Ger has a firm interior and concentrated nuttiness with floral notes. Washed with brine, Puigpedrós has a distinctive orange rind.

Manel Marcè of Mas Marcè produces Llanut, which means "woolly." Each piece of cheese is covered in a bit of sheep's wool for preserva-

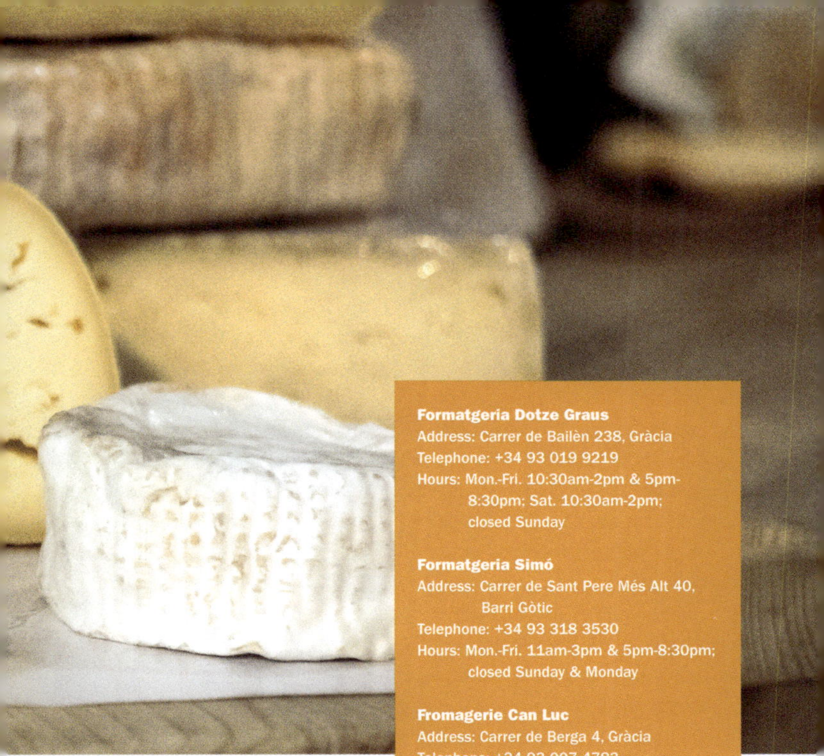

tion and presentation and must be very carefully cleaned before being served. This cheese is made from the raw milk of Mas Marcè's own sheep, as well as vegetable rennet, which results in a fresh, milky, barnyard flavor.

You can taste these and other artisan cheeses at markets, specialized shops, restaurants and bars in Barcelona, including those listed in the accompanying box.

Formatgeria Dotze Graus
Address: Carrer de Bailèn 238, Gràcia
Telephone: +34 93 019 9219
Hours: Mon.-Fri. 10:30am-2pm & 5pm-8:30pm; Sat. 10:30am-2pm; closed Sunday

Formatgeria Simó
Address: Carrer de Sant Pere Més Alt 40, Barri Gòtic
Telephone: +34 93 318 3530
Hours: Mon.-Fri. 11am-3pm & 5pm-8:30pm; closed Sunday & Monday

Fromagerie Can Luc
Address: Carrer de Berga 4, Gràcia
Telephone: +34 93 007 4783
Hours: 10am-2pm & 4:30pm-8pm; closed Sunday

Llet Crua
Address: Carrer de Càceres 14, Sants
Telephone: +34 93 503 1543
Hours: Tues.-Fri. 10am-2pm & 5pm-8:30pm; Sat. 10am-2pm; closed Sunday & Monday

La Teca de Vila Viniteca
Address: Carrer Agullers 9, La Ribera-El Born
Telephone: +34 93 777 7017
Hours: 8:30am-8:30pm (Sat. 8:30am-2:30pm in July & August); closed Sunday

CATALAN ICE CREAM & GELATO

The Real Scoop

As expected from a Mediterranean city with perpetually sunny weather, Barcelona always had plenty of excellent ice cream options, even in the dead of winter. The city's traditional spots have been the Valencian *turronerías* (p. 152) and *horchaterías* (*orxaterias* in Catalan, p. 140), where locals can get tasty *helados* with a more artisanal bent. **La Valenciana** offers wonderful ice creams with flavors like Xixona-style Marcona almond nougat and *leche merengada* (meringue milk). But as the city grows, many of these longstanding places have been disappearing, leaving stops like Sirvent in Sant Antoni, Planellas Donat in the Gotic, La Campana in Born, or Tío Che in Poblenou to hold down the old-school ice cream front. With that, a new generation of frozen dreams have stepped onto the summer dessert stage – more innovative, proudly handcrafted, and combining unique and local ingredients.

Take **Mamá Heladera**, where owner Irene Iborra turns childhood memories submitted by locals ("peaches washed in seawater at the beach" or "swinging under the pine tree with a popsicle") into ice cream flavors (salted peach or redcurrant with pine honey). The shop sits next to the aforementioned Tío Che, which opened in 1912. Irene is part of the fifth generation of Tío Che, and turned her fascination for her family's world of ice cream into a new business model. "I fell in love with what ice cream generates in people – the search for a perfect moment," she says.

The first memory Mamá Heladera recreated, still available to taste in-shop, is "Grandma sends you to the cherry tree for a snack" (*La abuela te manda al cerezo a merendar*). "We asked around about familiar smells from people's relatives, and the most mentioned one was lavender from the grandmas, which was used to aromatize closets and dressers back in the day," Irene explains. "We combined it with a touch of cherry, from the collective memory of climbing cherry trees."

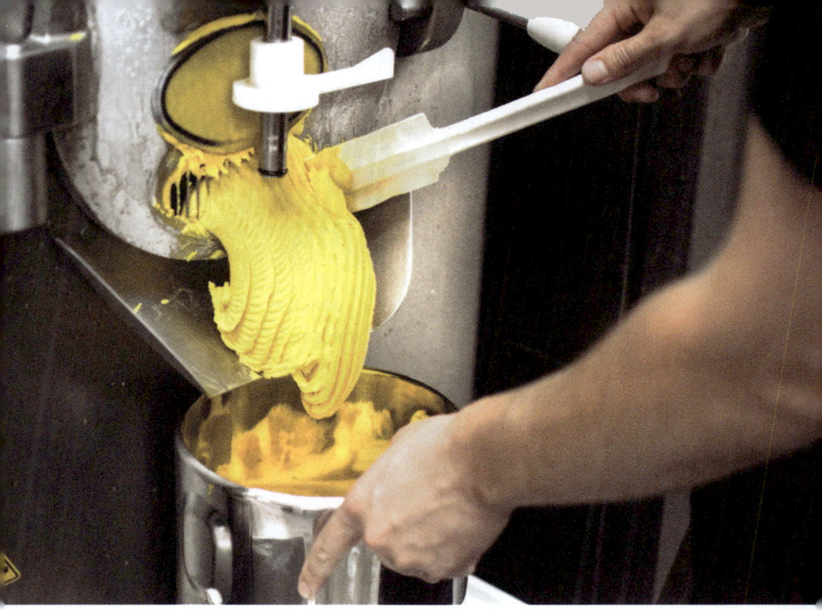

Like Mamá Heladera, the ice cream shops pushing a new wave of creation in Barcelona along exist at something of a cultural crossroads. They work with local Catalan ingredients of the highest quality (with a focus on organic, sustainable and seasonal materials), but they are also deeply influenced by Italian gelato techniques. When in 2010 Massimo Pignata introduced to Barcelona the Italian *pozzetti*, a well of deep stainless steel buckets that keeps gelato cold and preserved without the need for additives, his gelateria **DeLaCrem** became a reference point for some of the best gelato in the city. Its two locations produce gelatos and sorbets daily for around 30 shops and restaurants in the province. They range from well-known dessert flavors like carrot cake to boozy inspirations like Piña Colada, to more gastronomic combinations of savory and succulent ingredients like tomato gazpacho, ginger, chili, basil and watermelon.

Of course Delacrem has traditional flavors on offer, but the more creative (saffron or rosemary cream or EVOO lemon) are screaming to be sampled. Like at Mamá Heladera, the fascinating fir with cranberries evokes a walk in the piney woods. The Mediterra-

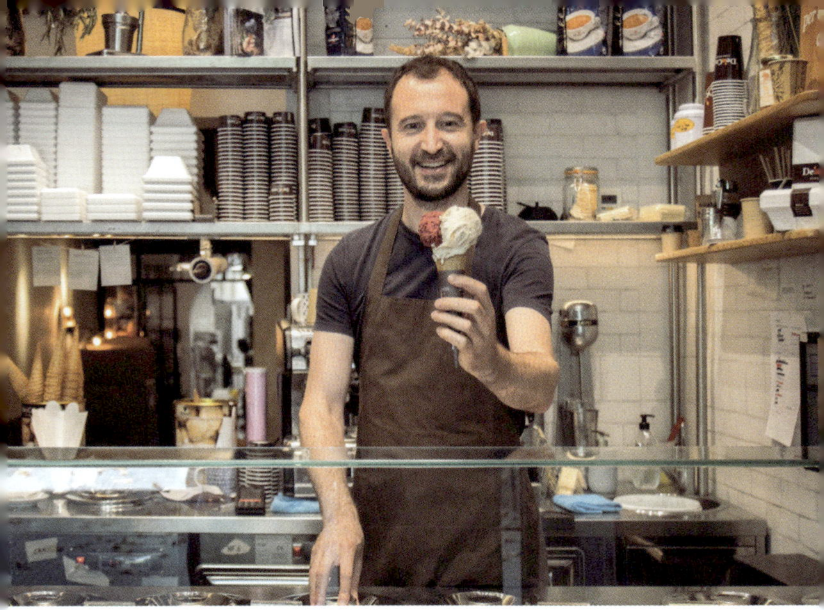

nean basil with lemon, one of our favorites, is refreshing and aromatic. And speaking of Mediterranean aromas, the seasonal fig leaf flavor is a can't-miss when available.

Paral·lelo is another best at Italian-Catalan gelatos. As the trio of Italian owners say, they offer "a parallel world" of flavors, intensity and creativity in gelatos, sorbets and premium popsicles. Their famous, old-school cart is parked inside the shop – a feature that both the grandpas and youngsters love for different reasons – and is whipped out for open-air events around the city. What makes their gelato so special is the careful selection of local suppliers for ingredients. Delectable seasonal creations include their refreshing gazpacho granita, made with cherry tomato and strawberries from El Maresme, with a subtle hint of cucumber. A close second is the Grana Padano cheese flavor, which they recommend combining with a Modena vinegar reduction, dried tomatoes and lyophilized raspberries. But their bestseller, the pistachio, is the landmark in a sea of pistachio gelatos, made with the tiny nut from the Lleida province and roasted with a bit of its husk, giving it an intense, wild taste.

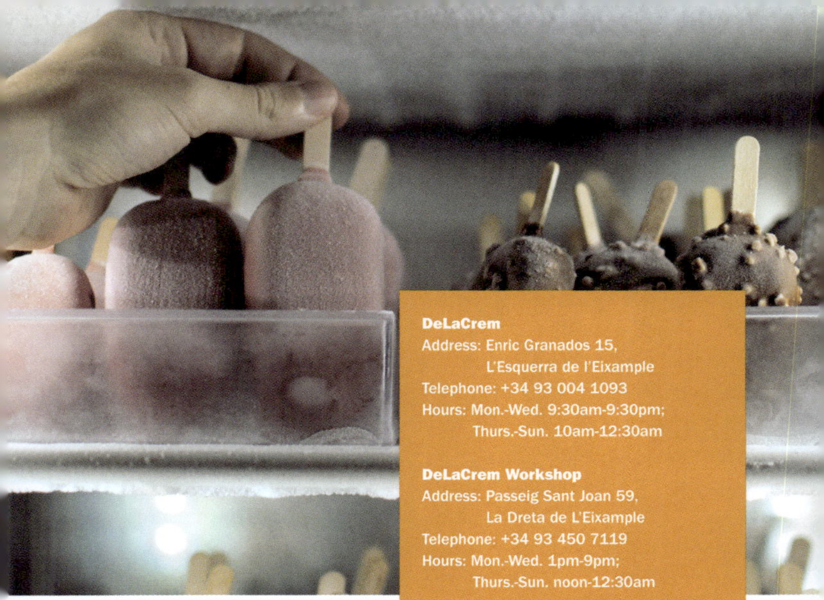

Many more ice cream spots abound, but **Rocambolesc** gets a special mention. Its name is a portmanteau meaning "bizarre" or "fanciful," and this is the ethos behind Catalan Michelin-starred pastry chef Jordi Roca's playful creations. The best example: a strawberry popsicle in the shape of his nose. Rocambolesc uses organic milk from the sustainable farm La Selvatana, crafting gelatos and sorbets with toppings like violet marshmallow, sablé butter cookie chips, pop rocks or fantastical clouds of cotton candy. Fortunately, Barcelona's surfeit of sunny days means there's plenty of opportunities to try them all.

DeLaCrem
Address: Enric Granados 15,
L'Esquerra de l'Eixample
Telephone: +34 93 004 1093
Hours: Mon.-Wed. 9:30am-9:30pm;
Thurs.-Sun. 10am-12:30am

DeLaCrem Workshop
Address: Passeig Sant Joan 59,
La Dreta de L'Eixample
Telephone: +34 93 450 7119
Hours: Mon.-Wed. 1pm-9pm;
Thurs.-Sun. noon-12:30am

La Valenciana
Address: Carrer de A'ribau 16, L'Eixample
Telephone: +34 93 317 2771
Hours: Mon.-Fri. 8am-11:30pm;
Sat.-Sun. 9am-2pm & 4pm-11:30pm

Mamá Heladera (and Tío Che)
Address: Rambla del Poblenou 44-46,
Poblenou
Telephone: +34 93 309 1872
Hours: Sun.-Thurs. noon-1pm;
Fri.-Sat. 1pm-11:30pm

Paral·lelo
Address: Carrer de Séneca 18, Gràcia
Telephone: +34 93 450 7119
Hours: Sun.-Thurs. noon-10:30pm;
Fri.-Sat. noon-midnight

Rocambolesc
Address: La Rambla 51-59, Raval
Telephone: +34 93 743 1125
Hours: 11:30am-11pm

COLMADOS

Gourmet Groceries

Colmados, queviures, mantequerías, ultramarinos... There are a number of names for Barcelona's traditional grocery shops, temples of specially curated items ranging from fine charcuterie to preserved seafood, wine, spirits and cheeses.

In the 19th century, Barcelona's large neighborhood markets were the main centers of food distribution in the city. The first colmados originally served as the place to get all the specialty delicatessen products and spices unavailable in the markets, and also supplied a variety of new jarred, packaged and canned products that industrialization introduced to Spain.

At the same time, the internationalization of food meant that more exotic delicacies were imported for the enjoyment of the wealthy classes – sugar and coffee from Cuba, chocolate from Mexico or Venezuela, caviar from Iran or pineapple from Costa Rica. Nothing was more fashionable on the Christmas tables of Barcelona families in the mid-20th century than a pineapple. These days, the shops that have managed to survive contain culinary wonders that can't be found in the supermarkets that have all but eradicated Barcelona's independent grocers. The colmados still standing are an iconic piece of the city's history – charming, beautiful old-school stores with highly specialized clerks wearing professional coats that seem to say: *I know what you are looking for, but here, we have something even better – let me show you.*

Any adult in Barcelona remembers the huge windows of **Colmado Quílez** filled with bottles, charcuterie and other sumptuous and colorful products from the best areas of Catalonia, Spain and abroad. The curator was a pioneer in many things and imported under his own brand: clams from Korea, pineapple "Del Monte" and other products which were very trendy in the mid-20th century. In 2014, high rent forced the shop, opened in 1906, to retreat to its back room, going from a 40-square-meter emporium of gourmet treasures to just 4. "It was a reduction, but only in space," says the current manager,

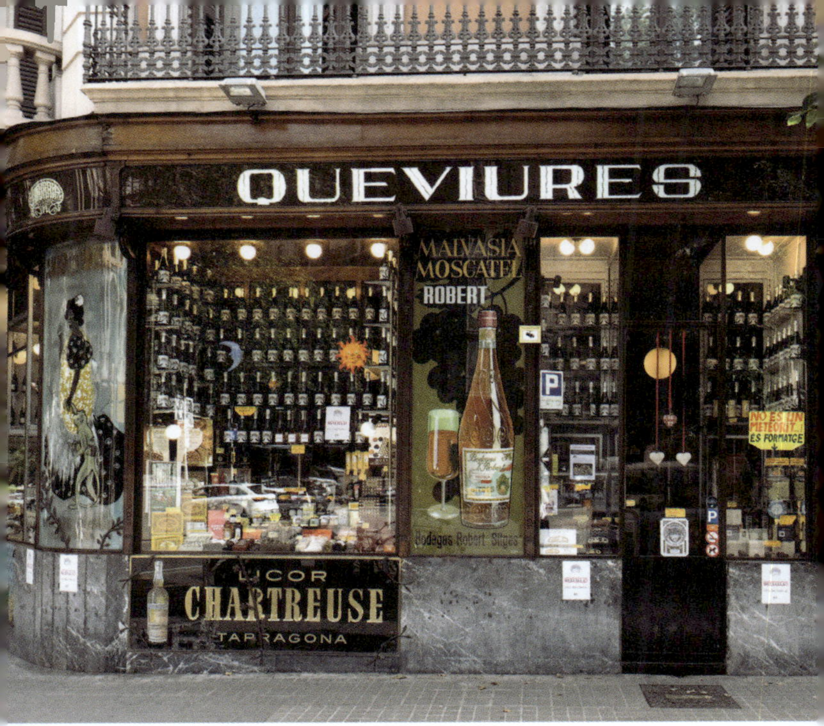

Faustino Muñoz. "The soul of Quílez is the same. Same products, same personnel. Over time, Quílez has only grown in prestige, and remains an iconic part of the city."

One of Barcelona's oldest colmados, **Queviures Múrria**, and its original Modernista-style facade, is under historical protection, having first opened in 1898 as Colmado La Purísima. Many of its original elements are still there, including the beautiful liquor advertisements outside, the wood and marble counters and the olive oil taps used to sell the oil in bulk. Its third-generation owner, Joan Múrria, can speak to customers about the history behind the shelves full of coffee and Bonilla chips, as well as the hypnotic variety of Manchego or the highly-regarded Norwegian Kraftkar.

A recent renovation means we can enjoy their gourmet products bodega-style in the adjoining Bar Murri. For a more clandestine affair,

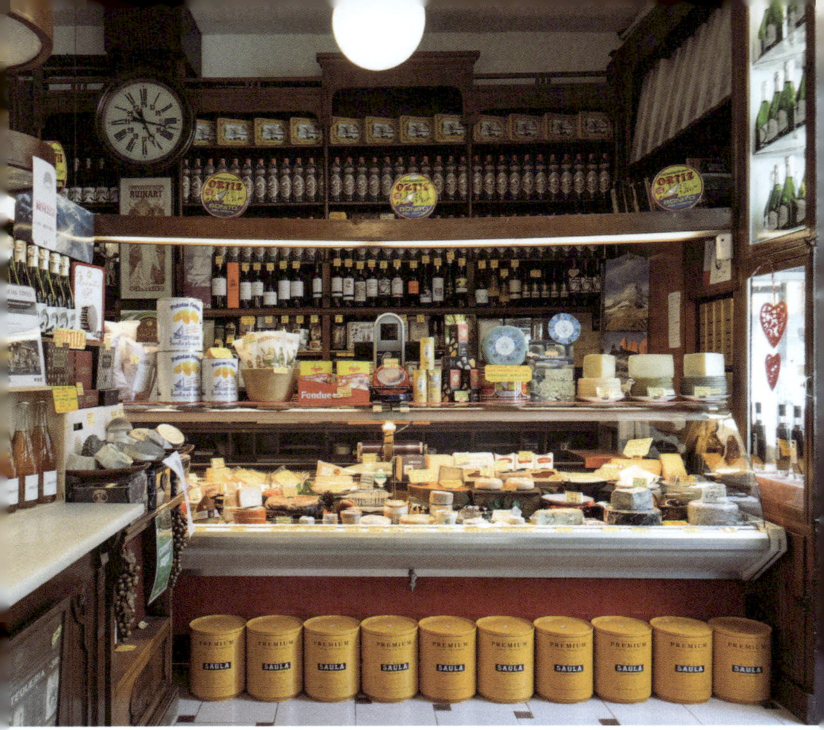

a tiny reservation-only restaurant is tucked away in what was once the storage attic.

The shop used to label everything in Catalan and – during the years of the Franco dictatorship, which had acted to suppress expressions of regional culture and made Spanish the mandatory national language – refused to change its sign. It remains *queviures*, meaning "food" in Catalan, as opposed to colmado, which is a Spanish word from Andalusia.

Third-generation colmado **Mantequería Lasierra**, run by Ramón Lasierra Valén, also maintains its name as an ode to its origins. It began as a mantequería, a typical 19th-century shop found in Barcelona, Madrid and other big Spanish cities which specialized in the sale of butter, cheese and other dairy products as they became more accessible to the urbanites of the time. Soon, the mantequerías started to include many other convenient products

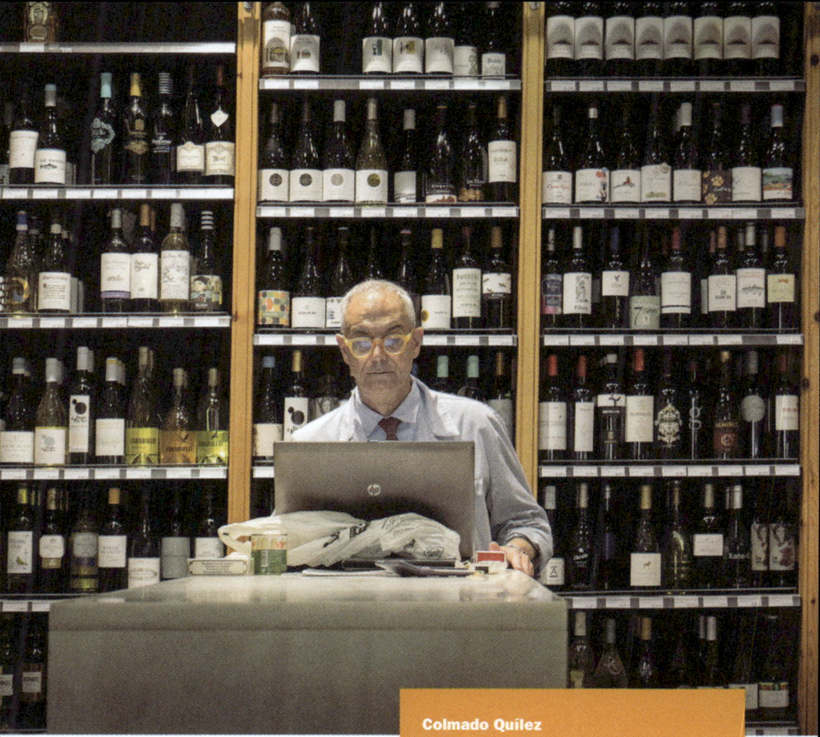

like cookies, detergent or legumes in bulk, until they became a kind of neighborhood colmado.

Instead of lowering prices in the '60s, when the supermarket boom struck, Ramón says his grandfather decided to get rid of all the basics and offer the most selective, hard-to-find products. "Our clientele really values what we have to offer and they let us advise them," Ramón says – it's what we love about colmados, after all.

Colmado Quílez
Address: Rambla de Catalunya 65, L'Eixample
Telephone: +34 93 215 8785
Hours: Mon.-Fri. 9am-2pm & 4:30pm-8:30pm; Sat. 9am-2pm

Mantequería Lasierra
Address: Carrer del Rosselló 160, L'Eixample
Telephone: +34 93 453 3575
Hours: Mon.-Fri. 10am-2pm & 5:15pm-8:30pm; Sat. 10am-2pm

Queviures Múrria
Address: Carrer de Roger de Llúria 85, L'Eixample
Telephone: +34 93 215 5789
Hours: Tues.-Sat. 10am-10:30pm

JAMÓN IBÉRICO

Spain's Leg-endary Ham

Ham is one of Spain's best-known culinary treasures, and different types of the cured meat offer their own flavors and characteristics, depending on the breed of pig, how the animal has been fed and raised, and how its meat has been processed and cured. The two major categories of Spanish ham are *jamón serrano* and *jamón ibérico*. The former comes from white or pink pigs normally raised on farms and fattened on grain, while the latter comes from the Iberian breed and is made according to very specific practices, yielding a special and often costly product.

The Iberian pig is an ancient breed of (usually) black pig that requires much more time to reach maturity and the right weight for slaughter than conventional breeds. Spain's best pork products – not just cured ham but also fresh cuts – come from pigs raised this way. The ham made from the black pig, *pata negra* ("black foot"), is easy to recognize by the black hoof, the distinctive shape of the leg and the intense maroon color of the meat.

The word "jamón" generally refers to the back leg, but the front legs are cured or cooked in the same way. When cured, the front leg is called the *paleta* or *paletilla* in Spanish and *espatlla* in Catalan. These tend to be smaller, less tender and juicy, often sold without the bone and less expensive than the other kind.

Jamón ibérico is produced mostly in the western-central and southern parts of Spain, with protected designations of origin guaranteeing the quality of the hams and the expertise that went into making them. Iberian pigs can be reared using industrial methods, but for the best meat, the pigs are raised in *dehesas*, or oak forests, where the animals can roam among the trees and forage for wild fruit, acorns and grass.

Jamón ibérico de cebo is the lowest subcategory and comes from grain-fed pigs. *Jamón ibérico de recebo* comes from animals fed a mixture of grain, pasture and acorns, while *jamón ibérico de bellota*, the most prized of all, comes from

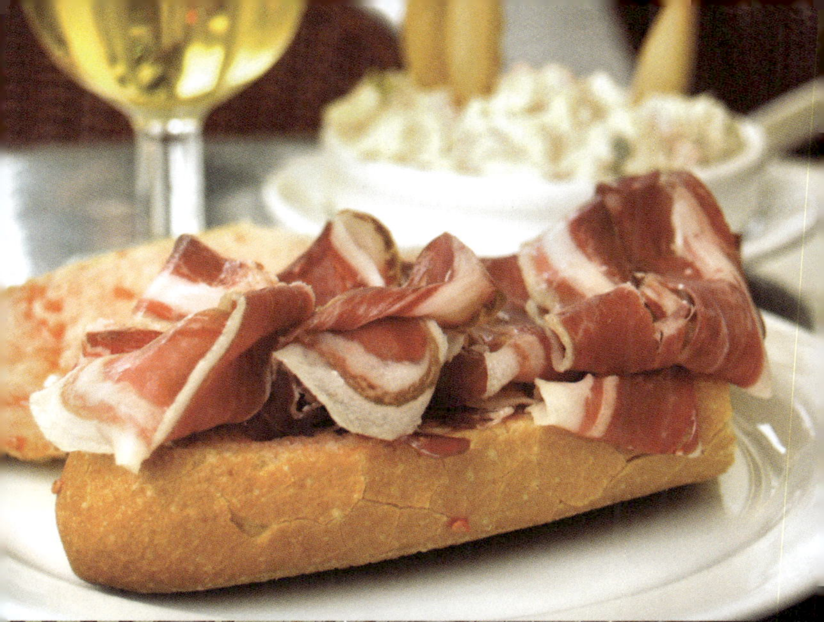

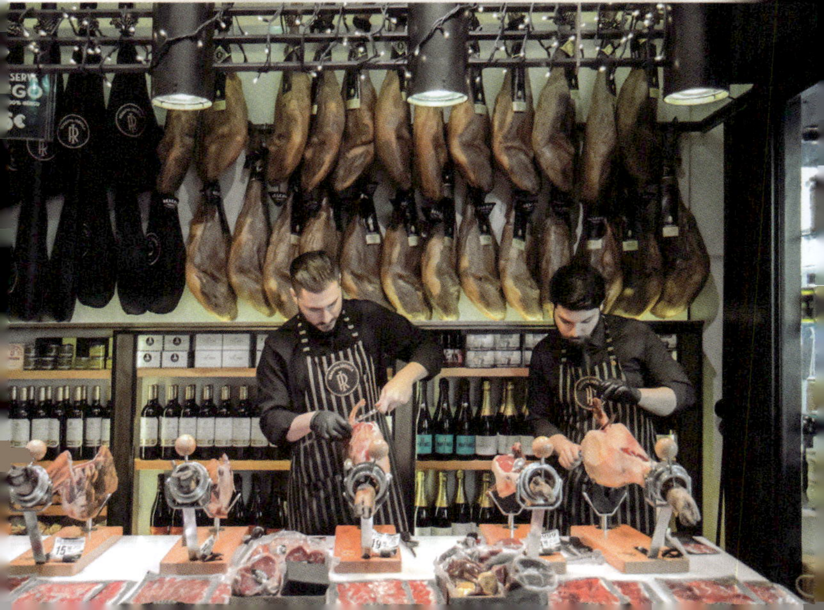

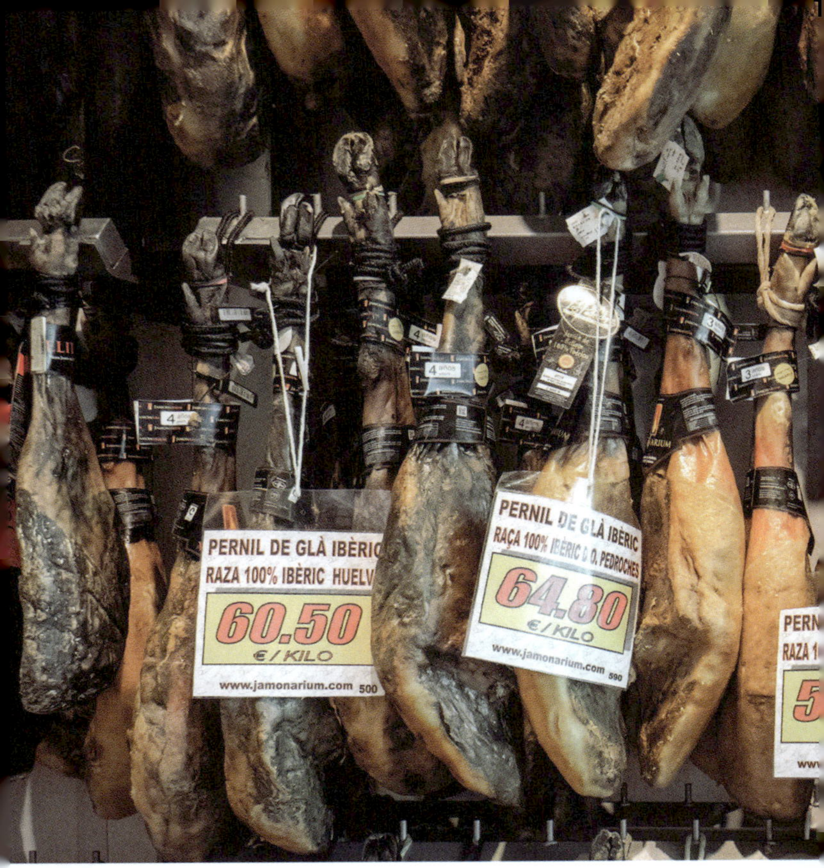

dehesa-raised pigs (*bellota* means "acorn") and boasts a luxurious amount of fat, an incredibly silky, melting texture and uniquely sweet-salty flavors. The definitive official code to recognize the best acorn Iberian ham is a series of colored seals: black (100% Iberian acorn-fed), red (75% or 50% Iberian purity and 100% acorn-fed), green (75% or 50% Iberian and free-range-fodder-fattened) and white (intensively fodder-fattened).

You can find jamón ibérico in bars, restaurants and food shops all over Barcelona (and Spain, for that matter), but the shops listed in the accompanying box are our favorite

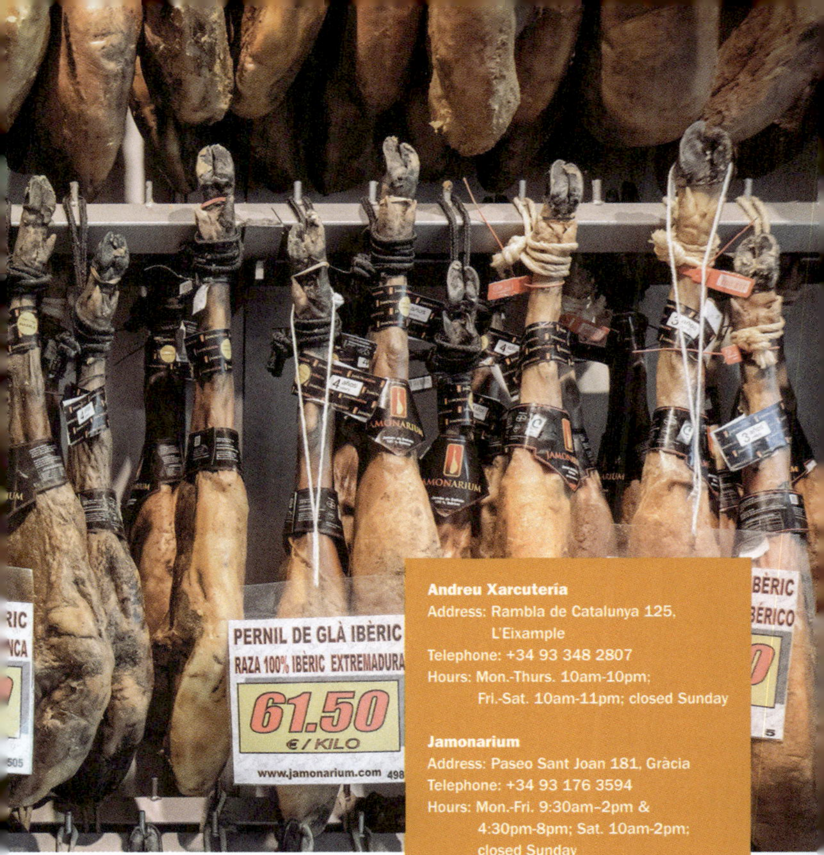

places in the city to get it. For jamón ibérico de bellota, look to specialized stalls in the markets, such as Aroma Ibèric stalls 183-5 in the Boquería market, or Can Marti Carles stalls 5-7 in the Santa Caterina market, as well as Enrique Tomás or Reserva Ibérica, both big chains with numerous shops across the city.

Andreu Xarcutería
Address: Rambla de Catalunya 125, L'Eixample
Telephone: +34 93 348 2807
Hours: Mon.-Thurs. 10am-10pm; Fri.-Sat. 10am-11pm; closed Sunday

Jamonarium
Address: Paseo Sant Joan 181, Gràcia
Telephone: +34 93 176 3594
Hours: Mon.-Fri. 9:30am-2pm & 4:30pm-8pm; Sat. 10am-2pm; closed Sunday

Moniberic
Address: Carrer de Mallorca 160 / Vía Laietana 46 / Carrer de Sants 180
Telephone: +34 93 451 0426
Hours: 9am-9pm; closed Sunday

Pernilería CEX
Address: Carrer de Cáceres 125, Sants
Telephone: +34 934 91 4662
Hours: Mon.-Fri. 9am-8:30pm; Sat. 9am-3pm; closed Sunday

OLIVE OIL

Spain's Liquid Gold

Olives arrived in the southern part of the Iberian Peninsula around 9th century B.C.E. with the Phoenicians, and Spain leads production of olive oil to this day, with 45 percent of the global total. In recent decades, the Spanish olive oil industry has become part of the wonderful culinary flowering the country is experiencing. It's a new golden (or, perhaps, greenish) age for Spanish olive oil.

Of the 260 different olive varieties in Spain, only about 20 are used for the best olive oil production. As with wine, the characteristics of an oil depend on raw materials, *terroir*, and harvesting and production methods. The trend in Spain right now is to produce greener and fresher single-variety extra-virgin olive oil and more organic ones.

Olives harvested early, when they are still a bit green, make oils with live polyphenols; intense, fresh, herbal and fruity aromas; some bitterness; and a peppery bite. These oils are best enjoyed raw, with bread or vegetables or as a finishing touch to point up the flavors of cooked dishes. More mature olives generally produce oil with more golden tones, a nuttier and sweeter flavor, and less bitterness and spiciness. This oil is less delicate, more stable and thus better for cooking.

Alongside the rise of excellent extra-virgin is the increasing number of specialty olive oil shops that have an important role as distributors, educators and curators of market trends, connecting consumers and producers.

Ana Segovia opened **Orolíquido** in Barcelona's Gothic quarter in 2005, when she decided to change careers and reconnect with her grandparents' land through olive oil. Ana was born in France after her grandfather and parents left their native Andalusia to flee the civil war and Franco's dictatorship. Located in the former antique shop that Ana's father opened after returning to Spain, Orolíquido sells some of the country's most prized and interesting

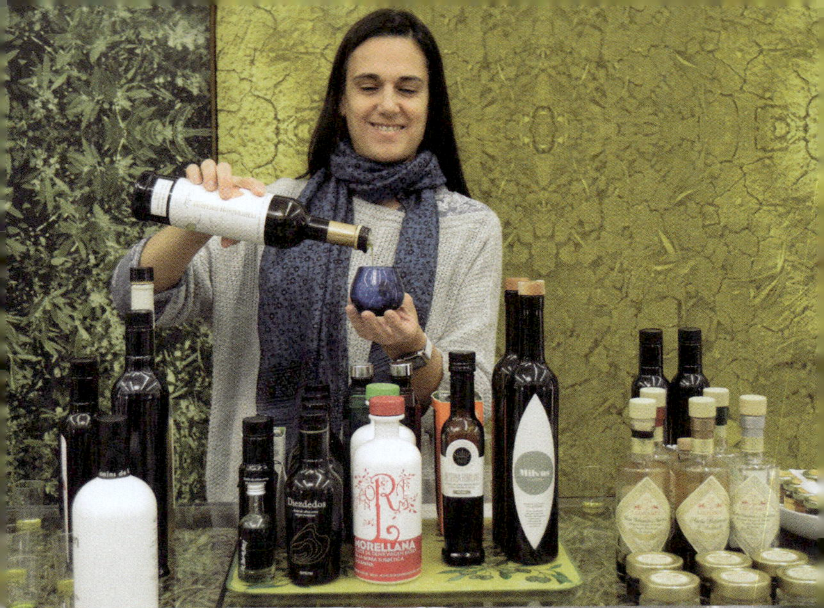
Diezdedos
MORELLANA
Milvus

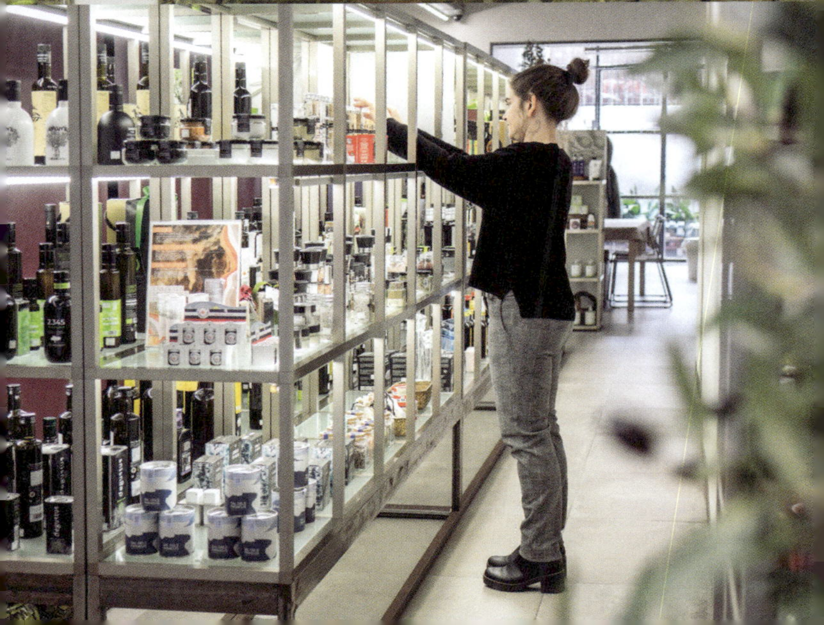

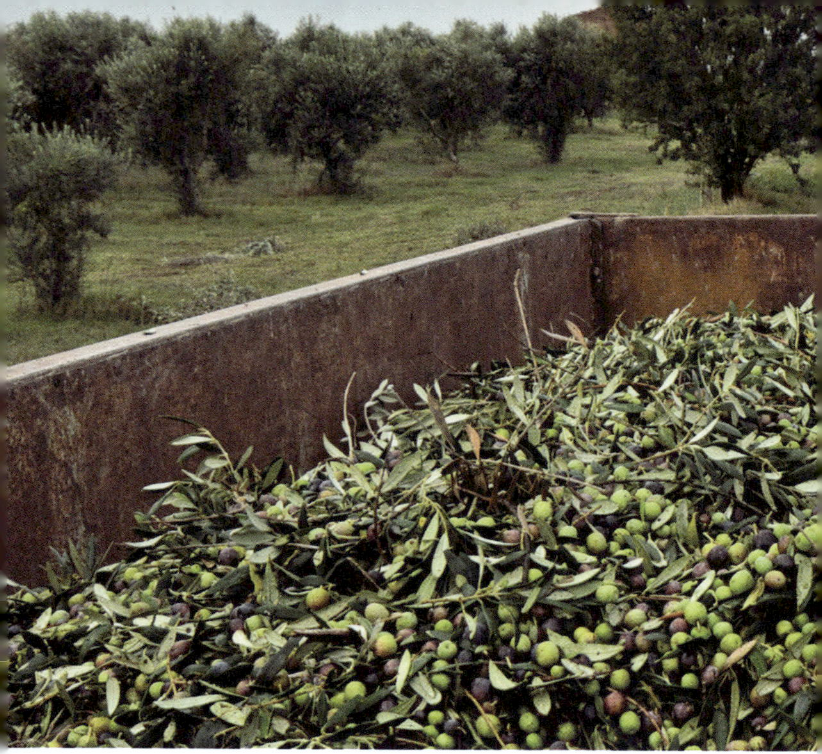

extra-virgin olive oils, along with a top-notch selection of those made by Catalan producers and a range of olive oil-based cosmetics.

Inspired by the wine shop concept, Sandra Stefani opened **Oli Sal** in Gràcia in 2006 with the idea of elevating Spanish extra-virgin olive oil to the gourmet level it deserves. Sandra works with high-quality and award-winning oils from all over Spain, but the shop concentrates on a wide and well-curated selection of Catalan brands. The oils range from the most precious bottles to economy-sized garrafas and cans. Here, you can also find olive-based cosmetic products, as well as an array of salts and vinegars as well. Sandra told us that the shop's best customers, besides chefs and food lovers, are many of the elderly women in the neighborhood.

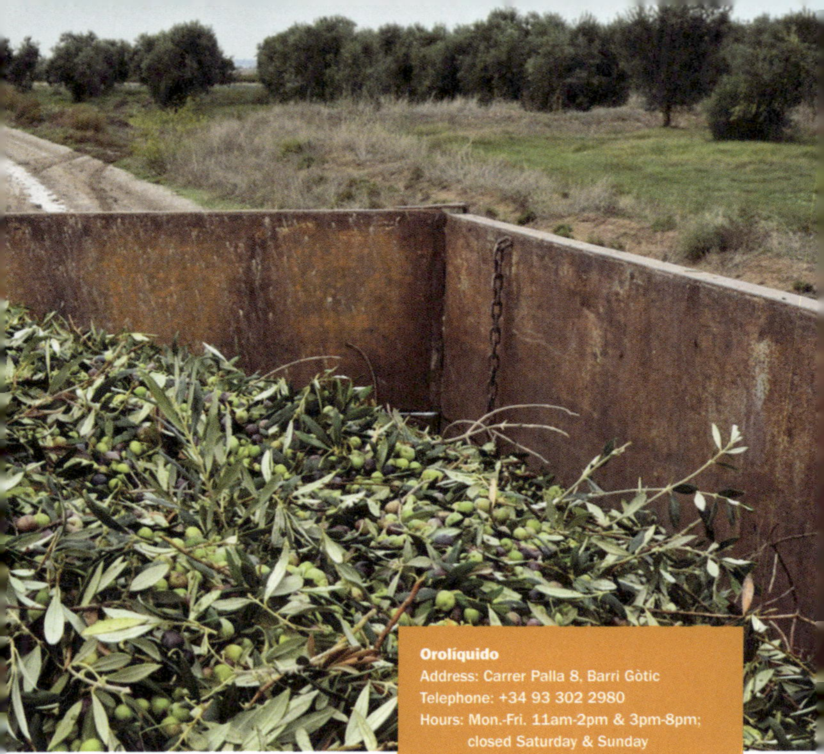

City markets are also excellent places to track down quality Spanish and Catalan extra-virgin olive oil. All of them are home to at least one stall dedicated to the stuff – among other products, like fresh olives, pickled vegetables and tinned wonders. **Olives i Conserves Torres** inside Santa Caterina Market is one such spot we can recommend. It's the perfect place to buy an edible or quaffable present.

Orolíquido
Address: Carrer Palla 8, Barri Gòtic
Telephone: +34 93 302 2980
Hours: Mon.-Fri. 11am-2pm & 3pm-8pm;
closed Saturday & Sunday

Oli Sal
Address: Travessera de Gràcia 149, Gràcia
Telephone: +34 93 415 0624
Hours: Mon. 6pm-8:30pm;
Tues.-Fri. 10:30am-1pm &
6pm-8:30pm;
Sat. 10:30am-1pm; closed Sunday

Olives i Conserves Torres
Address: Mercat de Santa Caterina,
Stalls 15-16
Avinguda de Francesc Cambó 16,
El Born-La Ribera
Telephone: +34 933 192 151
Hours: Mon-Thurs. & Sat. 7:30am-3pm;
Fri. 7:30am-8pm; closed Sunday

ORXATA

Nectar of the Gods

Be it *kvass* in Russia or *boza* in Turkey, every nation seems to have one of their own, a locally loved drink that to most outsiders comes off as a particularly strange brew. In Spain, that drink is called *horchata* (in Spanish) and *orxata* (in Catalan), a unique and deliciously refreshing concoction made from *chuflas/xufla* (tigernuts), water and sugar, and served chilled. In Barcelona, there's really only a handful of places to try the stuff, often at *orxaterias-torroneries* which specialize in one treat in the winter and the other in the summer (plus ice cream, always ice cream).

No visit to the city is complete without stopping by **Orxateria Sirvent**. A Barcelona institution founded in 1920 by Tomás Sirvent, its two locations are now managed by members of the third generation of the Sirvent family. The faithful line up here in droves during the summer months, waiting with ticket in hand to sip the best orxata de xufla in town. Sirvent's horchata is made the traditional way, that is, as it's made in Valencia. With its loose, sandy soil and moderate climate, Valencia boasts ideal conditions for growing tigernuts. The tigernut is not actually a nut, but a small tuber whose juice is used to make horchata, and chufas from Alboraya are renowned for their sweet, intense flavor.

Old-school ice cream spots **Planelles Donat** (also specialised in nougat, p. 152) , **Tío Che** and **La Valenciana** also serve up the best of both worlds, with their orxatas being just as well-loved. The line at Tío Che, opened in 1912 in Poblenou, can even rival that of Sirvent's original location.

To many an acquired taste, orxata goes down sweet with a slightly bitter aftertaste. Catalans routinely triple-park their cars to run in for a Venti-size cup to go or for larger, family-size containers. Horchata will keep in the refrigerator for two to three days.

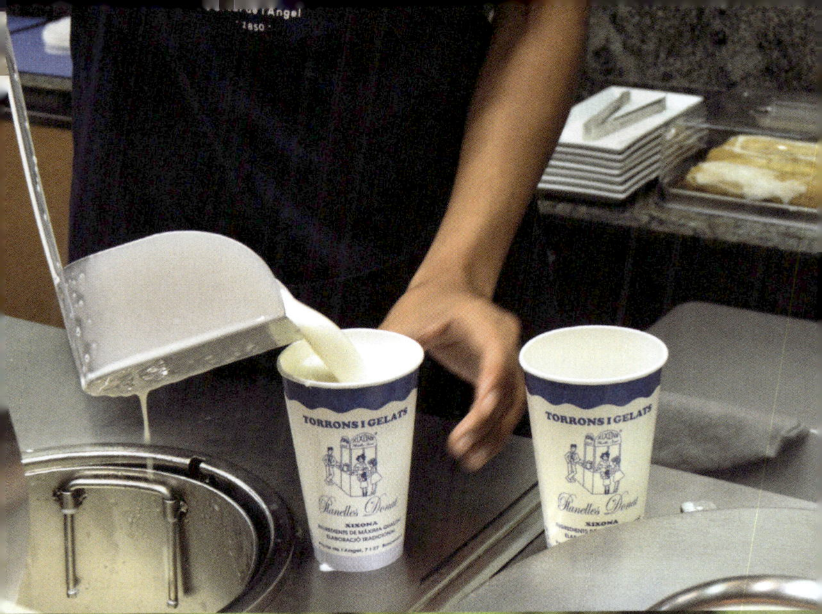

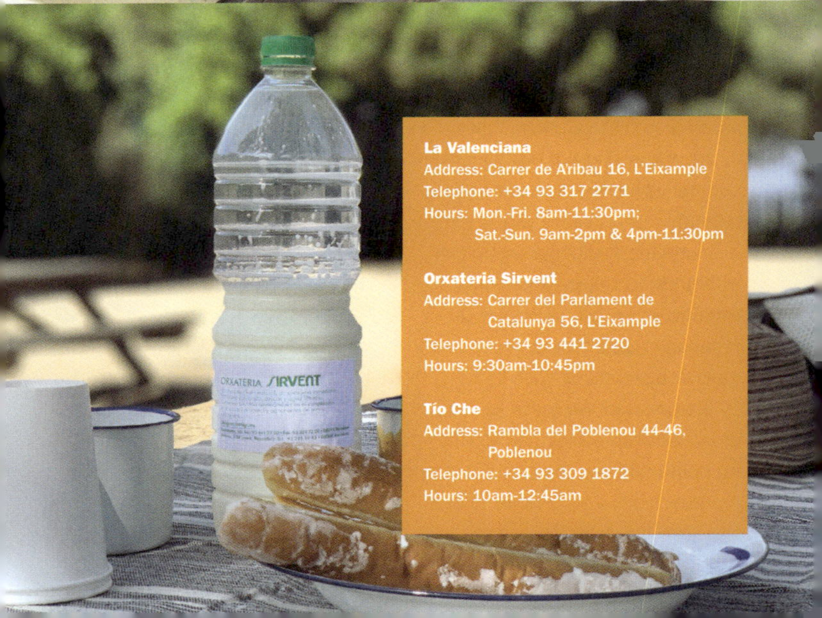

La Valenciana
Address: Carrer de A'ribau 16, L'Eixample
Telephone: +34 93 317 2771
Hours: Mon.-Fri. 8am-11:30pm;
Sat.-Sun. 9am-2pm & 4pm-11:30pm

Orxateria Sirvent
Address: Carrer del Parlament de Catalunya 56, L'Eixample
Telephone: +34 93 441 2720
Hours: 9:30am-10:45pm

Tío Che
Address: Rambla del Poblenou 44-46, Poblenou
Telephone: +34 93 309 1872
Hours: 10am-12:45am

PINTXOS

Small Basque Bites

Oriol's face lights up whenever a customer selects his favorite *pintxo* from one of the 49 different trays, beautifully displayed at **Euskal Etxea**, the bar where he works and the first in Barcelona to serve traditional Basque pintxos. One wonders how a small slice of bread topped with a chickpea fritter, *jamón serrano* and romesco sauce spiked with a toothpick can make someone so happy. We try one and we immediately see why.

A pintxo (literally "spike") is an individual bite-sized snack consisting of a combination of ingredients, placed on a small slice of bread, neatly pinned together with a toothpick or skewer. In the Basque Country, where pintxos originate, these diminutive snacks are the perfect excuse for socializing with friends while sipping a beer *zurito* (small glass), *txacolí* (local white wine) or cider.

Pintxos took Barcelona by storm a few years ago and Calle Blai in the Poble Sec district soon became a mecca for the tasty bites; these days, virtually every bar on the street now offers pintxos. **Koska** was one of the first pintxo bars to open in the area. "I would come here as a customer to get my daily fix of *gilda*," says Koska's manager, Nio, while pouring cider in the traditional northern Spanish way (his right arm stretched and pouring from as high as possible). "Eventually the owners asked me to come and work for them!" The gilda pintxo is comprised of an anchovy, a spicy *guindilla* pepper and a pitted olive, all secured by the customary skewer; this is probably the most classic pintxo of all time. Nio's current addiction, however, is the delicious *tortilla de txaca*, which consists of layers of potato omelet and crab salad. This cozy little bar also offers less conventional, more inventive pintxos using top-quality artisanal ingredients, such as Gorgonzola cheese with cardamom-pear compote.

Blai Tonight is just a stone's throw from Koska but serves up a very different take on pintxos; they specialize in what Spaniards call

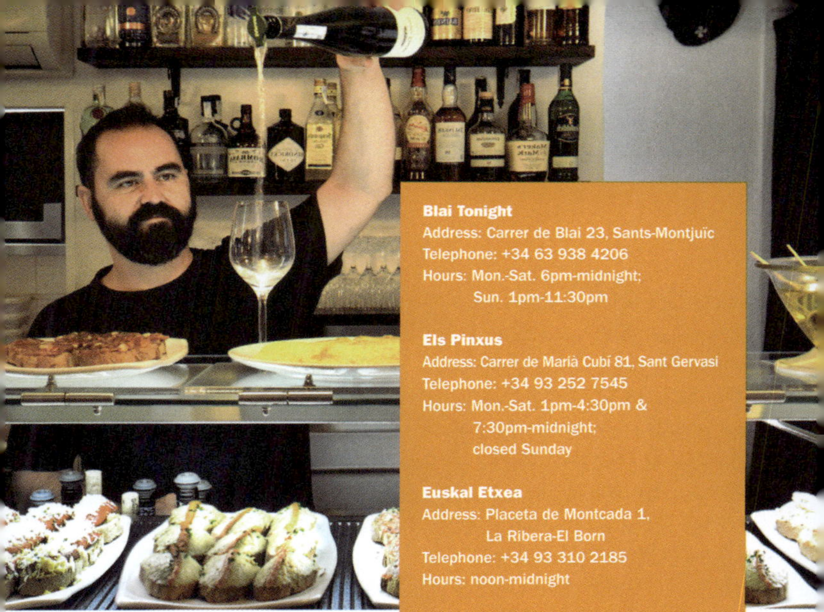

Blai Tonight
Address: Carrer de Blai 23, Sants-Montjuïc
Telephone: +34 63 938 4206
Hours: Mon.-Sat. 6pm-midnight;
Sun. 1pm-11:30pm

Els Pinxus
Address: Carrer de Marià Cubí 81, Sant Gervasi
Telephone: +34 93 252 7545
Hours: Mon.-Sat. 1pm-4:30pm &
7:30pm-midnight;
closed Sunday

Euskal Etxea
Address: Placeta de Montcada 1,
La Ribera-El Born
Telephone: +34 93 310 2185
Hours: noon-midnight

Koska
Address: Carrer de Blai 8, Sants-Montjuïc
Telephone: +34 93 127 0313
Hours: Wed.-Fri. 6pm-midnight;
Sat. noon-midnight; Sun. noon-4pm;
closed Monday & Tuesday

pintxos de batalla ("battle pintxos"): 40 different basic bites made with just a few ingredients. While not the most sophisticated in town, they certainly hit the spot. The mini-burger and the croquette are particular favorites with the hungry young crowds of locals, students and backpackers this noisy bar attracts.

Businesspeople with empty stomachs and more discerning palates usually head to the stylish **Els Pinxus Barra de Tapes**, in the business district of Diagonal. Toni, owner and chef, wanted to put a Catalan twist on the traditional Basque pintxos and created a range of 25 extremely elaborate masterpieces, such as his superb *tartar de fuet* (dry-cured pork sausage tartare) and his mouthwatering white sausage with sautéed mushrooms, caramelized onion and aioli mousse. Toni's mother, who helps behind the bar, told us how he served 600 servings of the tartar de fuet one year at Barcelona Fashion Week. "They vanished within minutes! Even the most calorie-obsessed models fell for them."

THE CATALAN MASÍA

Country Dining

As in many other rural parts of Europe, the Catalonian countryside is dotted with large, old farmhouses, legacies of feudalism that have since been converted into hotels, bed-and-breakfasts and restaurants. The origins of these *masías*, as they're known in Catalan, go back to the 11th century, but it was not until the end of feudalism in the 16th century that the former serfs turned masías into their own self-run farm holdings and homes. The buildings that survive today may be of a more recent vintage, built perhaps a century ago, sometimes older. Masías were usually named after the family who owned them; "Can Josep," for example, means "house of Josep."

The masía-restaurant is usually a rustic, down-to-earth eatery where local families and groups of friends gather together, especially during the weekends, to enjoy traditional and seasonal Catalan food at very affordable prices. (A few, however, currently hold Michelin stars.) Dishes visitors might tuck into include *mongetes amb botifarra* (beans and pork sausages), *escalivada* (grilled vegetables), *canelons* (cannelloni), *bacallà a la llauna* (fried and baked cod), *cargols* (cooked snails), *escudella* (stew), *embotits i pa amb tomàquet* (tomato spread on bread served with cured meats), *carn a la brasa amb allioli* (barbecued meats with garlic mayonnaise) or *calçots* (grilled green onions).

While masías were generally built far from towns and villages, there are a few that have been converted into restaurants in Barcelona. **Can Travi Nou** is a 17th-century masía with a spectacular flower-covered façade as well as a charming outdoor dining area where the fare is classic Catalan with a twist – such as sautéed lobster with chickpeas. The service is very attentive and the ambiance cozy. **Can Cortada**, an impressive building of Roman and medieval origins surrounded by peaceful gardens, serves fine

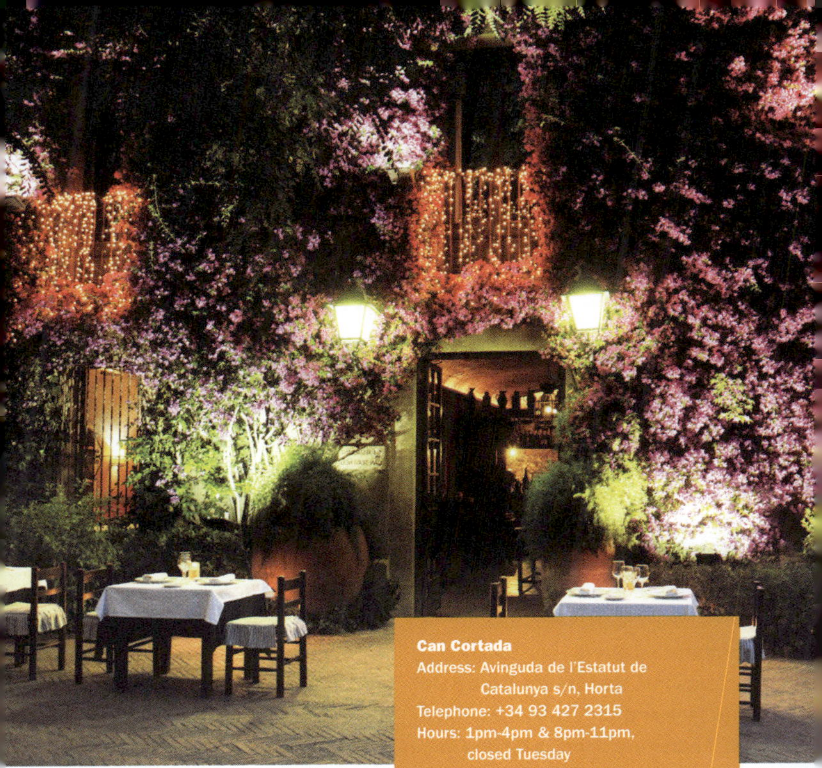

Can Cortada
Address: Avinguda de l'Estatut de Catalunya s/n, Horta
Telephone: +34 93 427 2315
Hours: 1pm-4pm & 8pm-11pm, closed Tuesday

Can Travi Nou
Address: Calle Jorge Manrique s/n, Horta
Telephone: +34 93 428 0301
Hours: 1pm-4pm & 8pm-11pm; closed Monday

Mediterranean cuisine and top-quality meats at higher prices. The restaurant is divided into different spacious lounges and private dining rooms, perfect for large groups. The Soler Ribatallada family, who have been in the hospitality business for decades, own both restaurants. (They also have two more restaurants in other emblematic spots of the city: El Pintor, in the Gothic quarter, and Xalet de Montjuïc, in Montjuïc's gardens.) Can Travi Nou and Can Cortada are both in the Horta neighborhood (walking distance from Mundet metro) and are the ideal way to get the rural masía experience without having to leave the city.

THE NEIGHBORHOOD MERCAT

Beyond the Boquería

Any guidebook to Barcelona is sure to sing the praises of the famous Boquería market, but although it's certainly worth a visit, you can avoid the swarms of tourists by heading to one of the city's smaller, more local food markets.

One of our favorites is the **Mercat de la Llibertat** in Gràcia. Designed in 1888 by Miguel Pascual, the brick and iron structure is an impressive example of Modernist architecture. With more than 40 stalls – a few of which have been in the same families for over 80 years – selling a variety of delicious-looking food products, the market can seem overwhelming at first. We can recommend *xarcuteria* Bragulat for *jamón* and sausages, Bordas for top-notch meats, Peix Fresc Esther for fish, and La Grana for *frutos secos*, including toasted hazelnuts, almonds, desiccated coconut, dried fruit, chocolate and delicious *torró* (nougat).

Not far away, in Barcelona's upscale Sant Gervasi-Galvany neighborhood, is the **Mercat de Galvany**, considered by many to be one of the most outstanding structures in Barcelona. The food stalls inside are also attractive but, since the market tends to be a bit on the pricey side, visitors might do just as well to remain outside and let the gorgeous façade serve as a feast for the eyes.

For take-home food shopping, head to the **Mercat de Santa Catarina** in the El Born–La Ribera neighborhood. Originally built in 1848, on the site of the previous Sant Caterina Convent, it was completely refurbished in 2005 by architects Enric Miralles and Benedetta Tagliabue. Inside the market, you'll find more than 70 stalls with high quality products and several bars and restaurants. The food stalls include groceries, butcheries, xarcuterias specializing in ham and cured sausages and cheeses, olives and conservas stalls, codfish stalls (*bacallanerias*), fresh fish, nuts, spices and much more. For olives, try Olives i Conservas Torres. For honey,

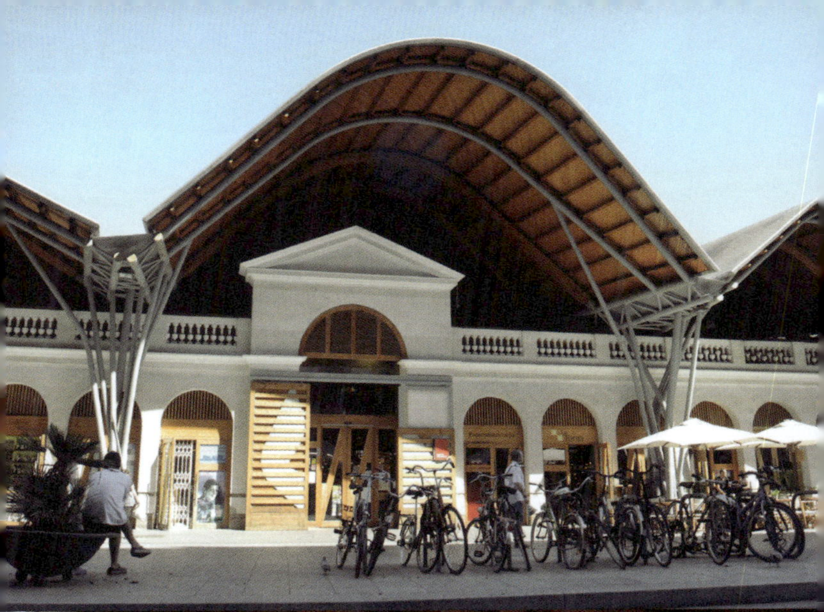

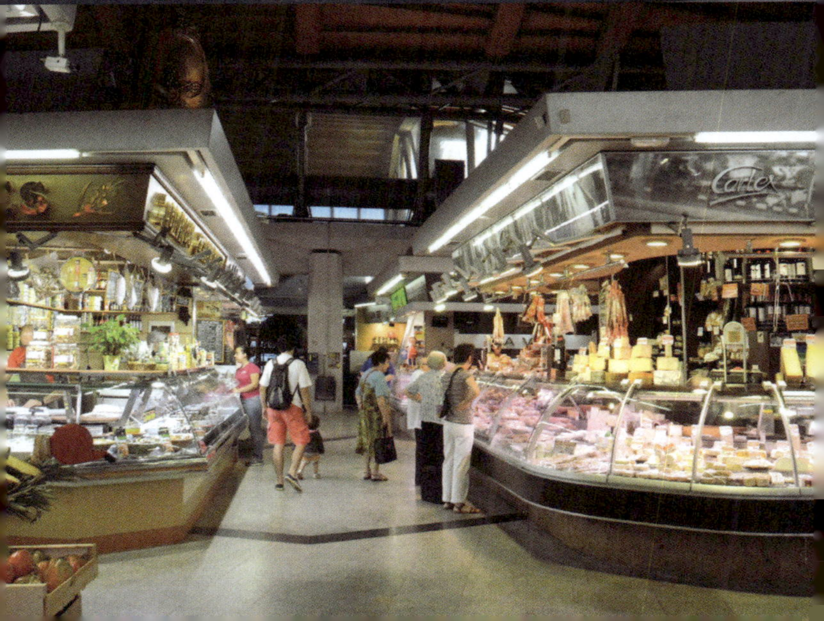
Carlex

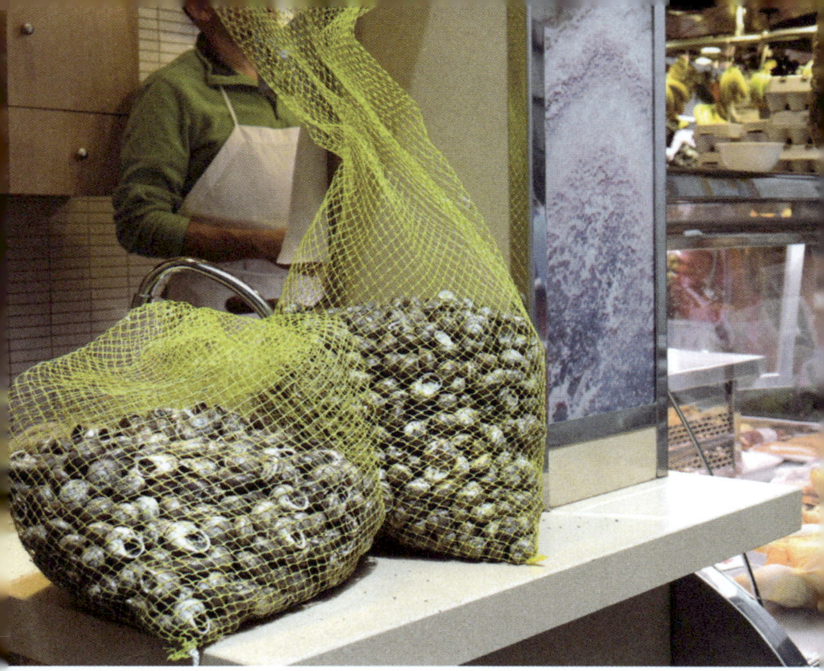

head to Manantial de Salud, who carry a range of artisanal honeys produced from different flowers like thyme, rosemary or orange blossom. Also look out for the LaMiel stall, for good honey, nuts and a cornucopia of spices.

In the L'Eixample district, the updated **Mercat del Ninot** ("Doll Market") now includes tasting bars and restaurants among the market stalls. Fish shops like La Medusa 73 or La Barra offer fresh oysters, clams, mussels, barnacles and prawns for eating on-site accompanied by a chilled glass of wine or cava, as well as daily specials like homey seafood rice and *ortiguillas* (battered and fried anemones).

There's confited tuna at Peixateria Ribera, and many of the fishmongers will even cook to order whatever fish you purchase – which you can then eat there with some wine or beer, of course. Perello, a classic (open since 1898) cod and conservas stall, serves the excellent Casa Mariol *vermut* alongside traditional dishes like *esqueixada*, a kind of Catalan ceviche made from salt

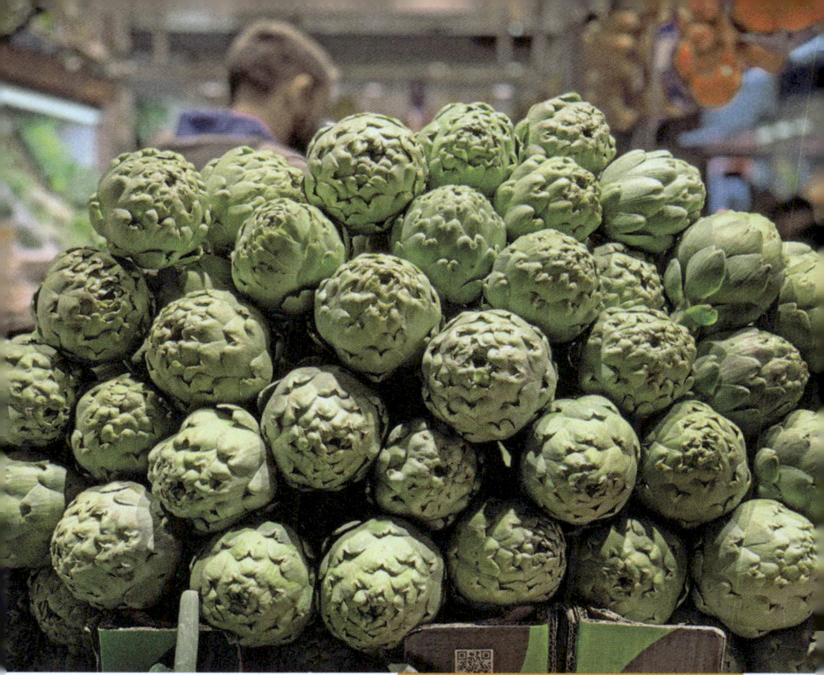

cod and dressed with tomato, fresh pepper, onions, olive oil and vinegar; cod *brandada* battered and fried in crispy pieces and served with aioli and romesco sauce; and smoked salmon and cod chops.

Another update that has made the Mercat del Ninot more accessible is to the weekday schedule, which now runs from 8 a.m. to 8 p.m. (it was previously open only in the morning). Even with all of them closed on Sunday, that's plenty of time to spend eating and drinking your way around any market.

Mercat de Galvany
Address: Carrer Santaló 55, Sant Gervasi
Hours: Mon.-Sat. 7am-2:30pm

Mercat de la Llibertat
Address: Plaça Llibertat 27, Gràcia
Hours: Mon.-Fri. 8am-8:30pm;
Sat. 8am-3pm

Mercat del Ninot
Address: Carrer del Mallorca 133-157, L'Eixample
Hours: Mon.-Fri. 8am-8pm; Sat. 8am-3pm

Mercat de Santa Caterina
Address: Avinguda de Francesc Cambó 16, El Born-La Ribera
Telephone: +34 933 19 5740
Hours: Mon-Thurs. & Sat. 7:30am-3pm;
Fri. 7:30am 8pm

TORTILLA DE PATATAS

The Hometown Favorite

It's the *tortilla española*, also known as *tortilla de patatas* (*truita de patata* in Catalan), and not paella, that really holds the place of honor in the hearts and stomachs of Spaniards. Often translated on menus as "potato omelet," this hearty round cake of potatoes, eggs, olive oil and salt has nothing to do with the traditional French omelet, nor does it have anything in common with a Mexican tortilla. At its most basic, the Spanish tortilla is made by frying up a thick mass of sliced potatoes and eggs in olive oil and then slicing it into savory wedges.

The tortilla is also incredibly versatile and can incorporate a dizzying array of supplementary ingredients, including (but certainly not limited to) spinach, garlic, leeks, parsley, asparagus and onions. It can be eaten for breakfast, lunch, dinner or a snack, and not only will you see it in every tapas bar you pass, but it also makes appearances on school lunch menus (at least once per week), at birthday parties and at picnics. You will even see this already carb-heavy dish stuffed between two slices of bread and served as a sandwich! In short, it is the ultimate go-to comfort food and the dish that Spaniards throughout the country most associate with home.

What makes a good tortilla? The answer depends on personal taste, and everyone will tell you something slightly different. There are debates on everything from whether or not a tortilla should include onions, to how the potatoes should be sliced (in thin rounds or in chunky squares), to just how runny the eggs in the middle should be, with some liking their tortillas *un poco crudito* (a little undercooked) on the inside and others preferring a more well-done version.

This classic Spanish dish is available virtually everywhere that serves food in Barcelona, and it is rare that you will come across one that falls flat. But there are exceptional versions to be found. **Taktika Berri**, a family-run Basque bar and restaurant

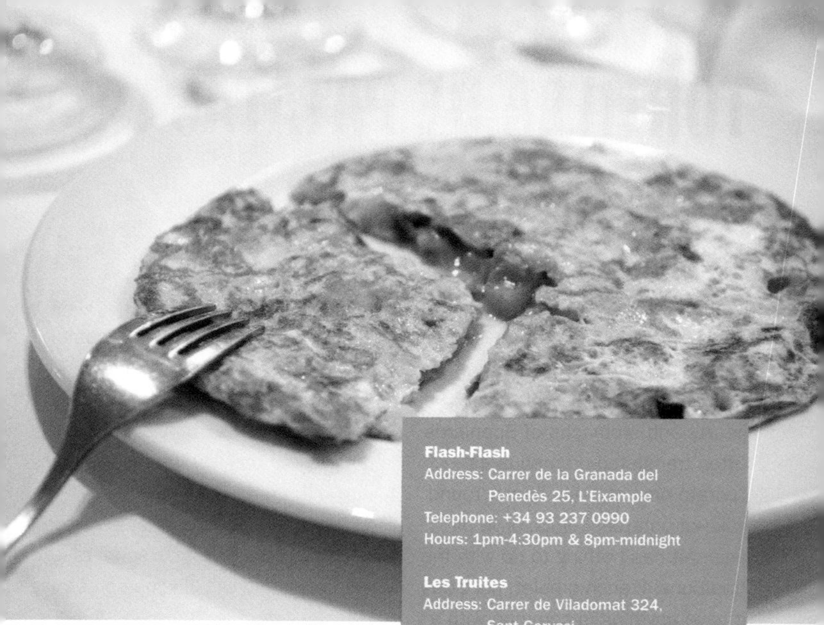

in L'Esquerra de l'Eixample, makes an especially good *tortilla de bacalao*. **Flash Flash**, the city's most famous *tortillería*, serves an astounding 70 varieties of tortilla, including ingredients such as *morcilla* (blood sausage), artichokes, black truffles and potato chips. (If in doubt, order the Catalan classic *tortilla de samfaina*, with a filling similar to ratatouille.)

Les Truites is another temple of tortillas experimenting with new ingredient combos and free-range eggs – from the most-conventional (mushroom or Iberian ham) to the most-unexpected (octopus, foie gras and even croissant). And finally, the tortilla at **Pollería Fontana** is a nostalgic taste of childhood: tender, juicy, anxiolytic and healing in general.

Flash-Flash
Address: Carrer de la Granada del Penedès 25, L'Eixample
Telephone: +34 93 237 0990
Hours: 1pm-4:30pm & 8pm-midnight

Les Truites
Address: Carrer de Viladomat 324, Sant Gervasi
Telephone: +34 93 418 0691
Hours: Tues.-Sat. 12:30pm-4:30pm & 8pm-11pm; closed Sunday & Monday

Pollería Fontana
Address: Carrer de Sant Lluís 9, Gràcia
Telephone: +34 93 217 3904
Hours: Tues.-Sat. 6pm-midnight; closed Sunday & Monday

Taktika Berri
Address: Carrer de València 169, L'Esquerra de l'Eixample
Telephone: +34 93 453 4759
Hours: 1pm-4pm & 8pm-11pm; closed Sat. night & Sunday

TURRÓN

A Tradition to Chew On

Typically eaten at Christmastime in Spain, *turrón*, a type of nougat, originated centuries ago. Traditionally produced in the region of Alicante, turrón comes in several varieties. Turrón de Alicante, or "hard turrón," is made with whole almonds set in a honey-egg white mixture so brittle that it's often broken with a kitchen mallet. The village of Jijona is famous as the main producer of turrón; in the old days, in the months leading up to Christmas, the inhabitants of Jijona would traverse the country, selling turrones from their horse carts. In the 19th century, Jijona artisans developed a delicate "soft turrón." This turrón de Jijona (or Xixona in Catalan and Valencian) is made with toasted, ground almonds combined with honey and egg white, the oil from the almonds lending a moist, chewy texture completely different from that of hard turrón.

At Christmastime, it is not uncommon to see lines of people at the city's most popular *maestros turroneros*, waiting to buy the hard Alicante variety, the soft Jijona kind, turrón *de yema tostada* (Catalonia's most typical nougat, made with egg yolk and a caramelized crust), contemporary adaptations made with chocolate truffle and many other types.

Since 1775, the Vicens family has produced *torró* (as the sweet is known in Catalan) in Agramunt, a village in the heart of Catalonia. This torró d'Agramunt has Protected Designation of Origin status. Vicens's nougat, which is similar to hard turrón, comes as a round disc made with toasted hazelnuts, sugar, egg whites and honey and sandwiched between thin wafers. **Torrons Vicens** has a number of shops in Barcelona.

In the entrances of **Casa Colomina** and **Planelles Donat**, two families have been selling turrón since the 19th century. Planelles Donat in particular makes some of the best nougat in town. Its soft turrón is chewy and buttery, has the right balance of sweetness and melts in the mouth.

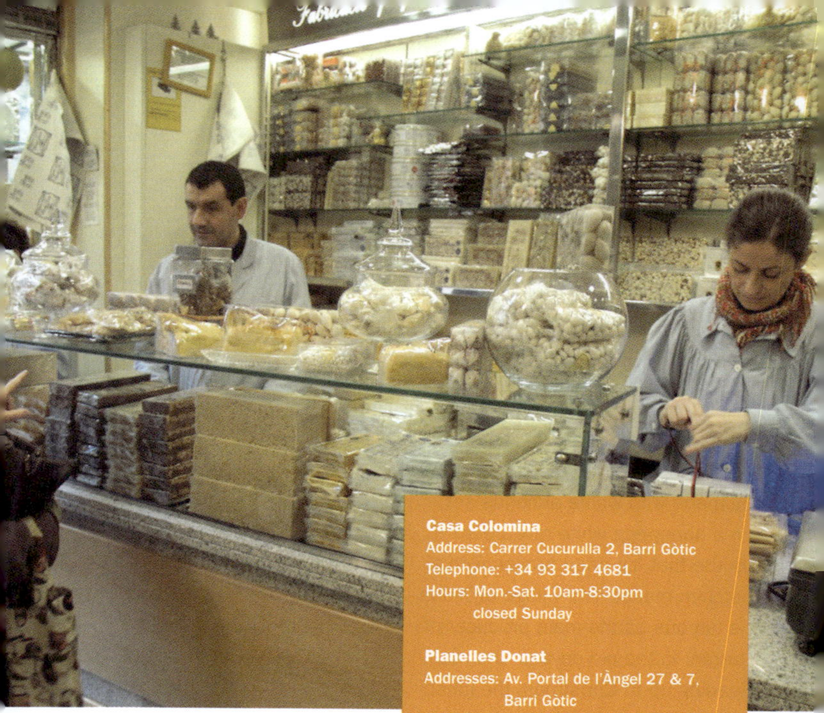

It's also known for its marzipan-like turrón de yema tostada.

La Campana, a lovely little patisserie founded in 1850 by Francisco Mira Miralles, a native of Jijona, uses top-quality raw materials to make turrón with concentrated flavors and textures, whether from the extra-crunchy caramelized sugar in the egg yolk nougat or the exceptionally smooth almond paste in the soft variety. While a special Christmas treat, we indulge in turrón any time of year. In summer, we particularly love grabbing a traditional ice cream at these *turronerías/torroneries* while shopping for our favorite nougat.

Casa Colomina
Address: Carrer Cucurulla 2, Barri Gòtic
Telephone: +34 93 317 4681
Hours: Mon.-Sat. 10am-8:30pm
closed Sunday

Planelles Donat
Addresses: Av. Portal de l'Àngel 27 & 7, Barri Gòtic
Telephone: +34 93 317 3439
Hours: 10am-8:30pm;
closed Sunday

Torrons La Campana
Address: Carrer de la Princesa 36, El Born
Telephone: +34 93 319 7296
Hours: 11am-11pm

Torrons Vicens
Address: La Boquería Market, stalls 405-409, La Rambla 100, El Raval
Hours: 9:30am-9:30pm; closed Sunday

VERMOUTH

Barcelona's Pre-lunch Aperitif Ritual

Why are you seeing colorful, 1960s-era carbonated water siphons everywhere in Barcelona? Because they're the symbol of our beloved *vermut* ritual – a fresh drink accompanied by tapas composed usually of preserved food, cold cuts, and cured or marinated fish and seafood – that has long served as a way to bring people together before meals.

The partners behind the **Morro Fi** project have put out their own line of vermuts (red, red reserve and white), made in a fresh style, with real love for the nostalgic ritual. Their original venue, Morro Fi, has a younger namesake inside La Illa Diagonal shopping mall, as well as two other bars. We also recommend their Sant Gervasi project, Dalt de Tot, which has a few tables on the street and a little kitchen that turns out more elaborate dishes, such as eggs, *butifarras,* omelets, croquettes and more.

More than a simple bar, **Casa Mariol** is a winery from Terra Alta that produces several kinds of wine and vermouth with accessible prices, available by the bottle or in bulk. Their Carrer Roselló shop near the Sagrada Familia also offers bar service with tables. Here you can have a glass of vermut made from *macabeu* grape and 150 different herbs in the company of a very good selection of cured and preserved foods – from cockles and stuffed olives to ham and cheese.

Established in 1937, **La Moderna** bodega in L'Eixample has survived just about everything, including the Spanish Civil War. In 2017, its new owners fell in love with the tapas bar and bulk-wine shop, deciding to keep it as is and only adding food to its offerings. Now you can show up for the vermouth hour and peruse their tasty menu of smoked oysters and sardines over *pan de cristal*, a thin and crusty bread, and the cod carpaccio with tomato, olives and delicate Santa Pau beans. We love a casual drink and a bite to eat in this simple, cozy and intimate space.

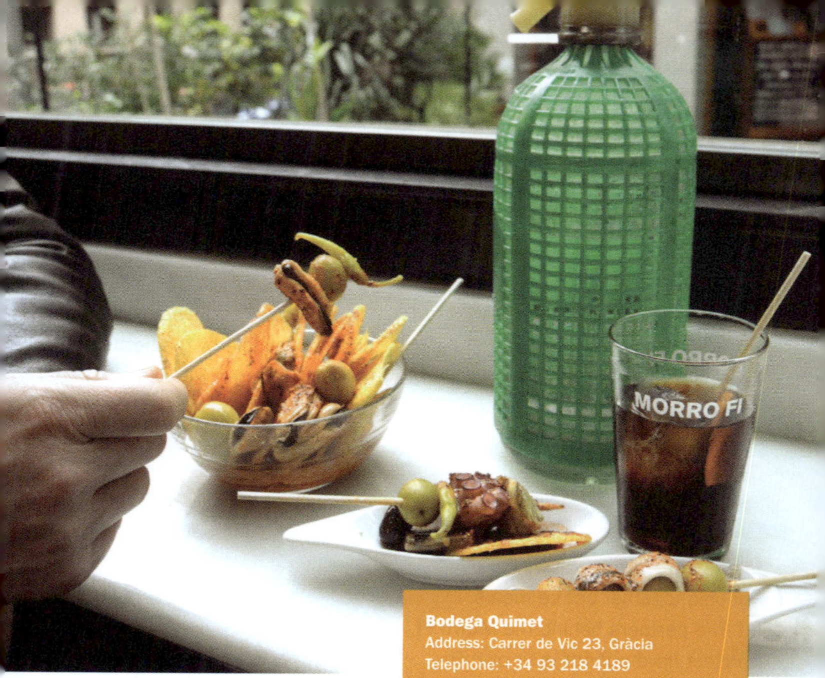

The original 1950s décor of **Bodega Quimet** (p. 56) is a large part of why this place feels so charmingly old-fashioned and welcoming. Quimet makes the classic combination for vermut, mixing cured anchovies, tuna, cockles or razor clams with the typical dressing of olive oil, vinegar and paprika. We also love the more elaborate tapas here, including baby fava beans with poached eggs and ham and scrambled eggs with chorizo. Besides vermut, there's also a wide selection of great wines and craft beers.

Bodega Quimet
Address: Carrer de Vic 23, Gràcia
Telephone: +34 93 218 4189
Hours: 11am-4pm & 6pm-11pm; closed Sun. & Mon. evenings

Casa Mariol
Address: Carrer Rosselló 442, L'Eixample
Telephone: +34 93 436 7628
Hours: Fri. 10am-10pm; Sat.-Mon. 10am-4pm

La Moderna
Address: Carrer Enric Granados, 110, L'Esquerra de l'Eixample
Telephone: +34 932 17 1351
Hours: Tues. 6:30pm-11:30pm; Wed.-Sat. 12:30pm-4pm & 7pm-midnight; closed Sunday

Morro Fi
Address: Carrer Consell de Cent 171, L'Eixample
Hours: noon-4pm & 6pm-11pm

XOCOLATA

Barcelona's Chocolate Artisans

In the weeks leading up to Easter, the best confectioners in Barcelona erect astonishing and fantastical chocolate constructions, known as *monas*, and display them in shop windows. Some of these wonderful visual confections – reproductions of monuments, scenes taken from classical history and abstract original creations – are on display at the **Museu de la Xocolata** in El Born, where you can also satisfy your craving for sweets in the museum shop. The practice has extended beyond the Easter season to become a professional expression of the local chocolate-making industry.

The chocolate artisans of **Bombonería Fargas** have been in business since 1827 and though they've had to move from their original location, the same intoxicating chocolate fragrance greets you at the door. Back in the day, the cacao was ground on the premises in a stone mill turned by a mule to make chocolate *a la piedra* (*xocolata a la pedra* in Catalan). The shop also used to offer hot chocolate customers could take home, adding sugar and spices according to their tastes. These practices are no more, but in the workshop, Fargas's artisans continue to hand-grind their cacao and turn it into a wide-ranging assortment of wonderful chocolates.

Oriol Balaguer, the author of three books about "sweet cuisine," is one of the best modern pastry chefs and chocolatiers of Barcelona. He has two shops in Les Corts as well as the cafeteria **Xocolatería Oriol Balaguer**, which is the place to taste his sophisticated hot chocolate along with a few churros, or some of his great chocolate candies.

Chocolatiers Ramón Morató and Quim Capdevila have created an excellent brand of Catalan chocolates, **Cacao Sampaka**. In their single shop in Barcelona, you'll find a whole world of cocoa: chocolate pastries and candies from different selected origins, hot chocolate,

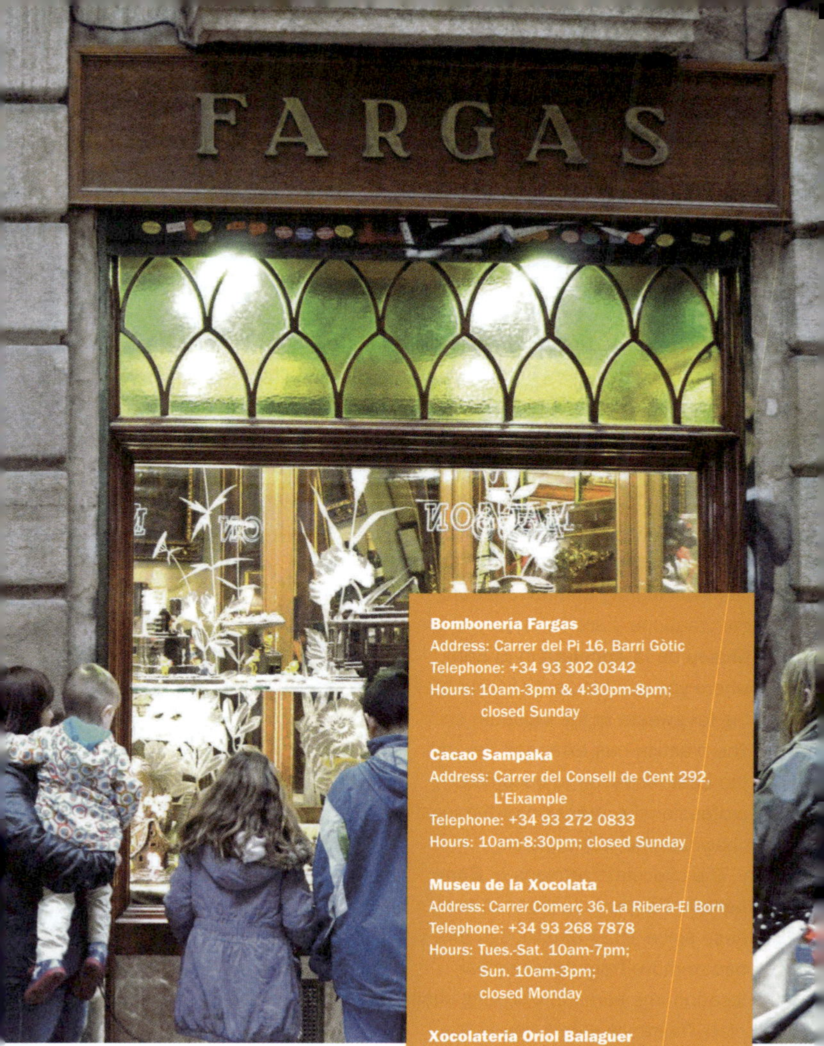

books on chocolate and some chocolate-making tools, along with a cozy cafeteria space.

Bomboneria Fargas
Address: Carrer del Pi 16, Barri Gòtic
Telephone: +34 93 302 0342
Hours: 10am-3pm & 4:30pm-8pm;
closed Sunday

Cacao Sampaka
Address: Carrer del Consell de Cent 292,
L'Eixample
Telephone: +34 93 272 0833
Hours: 10am-8:30pm; closed Sunday

Museu de la Xocolata
Address: Carrer Comerç 36, La Ribera-El Born
Telephone: +34 93 268 7878
Hours: Tues.-Sat. 10am-7pm;
Sun. 10am-3pm;
closed Monday

Xocolateria Oriol Balaguer
Address: Travessera de les Corts 340, Sarrià
Telephone: +34 93 363 2298
Hours: Mon.-Fri. 8am-2pm & 4pm-8pm;
Sat.-Sun. 9am-2:30pm

XURRERIAS

Where Every Day is Fryday

Churros, the long, skinny, crenelated, sweet fried crullers made from just flour, water and salt, have been enjoyed for centuries in Spain, with hot chocolate and without. However, in Barcelona, *xurros*, as they are called in Catalan, are becoming an endangered species. In recent years, more than half of the *xurrerias* in the city have disappeared. The best way to save this endangered species is to eat it, so here are our four favorites, all worth seeking out.

Churrería Manuel San Román opened back in 1968 and still makes crunchy, non-greasy, loop-shaped xurros with perfect consistency and at top speed, ensuring that you always get the freshest batch. Owner Manuel San Román, whose grandmother was a *xurrera*, has been making xurros for more than half a century, his son Luis for a third. Both belong to the trade union Gremi de Artesans Xurrers de Catalonia. Manuel makes his dough out of hard wheat flour, altering it as needed to account for the ambient temperature and humidity, and keeps a close eye on the heat of the oil (a combination of peanut, sunflower and olive oils that has a high smoke point). Manuel is widely acknowledged to be one of the city's masters of this craft.

The perfect spot for a coffee break, **Xurreria Laietana**, which opened in 1975, makes wonderful thin, light xurros and *porras*, which are similar but bigger, made with yeast and more commonly found in Madrid. José Ruz Martínez, a cheerful man with 43 years of xurrero experience, grew up in his father's xurreria. His cozy, bare-bones shop is frequented mostly by locals and area office workers, who come for good coffee or hot chocolate with xurros and porras for breakfast or on their breaks.

Xurreria J. Argilés is a street xurro icon. The stall's long, thin fried batons can come with sugar, extra salt or in any number of other delicious variations. José Argilés, who founded the operation in 1958, is also the president of the trade union. His

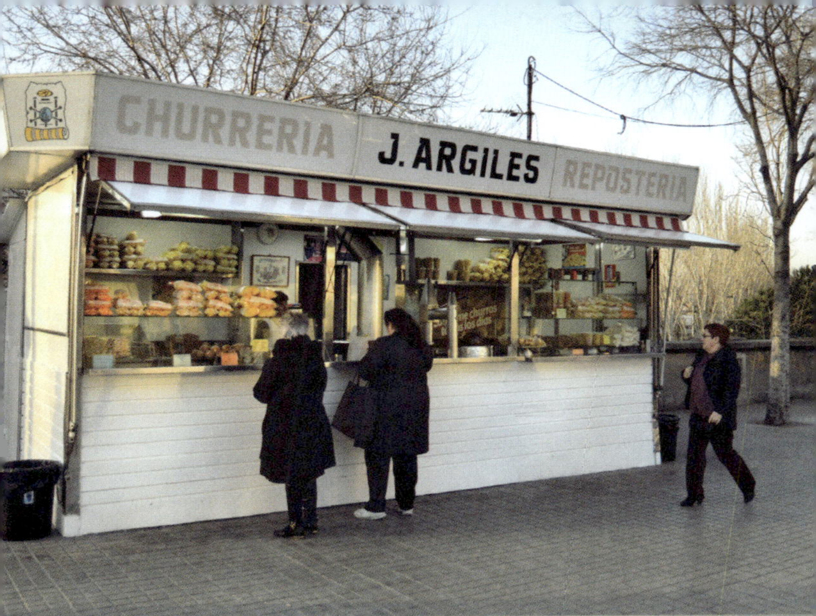
CHURRERIA
J. ARGILES
REPOSTERIA

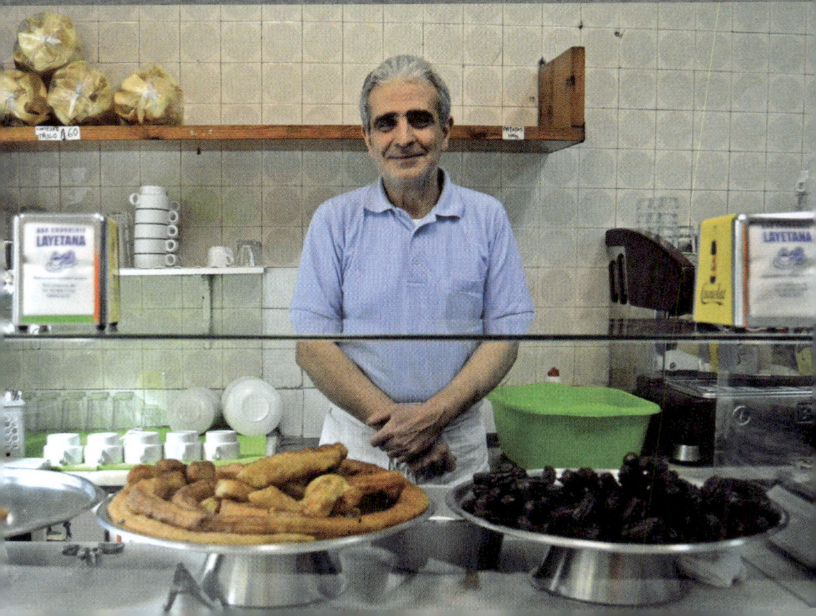
LAYETANA
LAYETANA

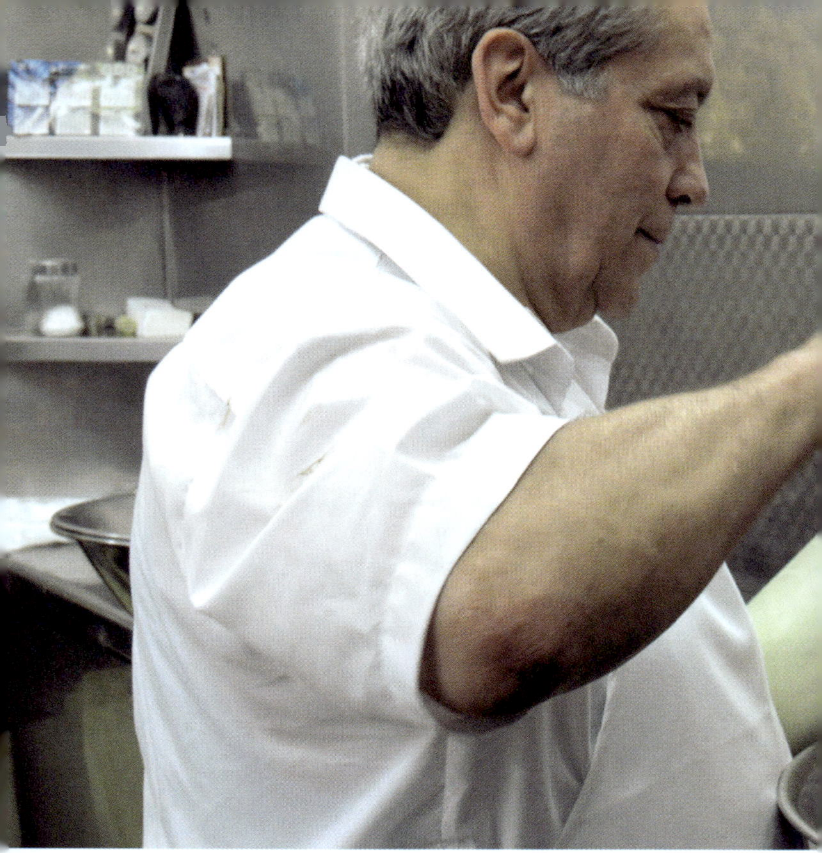

stand is now lovingly managed by Montse Roche, while Argilés runs a small factory that makes fried items such as potato chips and supplies the original stand as well as other shops throughout Catalonia. At the stand, Montse makes fresh xurros and great *xuxos*, soft crullers filled with a decadent cream and topped with sugar, and also serves hot chocolate and cold beverages.

The xurros at **Xurreria El Trebol** are extra long, thick and very crunchy, a bit on the toastier, well-done side. Cecilia Martínez and her husband, Juan Bacells, started making xurros in the 1940s, and around 1950 they opened this shop. El Trebol was the

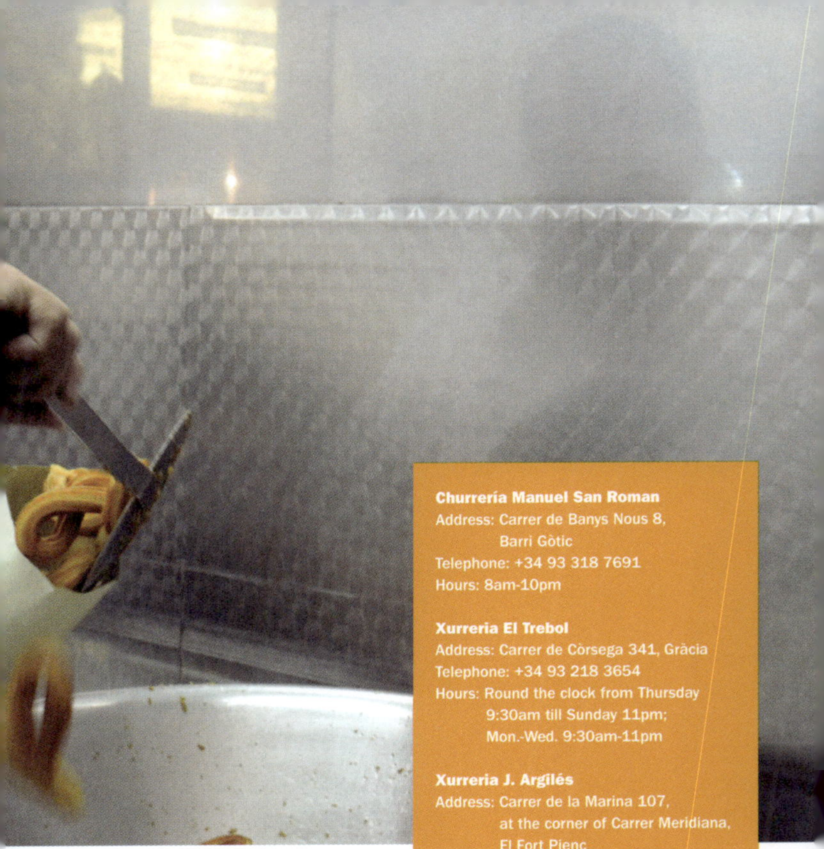

first xurreria in Barcelona to branch out to other fried items, such as cod fritters and *cañas* with Argentinian *dulce de leche*. Their son, Ramón Bacells, runs the business with grandson Alex, who is likely the one you'll find behind the counter. They also have good hot chocolate and sell cold drinks.

Churrería Manuel San Roman
Address: Carrer de Banys Nous 8,
Barri Gòtic
Telephone: +34 93 318 7691
Hours: 8am-10pm

Xurreria El Trebol
Address: Carrer de Còrsega 341, Gràcia
Telephone: +34 93 218 3654
Hours: Round the clock from Thursday
9:30am till Sunday 11pm;
Mon.-Wed. 9:30am-11pm

Xurreria J. Argilés
Address: Carrer de la Marina 107,
at the corner of Carrer Meridiana,
El Fort Pienc
Telephone: +34 93 232 4307
Hours: Round the clock from Friday 8am till
Sunday 9pm;
Tues.-Thurs. 8:15am-9pm;
closed Monday

Xurreria Laietana
Address: Via Laietana 46, El Born
Telephone: +34 93 268 1263
Hours: Mon.-Sat. 7am-1:30pm &
4:30pm-8:30pm; Sun. 7am-1:30pm;
closed for summer & holidays

WORDS TO EAT BY

Catalan

Bunyols: fritters
Butifarra: a type of sausage, usually white, plump and made from pork, garlic and spices
Calçot: winter scallion
Cargols: snails
Celler: cellar, tavern or wine bar that also offers wine in bulk and maybe some tapas
Coca: Catalan sweet or savory cake or bread of different kinds, normally flat and oval
Escalivada: traditional Catalan dish of coal-roasted and peeled red peppers, eggplant and onion
Escudella i carn de olla: A soupy stew made with a kind of pasta called "galets," vegetables and a big meatball called "pilota"
Esmorzars de forquilla: "fork breakfast," i.e. hearty breakfast items
Esqueixada: salad with fresh vegetables and salt cod
Fideuà: a noodle dish, similar to paella but made with short, thin noodles instead of rice
Fuet: Catalan cured pork and pepper sausage
Granja: farm, former dairy shops; currently cafeterias specializing in breakfast and lunch
Masía: countryside house or farmhouse
Olivada: olive paste or paté
Orxata: summer drink made from tiger nuts
Pa amb tomaquet: bread with tomato
Picada: literally "minced," a Catalan cooking base of nuts and day-old bread minced in a mortar with other ingredients
Pintxo: Basque-style tapas, usually served on a slice of bread
Porró: traditional glass wine jar or pitcher with a long spout to pour the wine directly into the mouth

Romescu: romesco, Catalan sauce made with nuts, tomato, capsicum, hard bread, garlic, olive oil and vinegar.
Samfaina: traditional Catalan dish of chopped and fried tomato, eggplant, red pepper, garlic and olive oil.
Sofregit: sofrito, a cooking base of olive oil, onion, garlic, tomato or other ingredients fried in a pan.
Suquet: traditional fish stew
Torró: turrón, nougat
Xipirons: chipirones, baby squid

Spanish

Anchoa: anchovy cured in salt
Banderilla: savory appetizer made of olives, chili peppers, anchovies or other pickles
Bodega: cellar, tavern or wine bar that also offers wine in bulk and maybe some tapas
Boquerón: fresh anchovy marinated in vinegar
Callos: tripe stew
Caña: glass of tap beer (33cl)
Cecina: cured cold cuts, normally made from beef
Chipirones: baby squids
Conserva: Canned or jarred goods
Garrafa: big plastic bottle, often used for wine or olive oil
Montadito: a slice of bread piled high with various toppings
Morcilla: blood sausage
Patatas bravas: literally "wild potatoes," fried potatoes doused in hot sauce
Plancha: flat grill
Platillo: small plate of food for sharing
Tapear: The act of eating tapas
Tapeo: a meal of tapas
Tortilla: omelet

INDEX

Alphabetically

Bakeries & Sweets

Catalan Classics

Bars, Bodegas & Vermuterias

Contemporary Spanish

Marisquerías & Seafood

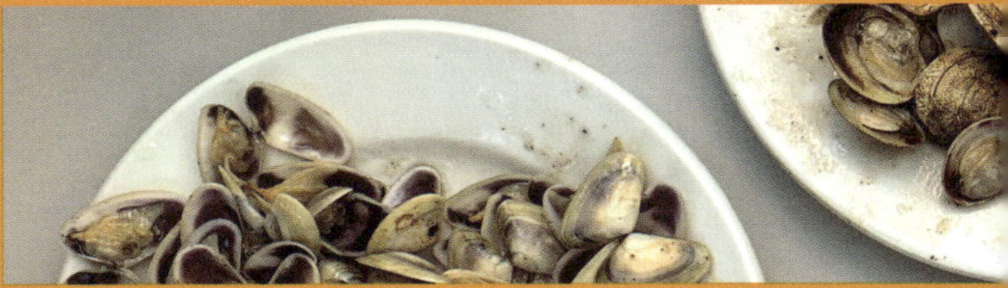

Regional Cuisine

Tapas & Pintxos

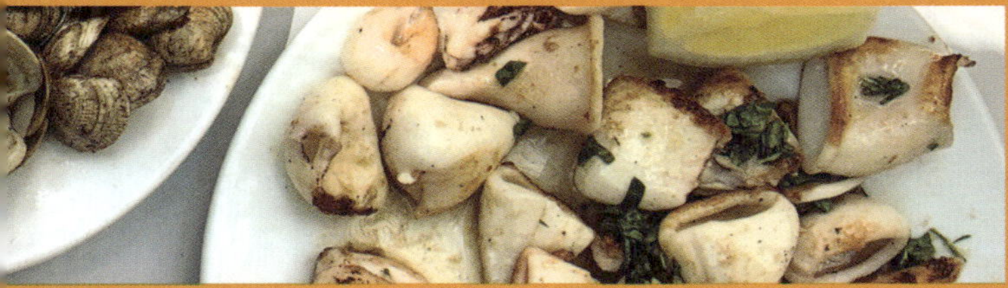

Specialty Shops & Markets

Vegetarian

THE OLD CITY

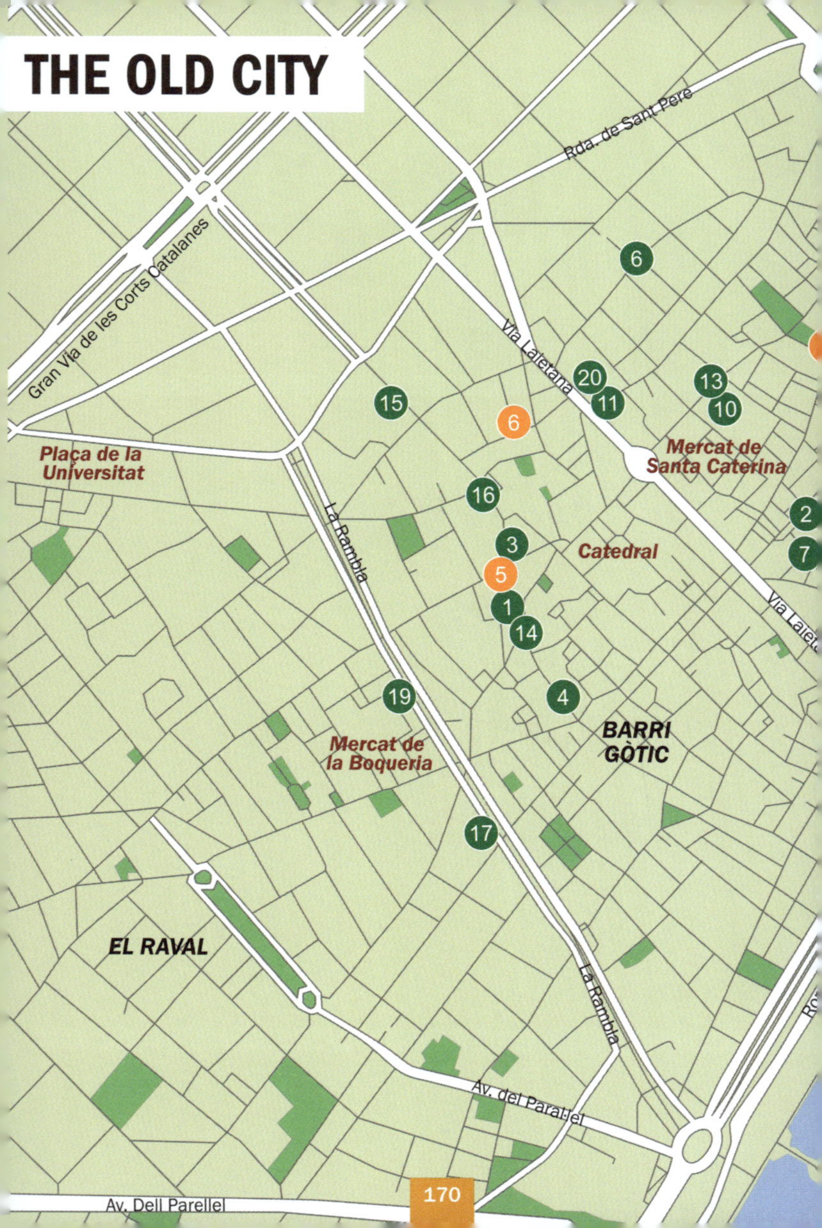

Rda. de Sant Pere
Gran Via de les Corts Catalanes
Via Laietana
Plaça de la Universitat
Mercat de Santa Caterina
La Rambla
Catedral
BARRI GÒTIC
Mercat de la Boqueria
EL RAVAL
Av. del Paral·lel
Av. Dell Parellel
6
20
11
13
10
15
6
16
2
3
7
5
1
14
19
4
17

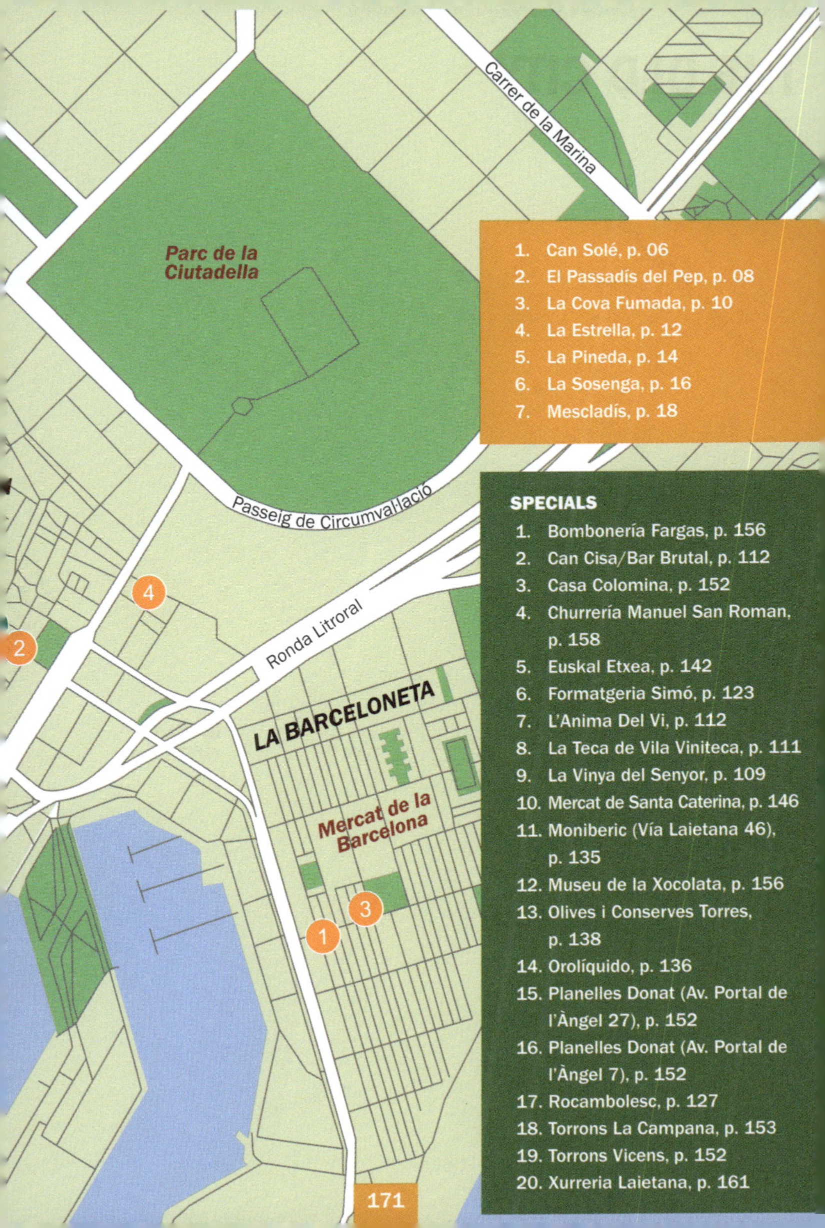

1. Can Solé, p. 06
2. El Passadís del Pep, p. 08
3. La Cova Fumada, p. 10
4. La Estrella, p. 12
5. La Pineda, p. 14
6. La Sosenga, p. 16
7. Mescladís, p. 18

SPECIALS

1. Bombonería Fargas, p. 156
2. Can Cisa/Bar Brutal, p. 112
3. Casa Colomina, p. 152
4. Churrería Manuel San Roman, p. 158
5. Euskal Etxea, p. 142
6. Formatgeria Simó, p. 123
7. L'Anima Del Vi, p. 112
8. La Teca de Vila Viniteca, p. 111
9. La Vinya del Senyor, p. 109
10. Mercat de Santa Caterina, p. 146
11. Moniberic (Vía Laietana 46), p. 135
12. Museu de la Xocolata, p. 156
13. Olives i Conserves Torres, p. 138
14. Orolíquido, p. 136
15. Planelles Donat (Av. Portal de l'Àngel 27), p. 152
16. Planelles Donat (Av. Portal de l'Àngel 7), p. 152
17. Rocambolesc, p. 127
18. Torrons La Campana, p. 153
19. Torrons Vicens, p. 152
20. Xurreria Laietana, p. 161

L'EIXAMPLE

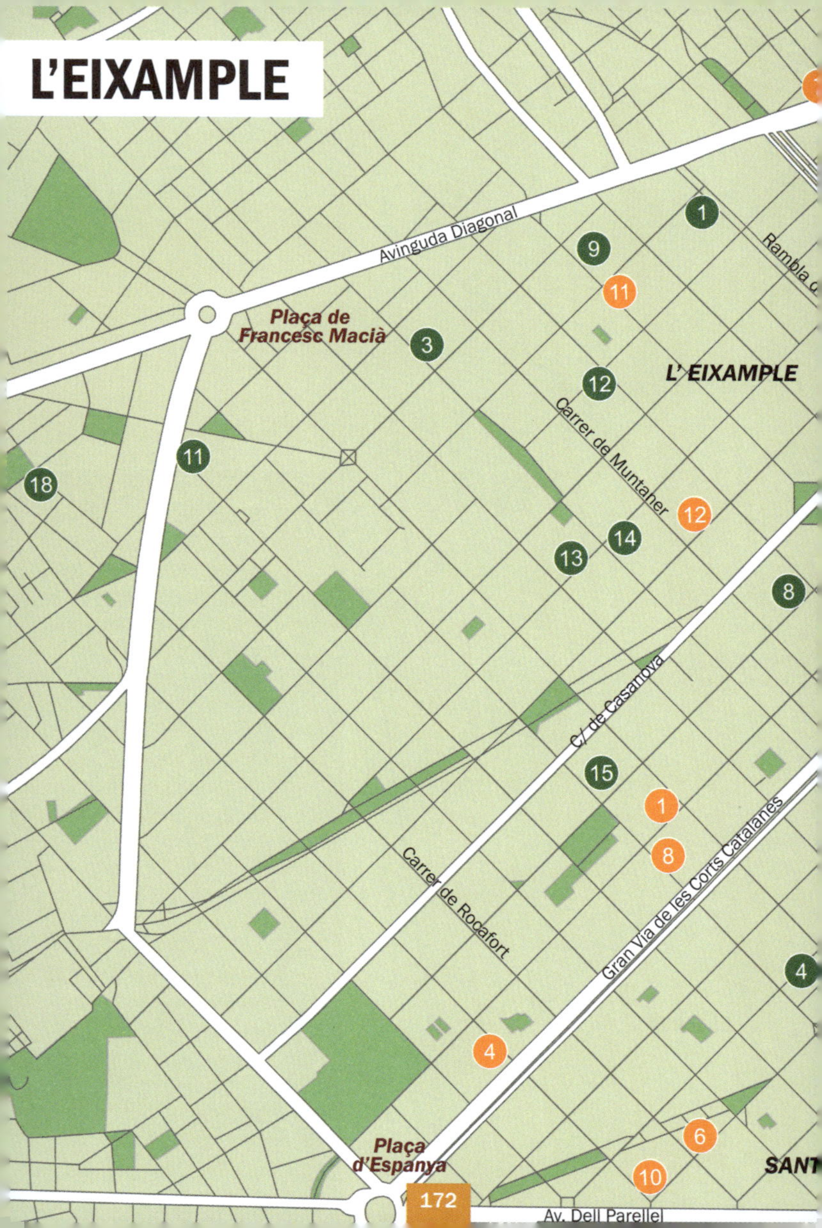
Avinguda Diagonal
Rambla d
Plaça de Francesc Macià
L' EIXAMPLE
Carrer de Muntaner
C/ de Casanova
Carrer de Rocafort
Gran Via de les Corts Catalanes
Plaça d'Espanya
Av. Dell Parellel
SANT
1
9
11
3
12
11
18
12
14
13
8
15
1
8
4
4
6
10

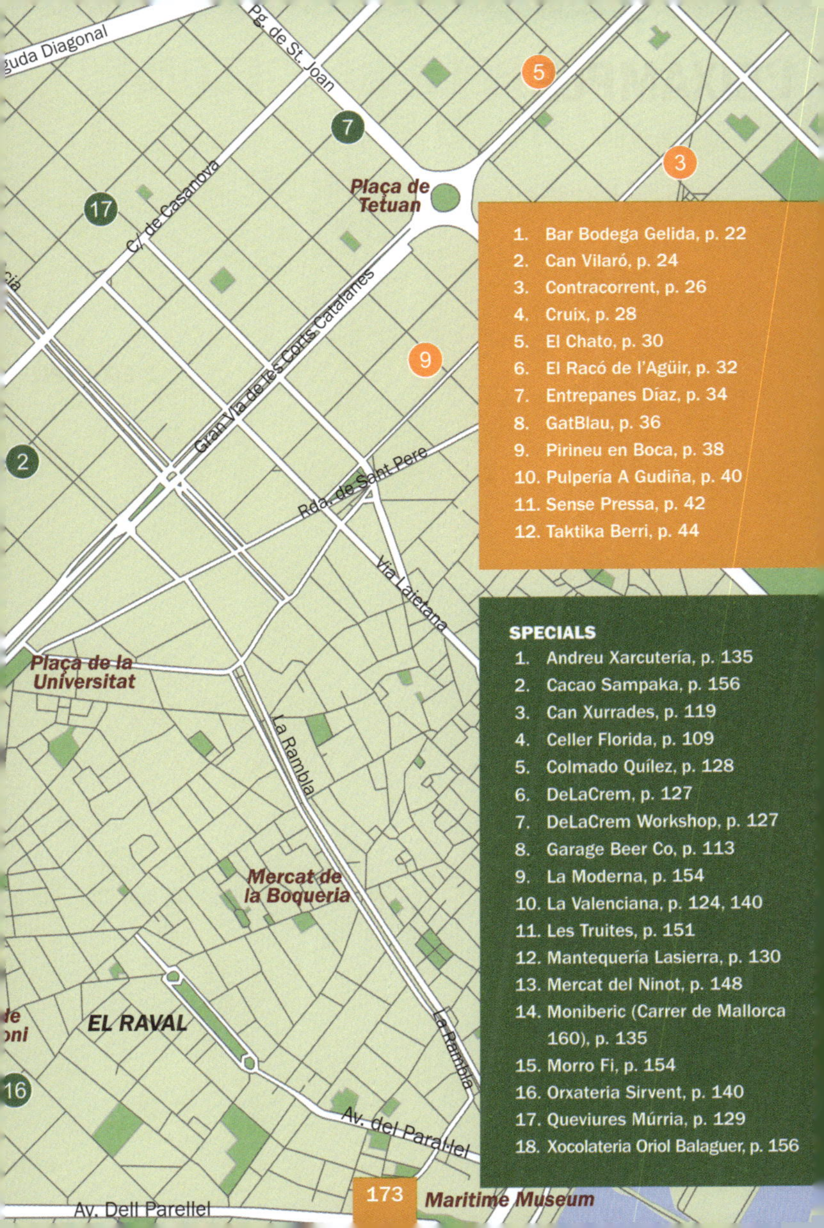

1. Bar Bodega Gelida, p. 22
2. Can Vilaró, p. 24
3. Contracorrent, p. 26
4. Cruix, p. 28
5. El Chato, p. 30
6. El Racó de l'Agüir, p. 32
7. Entrepanes Díaz, p. 34
8. GatBlau, p. 36
9. Pirineu en Boca, p. 38
10. Pulpería A Gudiña, p. 40
11. Sense Pressa, p. 42
12. Taktika Berri, p. 44

SPECIALS

1. Andreu Xarcutería, p. 135
2. Cacao Sampaka, p. 156
3. Can Xurrades, p. 119
4. Celler Florida, p. 109
5. Colmado Quílez, p. 128
6. DeLaCrem, p. 127
7. DeLaCrem Workshop, p. 127
8. Garage Beer Co, p. 113
9. La Moderna, p. 154
10. La Valenciana, p. 124, 140
11. Les Truites, p. 151
12. Mantequería Lasierra, p. 130
13. Mercat del Ninot, p. 148
14. Moniberic (Carrer de Mallorca 160), p. 135
15. Morro Fi, p. 154
16. Orxateria Sirvent, p. 140
17. Queviures Múrria, p. 129
18. Xocolateria Oriol Balaguer, p. 156

GRÀCIA & UPPER BARCELONA

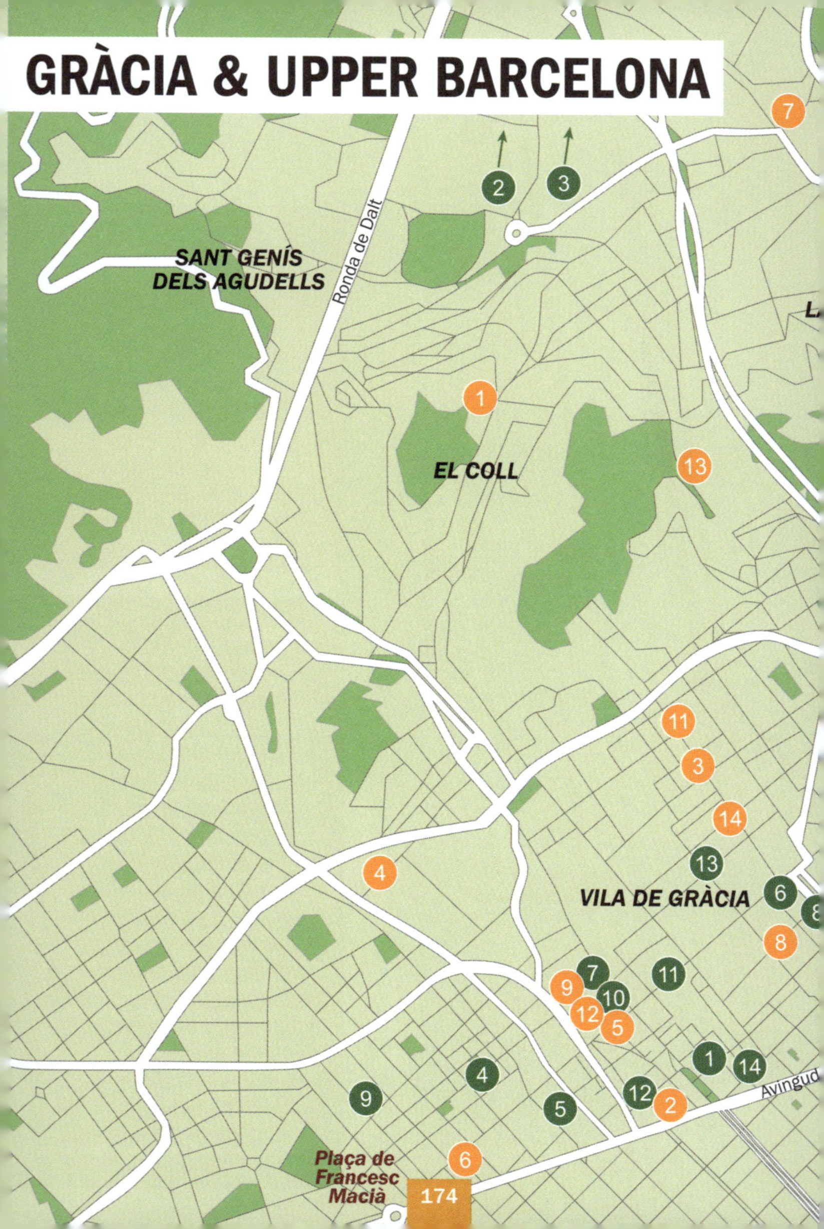

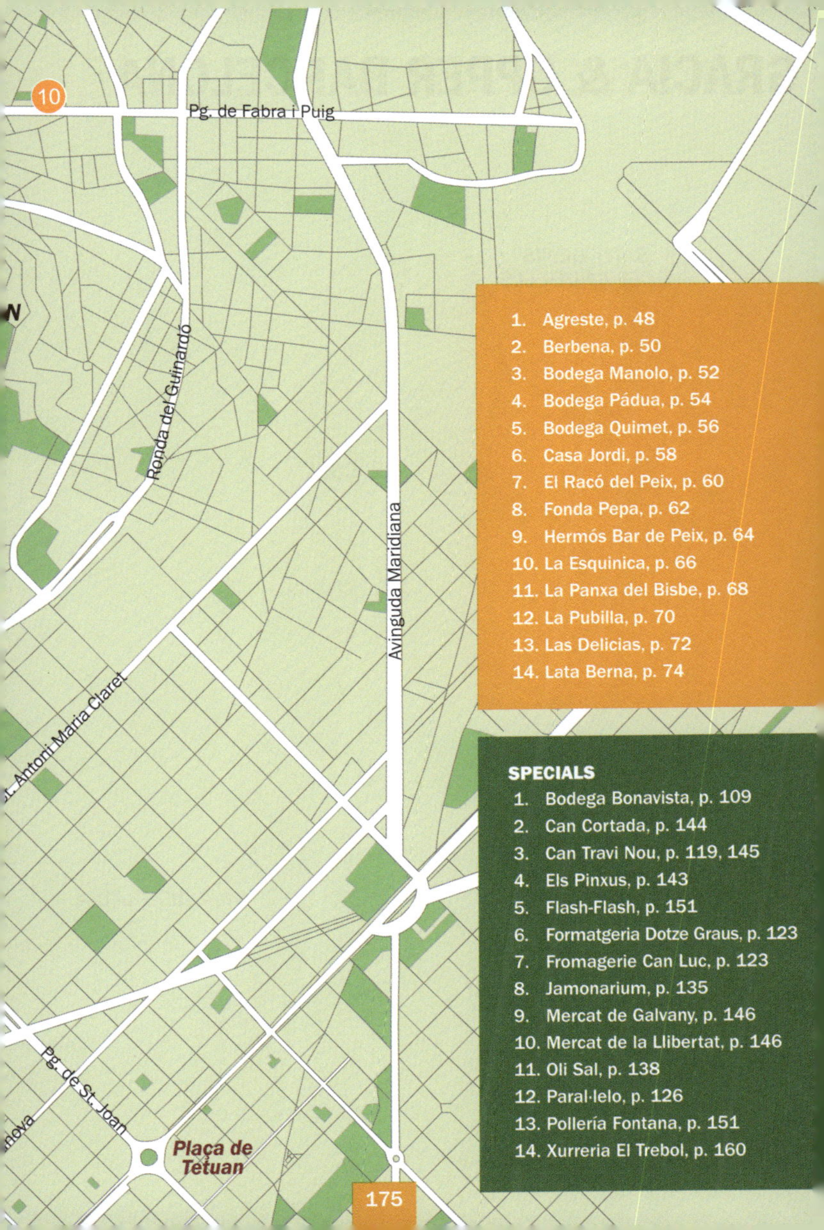

1. Agreste, p. 48
2. Berbena, p. 50
3. Bodega Manolo, p. 52
4. Bodega Pádua, p. 54
5. Bodega Quimet, p. 56
6. Casa Jordi, p. 58
7. El Racó del Peix, p. 60
8. Fonda Pepa, p. 62
9. Hermós Bar de Peix, p. 64
10. La Esquinica, p. 66
11. La Panxa del Bisbe, p. 68
12. La Pubilla, p. 70
13. Las Delicias, p. 72
14. Lata Berna, p. 74

SPECIALS

1. Bodega Bonavista, p. 109
2. Can Cortada, p. 144
3. Can Travi Nou, p. 119, 145
4. Els Pinxus, p. 143
5. Flash-Flash, p. 151
6. Formatgeria Dotze Graus, p. 123
7. Fromagerie Can Luc, p. 123
8. Jamonarium, p. 135
9. Mercat de Galvany, p. 146
10. Mercat de la Llibertat, p. 146
11. Oli Sal, p. 138
12. Paral·lelo, p. 126
13. Pollería Fontana, p. 151
14. Xurreria El Trebol, p. 160

SANTS-MONTJUÏC

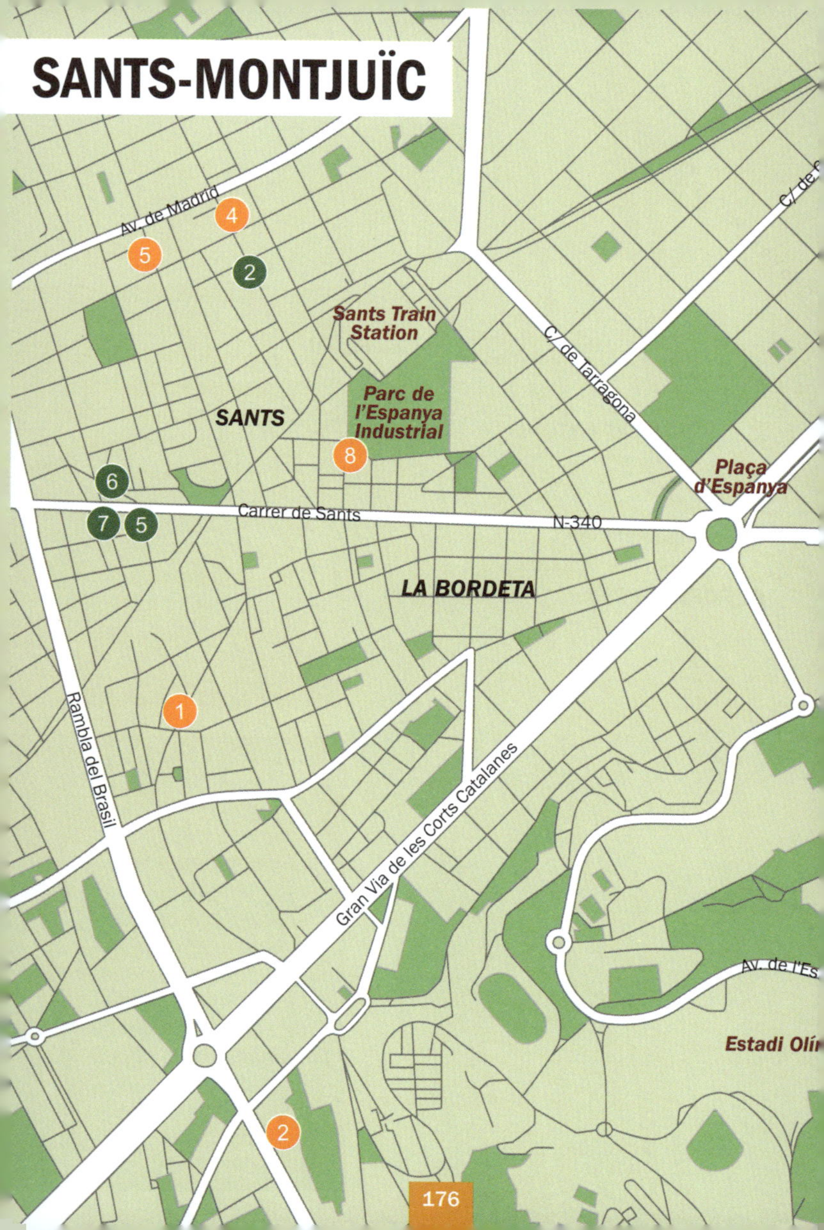

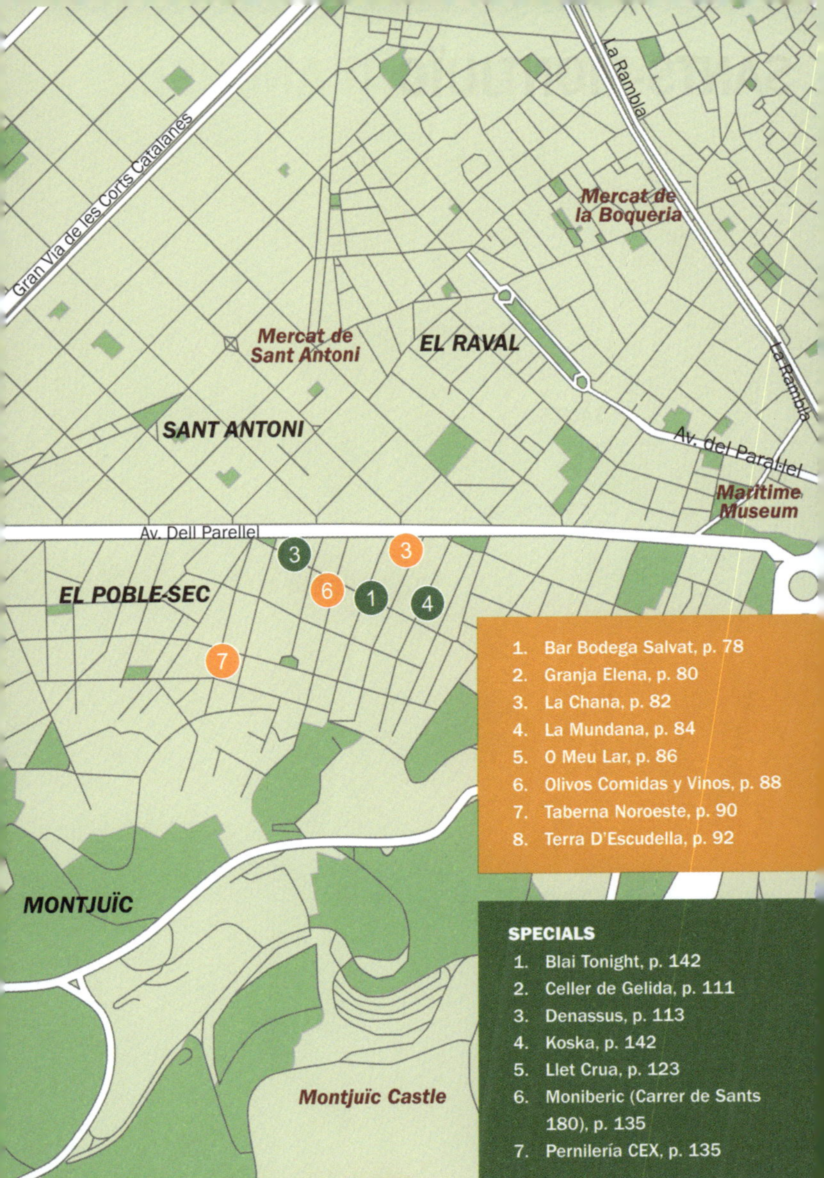
Gran Via de les Corts Catalanes
La Rambla
Mercat de la Boqueria
Mercat de Sant Antoni
EL RAVAL
SANT ANTONI
Av. del Paral·lel
Maritime Museum
Av. Dell Parellel
EL POBLE-SEC
MONTJUÏC
Montjuïc Castle
1. Bar Bodega Salvat, p. 78
2. Granja Elena, p. 80
3. La Chana, p. 82
4. La Mundana, p. 84
5. O Meu Lar, p. 86
6. Olivos Comidas y Vinos, p. 88
7. Taberna Noroeste, p. 90
8. Terra D'Escudella, p. 92
SPECIALS
1. Blai Tonight, p. 142
2. Celler de Gelida, p. 111
3. Denassus, p. 113
4. Koska, p. 142
5. Llet Crua, p. 123
6. Moniberic (Carrer de Sants 180), p. 135
7. Pernilería CEX, p. 135

SANT MARTÍ & SANT ANDREU

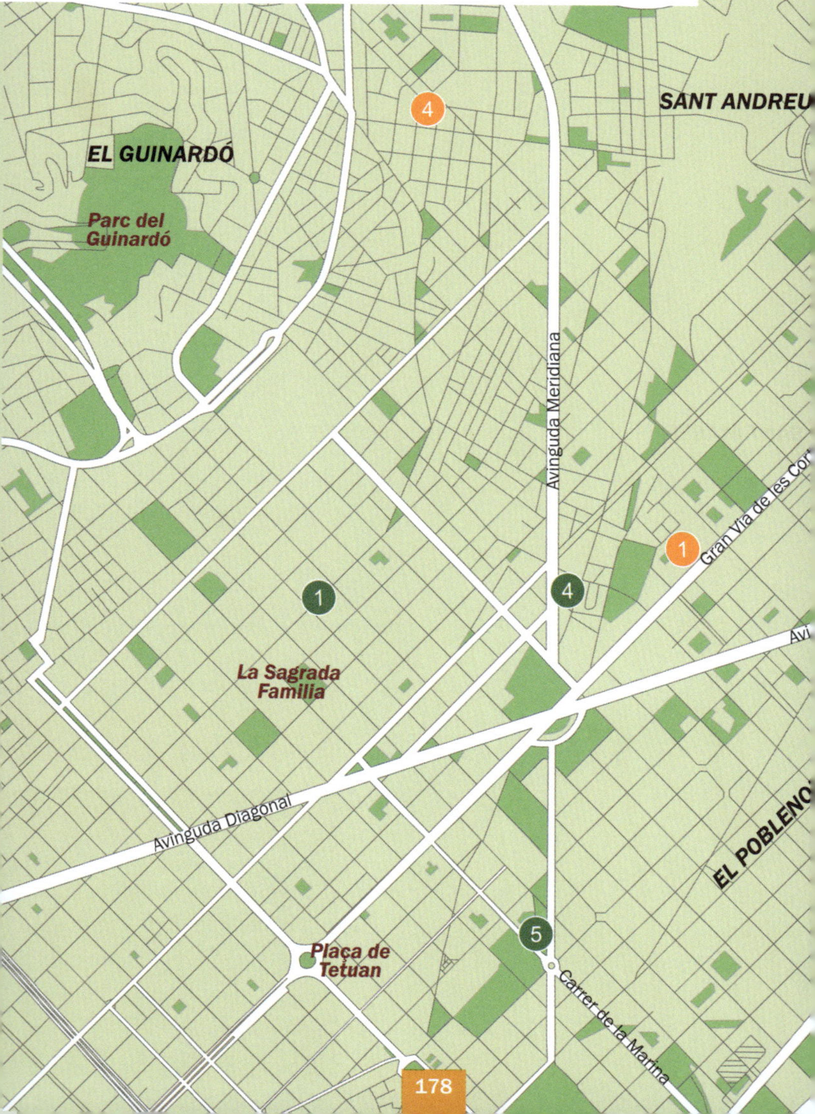

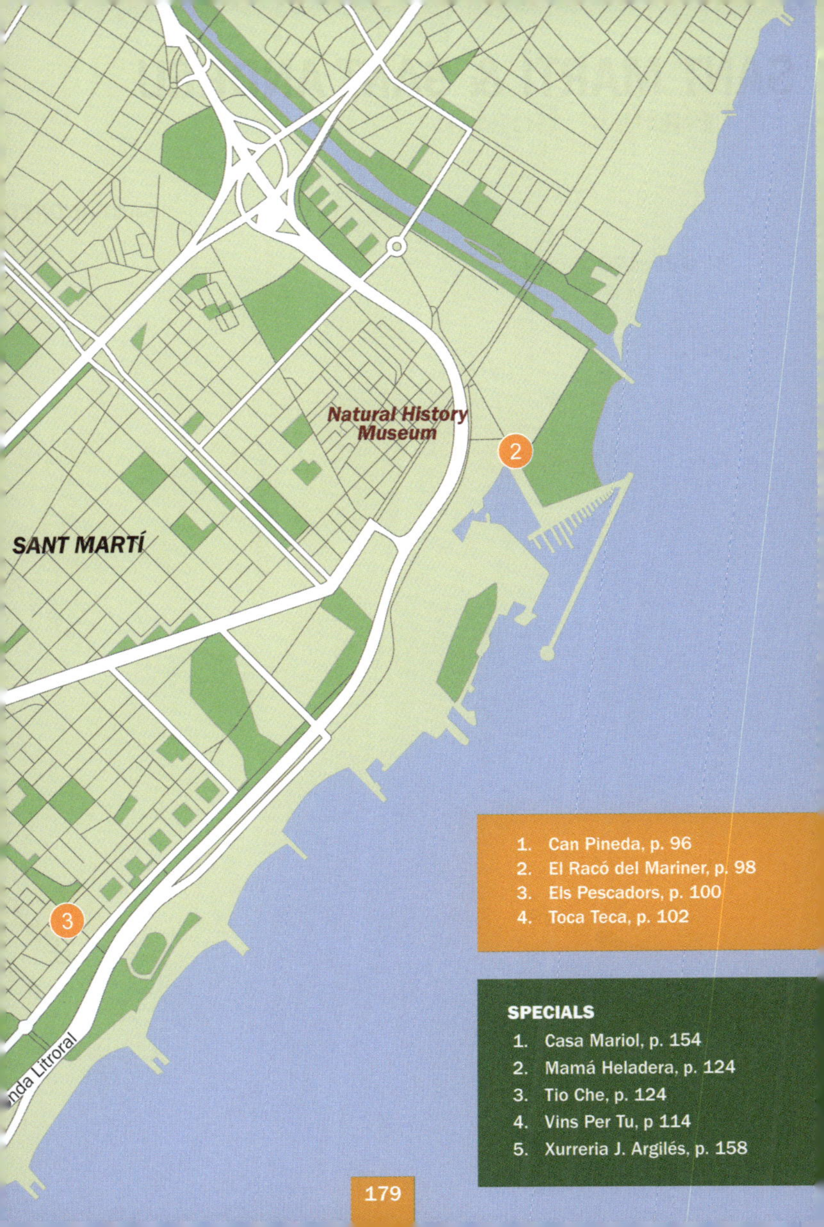

SPECIALS

Triangle▸Books

www.triangle.cat

TRIANGLE POSTALS SL
Carrer Pere Tudurí, 8
07710 Sant Lluís, Menorca

Printed by
Comgrafic
4 / 2024
Printed in Barcelona

ISBN 978-09-8632-900-5
D.L. Me 241-2024